THE OLD TESTAMENT SABBATH
A TRADITION-HISTORICAL INVESTIGATION

by

Niels-Erik A. Andreasen

Published by

SOCIETY OF BIBLICAL LITERATURE

for

The Form Criticism Seminar

DISSERTATION SERIES, NUMBER SEVEN

1972

THE OLD TESTAMENT SABBATH

A TRADITION-HISTORICAL INVESTIGATION

by

Niels-Erik A. Andreasen
Department of Religion
Pacific Union College
Angwin, California 94508

Ph.D., 1971
Vanderbilt University

Advisor:
J. Philip Hyatt

Copyright © 1972

by

The Society of Biblical Literature

Library of Congress Catalog Card Number: 72-88671

Printed in the United States of America
Printing Department, University of Montana, Missoula, Montana 59801

TABLE OF CONTENTS

v

PREFACE

The Sabbath has been the subject of many scholarly as well as popular writings during the last hundred years or so, and yet many questions regarding the Sabbath remain unsolved to the present time. Attempts have been made to discover the origin of the Sabbath, the history of its observance, its role in the life and thought of both the Jewish and Christian communities, and its relation to the week and to Sunday observance. The present study will attempt to contribute to our understanding of the Sabbath in yet another way. It is limited to a treatment of the Old Testament Sabbath, and as a tradition-historical investigation, its concern is primarily with the literature of the Old Testament. Its objective is to examine the form, content, function, and history of the Sabbath material within the Old Testament without insisting that the many questions we have regarding the Sabbath institution must necessarily be answered. In other words, the direct subject of this investigation is not the Old Testament Sabbath institution, but the Old Testament Sabbath literature.

The subject of this study was first suggested to me by Walter Harrelson, dean and professor of Old Testament at Vanderbilt Divinity School. In the execution of the task I have been guided by the pointed suggestions and kindly advice of Professor J. Philip Hyatt, also of Vanderbilt Divinity School. I appreciate the assistance of my teachers, not only while preparing this dissertation, but throughout my graduate studies.

Special thanks are due to the staff of the Joint University Libraries, especially those members in charge of interlibrary loans and of the divinity library. They have provided me with a great number of books, microfilms, and other matters.

In this study Biblical quotations in English have been taken from the _Revised Standard Version_ (New York: Oxford University Press, 1965), unless otherwise indicated. For the Hebrew Bible, I have followed the seventh edition of R. Kittel's _Biblia Hebraica_, and for the LXX the eighth edition of A. Rahlfs' _Septuaginta_, both published by Wüttenbergische Bibelanstalt, Stuttgart.

Finally, it should be said that my interest in the Sabbath is due, first of all, to my parents who long ago taught me by action, as well as by word, what the Sabbath is all about. This study is, therefore, dedicated to them.

ABBREVIATIONS

Commentaries

AB   . . . . The Anchor Bible, New York.
ATD   . . . . Das Alte Testament Deutsch, Göttingen.
BK   . . . . Biblischer Kommentar, Neukirchen.
HAT   . . . . Handbuch zum Alten Testament, Tübingen.
HK   . . . . Handkommentar zum Alten Testament, Göttingen.
HS   . . . . Die Heilige Schrift des Alten Testaments, Bonn.
ICC   . . . . The International Critical Commentary, Edinburgh.
KAT   . . . . Kommentar zum Alten Testament, Leipzig, Gütersloh.
KHC   . . . . Kurzer Hand-Commentar zum Alten Testament (Freiburg i. Br.,
              Leipzig), Tübingen.

Journals and series

AJSL . . . American Journal of Semitic Languages and Literatures,
            Chicago (Ill.).
AJTh . . . American Journal of Theology, Chicago (Ill.).
ANET . . . Ancient Near Eastern Texts Relating to the Old Testament,
            ed. by J. B. Pritchard, Princeton (New Jersey).
ASTI . . . Annual of the Swedish Theological Institute in Jerusalem,
            Leiden.
AThANT . . Abhandlungen zur Theologie des Alten und Neuen Testaments,
            Zürich.
BA   . . . . The Biblical Archaeologist, New Haven (Conn.).
BiOr . . . Bibliotheca Orientalis, Leiden.
BJRL . . . Bulletin of the John Rylands Library, Manchester.
BWANT . . . Beiträge zur Wissenschaft vom Alten und Neuen Testament
            (Leipzig), Stuttgart.
BZ   . . . . Biblische Zeitschrift (New Series from 1957), (Freiburg i.
            Br.), Paderborn.
BZAW . . . Beihefte zur Zeitschrift für die Alttestamentliche Wissen-
            schaft (Giessen), Berlin.
CBQ   . . . . Catholic Biblical Quarterly, Washington (D.C.).
CT   . . . . Cuneiform Texts from Babylonian Tablets in the British
            Museum, London.
CThM . . . Concordia Theological Monthly, St. Louis (Mo.).
CuW   . . . . Christentum und Wissenschaft, Dresden.
EvTh . . . Evangelische Theologie, München.
ExT   . . . . Expository Times, Edinburgh.
FRLANT . . Forschungen zur Religion und Literatur des Alten und Neuen
            Testaments, Göttingen.
HUCA . . . Hebrew Union College Annual, Cincinatti (Ohio).
IEJ   . . . . Israel Exploration Journal, Jerusalem.

JBL . . . . Journal of Biblical Literature (New York, New Haven
           [Conn.]), Philadelphia (Pa.).
JNES . . . Journal of Near Eastern Studies, Chicago (Ill.).
JQR . . . . Jewish Quarterly Review, Philadelphia (Pa.).
JRAS . . . Journal of the Royal Asiatic Society of Great Britain and
           Ireland, London.
JThC . . . Journal for Theology and the Church, New York.
JThS . . . Journal of Theological Studies, Oxford.
KuD . . . . Kerygma und Dogma, Göttingen.
MG . . . . Migne, Patrologia Graeca.
ML . . . . Migne, Patrologia Latina.
NThSt . . . Nieuwe Theologische Studiën, Groningen, Den Haag.
PSBA . . . Proceedings of the Society of Biblical Archaeology, Blums-
           bury (London).
RB . . . . Revue Biblique, Paris.
RHPhR . . . Revue d'Histoire et de Philosophie Religieuses, Strasbourg,
           Paris.
SBT . . . . Studies in Biblical Theology, London and Naperville (Ill.).
SEÅ . . . . Svensk Exegetisk Årsbok, Lund.
SVT . . . . Supplements to Vetus Testamentum, Leiden.
Syria . . . Syria. Revue d'Art Oriental et d'Archéologie, Paris.
ThLZ . . . Theologische Literaturzeitung, Leipzig, Berlin.
ThQ . . . . Theologische Quartalschrift, Tübingen, Stuttgart.
ThR . . . . Theologische Rundschau, Tübingen.
ThZ . . . . Theologische Zeitschrift, Basel.
VT . . . . Vetus Testamentum, Leiden.
WMANT . . . Wissenschaftliche Monographien zum Alten und Neuen Testa-
           ment, Neukirchen.
ZA . . . . Zeitschrift für Assyriologie (Leipzig), Berlin.
ZAW . . . . Zeitschrift für die Alttestamentliche Wissenschaft
           (Giessen), Berlin.
ZDMG . . . Zeitschrift der Deutschen Morgenländischen Gesellschaft
           (Leipzig), Wiesbaden.
ZDPV . . . Zeitschrift des Deutschen Palästina-Vereins (Leipzig,
           Stuttgart), Wiesbaden.
ZThK . . . Zeitschrift für Theologie und Kirche (Freiburg i. Br.,
           Leipzig), Tübingen.

I. INTRODUCTION

The Old Testament Sabbath in recent research

The great interest in the Sabbath among Old Testament scholars during the first third of this century is sometimes attributed to Wilhelm Lotz who in 1883 addressed the question of the origin of the Sabbath by means of some newly discovered Babylonian texts.[1] According to Lotz the Hebrew šabbāt and the Babylonian šabattu are identical, namely a day of rest.[2] Although the characterization of šabattu as a

---

[1]Questiones de Historia Sabbati (Leipzig: J. C. Hinrichs, 1883). The significance of the Babylonian origin of the Sabbath followed on the heels of the rejection of the historicity of the Pentateuchal literature. Conservative scholars who accept its historicity have naturally never been very much impressed with the attempts to find an origin of the Sabbath in Babylonian literature, for they have consistently asked the question of origin from within the Old Testament itself. Thus more than seventy years after Lotz's thesis, the following exchange concerning the origin of the Sabbath could be made by Biblical scholars in doctoral dissertations: "There is absolutely no mention of the Sabbath before the Lord said to Moses. . . . These words indicate that the event was bound to the Decalogue of Sinai. The quoted words are recorded in Exodus 16:4. The first mention of the Sabbath in the Bible and the first known chronological use of the word in all history is in Exodus 16:23." Roger D. Congdon, "Sabbatic Theology" (unpublished Th.D. dissertation, Dallas Theological Seminary, 1949), pp. 122-123. "When the first Sabbath came to earth, only God had worked the six previous days of the week. The angels had looked on in praise and admiration, but they had not created. . . ." "Therefore, it can only mean that the Sabbath of the fourth commandment and the Sabbath of Exodus 16:23, and the rest of Gen. 2:2-3 are one and the same in the original." George Yamashiro, "A Study of the Hebrew Word Sabbath in Biblical and Talmudic Literatures" (unpublished Ph.D. dissertation, Harvard University, 1955), pp. 6-7, 9.

[2]Lotz, Questiones, p. 58. ". . . sjabattu, quod sine ulla dubitatione idem sit atque שבת Hebraerum. . . ." The occurrence of sabattu on which Lotz relied identifies it with the expression ûm nûh libbi (lit., a day of the heart's rest). See below, n. 3, p. 2 and n. 1, pp. 96-97.

1

"rest day" was soon abandoned,[1] there were other arguments supporting a Babylonian origin of the Old Testament Sabbath; e.g., the close similarity between šabbāt and šabattu,[2] the newly discovered ûmê lemnûti (evil days) which occurred approximately every seventh day in an Assyrian calendar,[3] and the characterization of the šabattu as a day of propitiation rather than of rest.[4] Consequently Lotz's basic conclusions concerning the origin of the Sabbath were very much celebrated around the turn of the century.[5]

---

[1] In 1889 P. Jensen pointed out that ûm nûḫ libbi cannot be translated "Tag der Ruhe des Herzens," that it means "Tag der Beruhigung des Herzens," and that the corresponding verb šabātu does not mean "to rest." "Assyrio-hebraica," ZA, IV (1889), 274, 278. See below, pp. 101-02.

[2] See below, n. 1, pp. 96-97.

[3] First discovered in 1869 by George Smith. He writes: "In the year 1869, I discovered among other things a curious religious calendar of the Assyrians, in which every month is divided into four weeks, and the seventh days, or 'Sabbaths,' are marked out as days on which no work should be undertaken." George Smith, Assyrian Discoveries: An Account of Explorations and Discoveries on the Site of Nineveh, During 1873 and 1874 (New York: Scribner, Armstrong and Co., 1875), p. 12. See below, n. 1, pp. 96-97.

[4] The ûm nûḫ libbi was a day on which the god's heart was at rest; i.e., a day of pacification or propitiation. The similarity on this point between the Hebrew šabbāt and the Babylonian šabattu has been explored in particular by Morris Jastrow, "The Original Character of the Hebrew Sabbath," AJTh, II (1898), 312-352.

[5] Cf. Friedrich Delitzsch, Babel und Bibel (3rd ed.; Leipzig: J. C. Hinrichs'sche Buchhandlung, 1903), pp. 60-61; Hermann Gunkel, Schöpfung und Chaos in Urzeit und Endzeit: Eine religionsgeschichtliche Untersuchung über Gen 1 und Ap Joh 12 (Göttingen: Vandenhoeck & Ruprecht, 1895), p. 155; Morris Jastrow, "The Original Character," pp. 313ff.; A. H. Sayce, The "Higher Criticism" and the Verdict of the Monuments (3rd ed., rev.; New York: E. & J. B. Young & Co., 1894), p. 74; Crawford H. Toy, "The Earliest Form of the Sabbath," JBL, XVIII (1899), 190-94; Heinrich Zimmern, "Sabbath," ZDMG, LVIII (1904), 201-2; et al.

In 1904 a new text published by Theophilus G. Pinches threw additional light on the Babylonian origin of the Sabbath.[1] In it the Babylonian šabattu[2] is identified as the fifteenth day of the month, an identification which is now generally accepted.[3] Consequently there was no longer any direct evidence for associating the Babylonian word šabattu with the ûmê lemnûti, or any other weekly day.[4] It was as a direct result of this observation that one of the most amazing theories regarding the origin of the Sabbath was developed. After an initial suggestion by Zimmern in 1904,[5] Johannes Meinhold proposed in a number

[1] "Šapattu, the Babylonian Sabbath," PSBA, XXVI (1904), 51-56.

[2] The second radical in Pinches' text is p rather than b. Most scholars consider šapattu and šabattu to be alternative readings of the same word. For a contrary opinion, see Delitzsch, Babel und Bibel (5th ed.; Leipzig: J. C. Hinrichs'sche Buchhandlung, 1905), p. 65; E. J. Kraeling, "The Present Status of the Sabbath Question," AJSL, XLIX (1932-33), 221.

[3] See below, n. 2, pp. 94-95.

[4] This conclusion had been maintained by some conservative scholars all along. Cf. Francis Brown, "The Sabbath in the Cuneiform Records," The Presbyterian Review, III (1882), pp. 688-700. It is possible, of course, that the šabattu, assuming that it was the day of the full moon, might also fall on the fourteenth day of the month, i.e., on an ûmu lemnu (see below, n. 2, pp. 94-95), but any attempt to identify the ûmê lemnûti with šabattu is purely hypothetical. Cf. Zimmern, "Sabbath," p. 201: "Von hier aus wäre es nun allerdings doch recht wohl denkbar, dass in der Tat bei Vierteilung (statt Sechsteilung) des babylonischen Monats, . . . zunächst der 14. Monatstag als šapattu gegolten hätte und dass von ihm ausgehend auch der 7., 21., 28., (und 19. als der 7×7. des vorhergehenden Monats) als šapattu-Tage bezeichnet and gefeirt worden wären, so dass wir also in den vielbesprochenen siebener-Tagen der babylonischen Hemerologien doch babylonische šapattu-Tage zu erblicken hätten." This opinion published shortly after Pinches' article evidences the frustrations of someone whose position has just been undermined.

[5] Zimmern, "Sabbath," p. 202.

of publications beginning in 1905[1] that the Sabbath was originally the
day of the full moon both in Babylonia and in pre-exilic Old Testament
literature, and that it became a weekly day only under the influence of
Ezekiel, or in postexilic times.[2] Though this hypothesis met with oppo-
sition from the start,[3] it gained remarkable acceptance among many Old

---

[1]Sabbat und Woche im Alten Testament (Göttingen: Vandenhoeck und
Ruprecht, 1905); Sabbat und Sonntag, Wissenschaft und Bildung, Vol. 45
(Leipzig: Verlag von Quelle & Meyer, 1909); "Die Entstehung des
Sabbats," ZAW, XXIX (1909), 81-112; "Zur Sabbatfrage," ZAW, XLVIII
(1930), 121-38.

[2]Under the impact of the Deuteronomic reform the full moon Sabbath was dissolved, and its name was transferred to the seventh day of
the week which was originally a rest day in the old harvest week (Ex.
34:21), but which now, under the influence of the Sabbath, came to run
uninterrupted throughout the year. In Meinhold's early study, Sabbat
und Woche, pp. 9, 34, this transformation is attributed to Ezekiel, but
in the later essay, "Zur Sabbatfrage" (pp. 128ff.), this process is
placed in postexilic times, in connection with the reform of Nehemiah.
In doing so Meinhold replied to his critics who charged that Ezekiel
gives no evidence of having created a new kind of Sabbath. He now
claimed that the Sabbath texts in Ezekiel are secondary, and were inserted in postexilic times, after the development of the seventh-day
Sabbath.

[3]Cf. Wilhelm Lotz, "Sabbat," Realencyklopädie für protestantische
Theologie und Kirche, ed. by A. Hauck (Leipzig: J. C. Hinrichs'sche
Buchhandlung, 1906), XVII, 283-91; Johannes Hehn, Siebenzahl und Sabbat
bei den Babyloniern und im Alten Testament (Leipzig: J. C.
Hinrichs'sche Buchhandlung, 1907), pp. 115-20; Eduard König, Geschichte
der alttestamentlichen Religion (2nd ed.: Gütersloh: Druck und Verlag
von C. Bertelsmann, 1915), pp. 294-96; Rudolf Kittel, Geschichte des
Volkes Israel (6th ed.; Stuttgart: Verlag Friedrich Andreas Perthes
A.-G., 1923), pp. 447-48; Povl O. Bostrup, Den israelitiske Sabbats
Oprindelse og Karakter i Foreksilsk Tid (Copenhagen: G. E. C. Gads
Forlag, 1923), p. 56; Aage Bentzen, Den israelitiske Sabbats Oprindelse
og Historie indtil Jerusalems Erobring aar 70 e. Kr. (Copenhagen:
J. H. Schultz Forlagsboghandel A/S, 1923), pp. 26ff.; Benno Jacob, "The
Decalogue," JQR, XIV (1923-24), 157ff.; Bernardus D. Eerdmans, "Der
Sabbath," in Vom Alten Testament: Festschrift Karl Marti, ed. by Karl
Budde, BZAW, No. 41 (Giessen: Verlag von Alfred Töpelmann, 1925), pp.
79-83; Karl Budde, "The Sabbath and the Week: Their Origin and their
Nature," JThS, XXX (1929), 1-15; "Antwort auf Johannes Meinholds 'Zur
Frage,'" ZAW, XLVIII (1930), 138-45; Kaufmann Kohler, "The Sabbath and
Festivals in Pre-Exilic and Exilic Times," in Studies, Addresses, and

Testament scholars during the succeeding years.[1] In time, however, it proved untenable,[2] and gave way to other hypotheses regarding the origin and history of the Sabbath.

One such hypothesis, traced back to Kuenen,[3] derives the week from planet worship in Mosaic times. It was developed in the hands of Eerdmans,[4] Budde,[5] and Rowley[6] into the so-called Kenite hypothesis concerning the origin of the Sabbath. However, since there is very little evidence in support of this hypothesis, it has not gained wide acceptance.[7]

Personal Papers (New York: Bloch Publishing Co., 1931), p. 87; Th. C. Vriezen, "Kalender en Sabbat," NThSt, XXIII (1940), 182-83; et al.

[1]See below, n. 1, pp. 95-96.

[2]See especially the arguments by Budde (above, n. 3, p. 4). The main points of contention are: (1) There is no evidence that Ezekiel radically transformed the nature of the Sabbath; in fact he appears to assume the existence of a weekly Sabbath. (2) The association of Sabbath and new moon in the Old Testament (2 Kg. 4:23; Am. 8:5; Hos. 2:11; Is. 1:13, 66:23; Ezek. 46:1) does not imply that the Sabbath is the full moon, nor that the two days occurred with the same frequency. (3) There is definite evidence of a weekly Sabbath in pre-exilic literature (see below, pp. 108-21.   (4) The etymological relationship between šabattu and šabbāt is not as simple as Meinhold's theory would make it (see below, pp. 101-2.

[3]Abraham Kuenen, The Religion of Israel, trans. by A. H. May (London: Williams and Norgate, 1874), p. 276.

[4]See above, n. 3, p. 4.

[5]See above, n. 3, p. 4.

[6]H. H. Rowley, "Moses and the Decalogue," BJRL, XXXIV (1951-52), 81-118. Also in Men of God: Studies in Old Testament History and Prophecy (London: Thomas Nelson and Sons Ltd., 1963), pp. 1-36.

[7]Cf. Roland de Vaux, Ancient Israel, Vol. II: Religious Institutions (New York: McGraw-Hill Book Company, 1965), p. 480. ". . . If the Qenite hypothesis looks the least unlikely, this may be merely because we have no documents at all which contradict it." Moreover, the

Various attempts have been made to derive the Sabbath from the lunar phases, either directly,[1] or as a secondary development from the Babylonian šabattu and the ûmê lemnûti, both of which were undoubtedly connected with the lunar phases originally, or from the sacred number seven which was perhaps also associated with the moon at one stage.[2] However plausible these explanations are, they fall short of taking account of the Old Testament Sabbath which is completely independent of the moon and the lunar month.[3]

Another hypothesis proposes that the regularly recurring weekly Sabbath may have originated as a market day on which the community stopped regular activities and attended market in the city. Various forms of taboo as well as religious functions may have been associated

---

association of the Sabbath and planetary worship (Saturn worship) on the one hand, and of Saturn worship and pre-Mosaic Kenites (Am. 5:26) on the other hand, is now discredited by most scholars. The planetary week is a late development which cannot be held responsible for the origin of the week or for the seventh day of rest. For a recent review of this problem, see Willy Rordorf, Sunday: The History of the Day of Rest and Worship in the Earliest Centuries of the Christian Church, trans. by A. A. K. Graham (Philadelphia: Westminster Press, 1968), pp. 20ff. One last piece of evidence (the prohibition against fire making, Ex. 35:3) could once have applied to Kenites (smiths), but also to any other ancient people who cooked food and worked in metal, and it is therefore not conclusive.

[1]Cf. Ditlef Nielsen, Die altarabische Mondreligion und die mosäische Uberlieferung (Strassburg: Verlag von Karl J. Trübner, 1904), pp. 52-88.

[2]Cf. Hehn, Siebenzahl und Sabbat, pp. 59-61. See below, pp. 102-4.

[3]See below, pp. 97, 100-1.

with such a day.[1] Days of this type have been found in various parts of the world, but no trace of them has appeared in the Near East.[2]

Two final hypotheses show some similarity and may be examined together. According to the first, the Sabbath and the seven-day week are derived from a particular type of calendar (the pentecontad calendar), which supposedly was in existence in very ancient times.[3] This calendar is based on seven fifty-day periods,[4] totaling 350 days, which would require fifteen additional days, or approximately two weeks to fill out a solar year. These fifteen days, if they were inserted in two install- ments, each a week long, could have started the development of the continuous seven-day week.[5] According to the second hypothesis the one or two seven-day periods which inspired the continuous week were festi- val periods, viz., the feast of unleavened bread and the feast of booths, or their predecessors, and the week (and the Sabbath) was developed as a means of measuring the proper interval between these festivals.[6]

---

[1]See the important study by Hutton Webster, Rest Days: A Study in Early Law and Morality (New York: Macmillan Company, 1916), pp. 102- 23.

[2]See below, n. 5, pp. 97-98; pp. 123-24.

[3]Julius Lewy and Hildegard Lewy, "The Origin of the Week and the Oldest West Asiatic Calendar," HUCA, XVII (1942-43), 1-152.

[4]The fifty-day period in question is derived from the word ḫamuštum. It is a serious question, however, if this word refers to a period of fifty days (see below, n. 5, pp. 97-98).

[5]This theory concerning the origin of the Sabbath has been popularized by Julian Morgenstern, "Sabbath," Interpreter's Dictionary of the Bible, ed. by G. A. Buttrick, et al. (New York: Abingdon Press, 1962), IV, 135-41.

[6]See below, pp. 97-98; 113-16.

The interest in extra-Biblical origins of the Sabbath has now subsided. It is generally agreed that the seventh-day Sabbath is old, dating back to premonarchical, and undoubtedly to Mosaic times.[1] Beyond this point scholars now proceed with a great deal of tentativeness. It is recognized that the various hypotheses regarding Sabbath origins have exhausted the available source material without providing any final conclusions.[2] The origin and early history of the Sabbath thus continue to lie in the dark. This does not mean that the quest for the original Sabbath has been completely in vain, for it has provided illustrations of special days which demonstrate some similarity to the Biblical seventh-day Sabbath,[3] and which may have influenced it, or even helped

---

[1]See below, pp. 117-21.

[2]This was realized already in Kraeling's survey of the various hypotheses ("The Present Status of the Sabbath Question," pp. 218-28), and the situation had not changed markedly twenty-five years later. Cf. de Vaux, Ancient Israel, II, 475-83. Robert North makes the same confession when, after reviewing the various hypotheses, he includes most of them in his concluding statement (one-half page long) of the origin of the Sabbath ("The Derivation of Sabbath," Biblica, XXXVI (1955), 182-201. It is quite possible that the coup de grâce has been given to all the presently known hypotheses regarding the extra-Biblical origin of the Sabbath by J. H. Meesters, Op zoek naar de oorsprong van de Sabbat, Studia Semitica Neerlandica, No. 7 (Assen: Van Gorcum & Comp. N. V., 1966), pp. 1-82. Apparently unaware of Meesters' study, Charles W. Kiker came to the same conclusion in his much less persuasive survey of the theories regarding the original Sabbath. "The Sabbath in the Old Testament Cult" (unpublished Th.D. dissertation, Southern Baptist Theological Seminary, 1968), pp. 1-66. See also Vriezen, "Kalender en Sabbat," pp. 172-95; N. H. Tur-Sinai, "Sabbat und Woche," BiOr, VIII (1951), 14-24; G. Joh. Botterweck, "Der Sabbat im Alten Testamente," ThQ, CXXXIV (1954), 448-59; Theodore H. Gaster, "Le jour du repos," Evidences, XLIII (1954), 43-48.

[3]In 1923 Bentzen pointed out that the comparative studies, as carried out by Webster for example (see above, n. 1, p. 7), do not provide explanations of the Old Testament phenomenon, but "illustrations" of more or less similar phenomena (Den israelitiske Sabbats Oprindelse og Historie, pp. 39ff.).

formulate it, but this latter process is unknown. It is not surprising, therefore, that Sabbath studies should shift their attention from the extra-Biblical to the Biblical sources, and that is precisely what has happened.

Within the Old Testament literature, one of the first questions which claims attention concerns the word šabbāt itself. A number of etymological explanations have been proposed for this word. (1) According to one view it is derived from the Arabic thabat, a noun referring to the stations of the moon in its four phases. This explanation is now largely discredited on the ground that Arabic culture had little impact on ancient Israel, and that the Sabbath had little or nothing to do originally with the lunar phases. (2) A derivation of šabbāt from the Accadian šabattu (the fifteenth day of the month, or the day of the full moon) is unlikely for two reasons. Firstly, the words are not quite as much alike as they sound and, secondly, šabbāt refers exclusively to a weekly day, while šabattu refers to a monthly day, and the former is not known to have been derived from the latter. (3) A classical etymology derives šabbāt from šebaᶜ (seven). This seems rather plausible since the Sabbath is so closely associated with the number seven, but the difficulties involved in deriving šbt from šbᶜ, even if it occurred in Accadian, are not easily overcome. (4) Finally, it is possible that šabbāt is a genuine Hebrew word derived from the common verbal root šbt meaning "to cease" or "to stop." This is a plausible solution to the etymological question, and one which we shall suggest to be the most likely.[1]

---

[1] For a fuller discussion of the etymological question, see below, pp. 100-4.

Since the shortcoming of most of these hypotheses regarding the original Sabbath is their inability to take adequate account of the particular nature of the Old Testament Sabbath, the second important question addressed to the Old Testament Sabbath literature concerns the nature of the Sabbath institution. Unfortunately, an examination of the Sabbath institution is confronted with some problems all of its own. Firstly, we have few and only sketchy descriptions of Sabbath keeping in the Old Testament; secondly, most of the laws regulating Sabbath observance are late, according to the history of the Old Testament literature. Nevertheless, attempts to understand the Sabbath institution in the Old Testament literature have been made, with or without the assistance of extra-Biblical sources.[1]

In 1903 Friedrich Bohn published a "readable book" (lesbares Buch) on the Sabbath.[2] He proposed that the earliest Sabbath is an

---

[1] In actuality the efforts to examine the Old Testament institution and the extra-Biblical "Sabbath" cannot be completely separated, nor should they be. In fact, some efforts to understand the Old Testament institution are heavily influenced by extra-Biblical information. An illustration of this is provided by Meinhold's reconstruction of the history of the Old Testament Sabbath (see below), and a few years earlier by Jastrow ("The Original Character of the Hebrew Sabbath") who argued that the Hebrew Sabbath (šabbātôn) was basically a day of propitiation and pacification of the god's anger in early times, like its Babylonian counterpart (šabattum). The flaws in this proposition were demonstrated by Crawford H. Toy in his reply to Jastrow the following year. The essential idea in the Old Testament Sabbath is not, according to Toy, propitiation, but abstinence from work. (Toy, "The Earliest Form of the Sabbath," pp. 190-94). We are, however, justified in distinguishing formally between the pure question of origin (where did it come from?) and the question of its essential nature (what is it really like?). This distinction will help us to focus on a further aspect of Old Testament Sabbath studies.

[2] Der Sabbat im Alten Testament und im altjüdischen religiösen Aberglauben (Gütersloh: Druck und Verlag von C. Bertelsmann, 1903), p. 5.

example of the holy days in primitive (pre-Mosaic) religion,[1] but that
it was transformed through revelation (the peculiar quality of Old Testament religion) and became the one joyous rest day in Israel.[2] As such,
it shows no historical development; it is always the same.[3]

A very different view of the Sabbath institution was developed
by Johannes Meinhold, and subsequently adopted by many scholars.[4]
According to Meinhold, the pre-exilic Sabbath was a full moon feast day
with sacrifices and holy assemblies, and it naturally occurred only once
a month.[5] In exilic or postexilic times[6] this day had lost its astro-
nomical connections, and gave name to the last day (a rest day) of a
seven-day week which was now running throughout the year.[7] This seventh
day became the Sabbath of postexilic Judaism and was identified as
Yahweh's Sabbath, a sign, and a day on which all work was prohibited.[8]
We have already noted the difficulties with this reconstruction,[9] but we
must not underestimate its important emphasis on development in the Old
Testament Sabbath literature.

---

[1]Ibid., p. 91.   [2]Ibid., pp. 91, 97.

[3]Ibid., p. 11.

[4]See above, pp. 3-5.

[5]Meinhold, Sabbat und Woche, pp. 3ff.; "Zur Sabbatfrage,"
pp. 122ff.

[6]See above, n. 2, p. 4.

[7]Meinhold, Sabbat und Woche, p. 34; "Zur Sabbatfrage," pp. 132-133.

[8]Meinhold, Sabbat und Woche, pp. 35ff.; "Zur Sabbatfrage,"
pp. 131, 133.

[9]See above, n. 2, p. 5.

In 1923 two additional studies on the Sabbath appeared.[1]
Bostrup's book examines the pre-exilic Sabbath in the light of ancient
Near Eastern "Sabbaths," and concluded that there probably was a pre-
Mosaic seventh-day Sabbath governed by a taboo, perhaps connected with
the changing phases of the moon.[2] However, it was released from the
lunar phases as early as Mosaic times and became an independent seventh-
day Sabbath, dedicated to Yahweh, on which work was prohibited.
Moreover, in pre-exilic times it received an ethical content (Dt. 5:12-
15) and became a religious festival.[3] Bentzen's book is devoted entirely
to a history of the Sabbath institution based on Biblical literature.
The extra-Biblical evidence is referred to in the introduction, but
dismissed, and the hypotheses based on it, notably Meinhold's, regarding
the origin of the Sabbath are rejected.[4] This means, according to
Bentzen, that although the Sabbath is probably pre-Mosaic (in the form
of a taboo day related to the lunar phases), its pre-Mosaic history is
unknown. We have access to it only through analogies gathered from
extra-Biblical sources, but these do not explain how the primitive lunar
day, market day, et cetera, became the seventh-day Sabbath of the Old

---

[1]Bostrup, Den israelitiske Sabbats Oprindelse og Karakter;
Bentzen, Den israelitiske Sabbats Oprindelse og Historie. Both studies
were originally prepared in competition for a position at the University
of Copenhagen.

[2]Bostrup, Den israelitiske Sabbats Oprindelse og Karakter,
pp. 50-55.

[3]Ibid., pp. 58-62.

[4]Bentzen, Den israelitiske Sabbats Oprindelse og Historie,
pp. 2-35.

Testament.[1] In pre-exilic times the Sabbath developed into a feast day with humanitarian overtones.[2] During the exile it was changed into a day of enforced rest,[3] which in postexilic times was strictly enforced with taboo-like regulations.[4] In the Hellenistic period dispensations were given to place practicable Sabbath observance in agreement with the strict regulations. Finally Christianity returned the Sabbath institution to the prophetic ideals, i.e., a day of good works.[5] This schematization of the development of the institution is of course artificial, and the various stages overlap each other,[6] but this does not minimize the importance of Bentzen's attempt to show the growth of the Sabbath institution and its relationship to the history and religion of Israel.

---

[1]Ibid., pp. 39ff., 50-51.   [2]Ibid., pp. 52-58.

[3]Ibid., p. 69.

[4]Ibid., pp. 79-85.

[5]Ibid., p. 150.

[6]Ibid., p. 9. Bentzen summarizes his position on this point as follows: "The main point, as we have said, is that the Sabbath in historical time must be understood essentially as an internal Jewish phenomenon, whose history finds its determinating turning point in the Babylonian exile. At this time the emphasis on what Sabbath keeping really means is changed in such a way that a plain and obvious distinction exists between the pre-exilic temple feast and the postexilic rest day. Nevertheless, nothing completely new is introduced, for the idea of rest was already presented in pre-exilic time by the humanitarian concern, which we presumably meet already early in history, but which is not of the same importance as the other, namely, the festive aspect of the Sabbath. The idea of rest becomes central only in and after the exile. But by then the humanitarian orientation is no longer as essential as the theological orientation now is, namely, that God rested, kept Sabbath on the seventh day, wherefore man should also do so, if he wants to belong to God's people." (Translation mine.)

These and other examinations[1] of the history of the Sabbath institution have demonstrated not only that this institution went through a development related to the historical and religious process in ancient Israel, but also that it became the source of various traditions which became part of Israel's theological heritage; that is, Israel not only kept the Sabbath, she also contemplated it, and strangely enough it is the record of her contemplation rather than of her observation which

---

[1]Cf. Botterweck, "Der Sabbat im Alten Testamente," pp. 134-47; Vriezen, "Kalender en Sabbat," pp. 172-95; Eduard Mahler, "Der Sabbat: Seine etymologische und chronologisch-historische Bedeutung," ZDMG, LXII (1908), 33-79. The same information is found in Mahler's book, Handbuch der jüdischen Chronologie (Leipzig: Buchhandlung Gustav Fock, G.m.b.H., 1916), pp. 30-91. Tur-Sinai, "Sabbat und Woche," pp. 14-24; A.-M. Dubarle, "La signification religieuse de Sabbat dans la Bible," in A.-M. Dubarle, et al., Le dimanche, Lex orandi, Vol. XXXIX (Paris: Les éditions du Cerf, 1965), pp. 43-59; Walter Kornfeld, "Der Sabbath im Alten Testament," in Der Tag des Hern, ed. by Hermal Peichl (Vienna: Verlag Herder, 1958), pp. 11-31; Ernst Jenni, Die theologische Begründung des Sabbatgebotes im Alten Testament, Theologische Studien, No. 46 (Zollikon-Zürich: Evangelischer Verlag AG., 1956); H. M. Feret, "Le sources bibliques," in Le jour du Seigneur: Mystique et pratique du dimanche, Congrès (2e) National de Pastorale Liturgique, Lyon, 1947 (Paris: R. Laffont, 1948), pp. 39-104. In addition to these there are numerous dictionary articles (see bibliography), most of which treat the origin and history of the Sabbath institution. Some lengthy studies have also appeared: Rordorf's book (Sunday) deals with the Sabbath (Sunday) in New Testament and early Christian times, with only an intro-ductory treatment of the Old Testament period. Roger Campiche, "Le Sabbat dans l'Ancient Testament," (dissertation, University of Geneva, 1935), has not yet been accessible to me. In addition to these we have already mentioned Congdon, "Sabbatic Theology," Yamashiro, "A Study of the Hebrew Word Sabbath in Biblical and Talmudic Literatures"; Meesters, Op zoek naar de oorsprong van de Sabbat, pp. 84-164. These three studies, though very extensive, commit the mistake of examining the Sab-bath texts according to their order in the canon, rather than in the sequence of their historical and theological development. Consequently, they have degenerated to becoming simply running commentaries on the texts in question. More recently Kiker ("The Sabbath in the Old Testa-ment Cult") has addressed the more limited question of the origin and early history of the Sabbath in relationship to the Old Testament cultic calendars. For an examination of this treatment, see below, pp. 114-21.

predominates in the Old Testament Sabbath literature.[1] It would be
essential, therefore, to shift the emphasis from an examination of the
Sabbath institution and its observance to an examination of Israel's
contemplation and understanding of it, and the relationship of these to
her historical and religious process. Such is the aim of the present
investigation.

This is not entirely innovative, as we have already noted. It
has frequently enough been suggested that Israel's theological genius in
Mosaic times transformed a taboo day of some kind into a Sabbath for
Yahweh,[2] and that the exilic and postexilic communities came to understand its covenant in terms of the Sabbath and, consequently, made it
into something of a taboo day again.[3] These limited efforts have not,
however, been satisfactory. For example, it is now seriously questioned
if the exile with its defeat, deportation, and cultic deprivation was
really responsible for so many new thoughts about the Sabbath, and its
new strict observance.[4] Secondly, some of the early examinations of the

---

[1]It is also interesting that some of the very early Sabbath
texts (Ex. 23:12; 34:21; Hos. 2:11; Am. 8:5; Is. 1:13) indicate that the
Sabbath is being contemplated, whereas some later texts (Neh. 13:15-22
and most of the texts in Chronicles) merely inform us about Sabbath
observance.

[2]Cf. Bohn, Der Sabbat im Alten Testament, pp. 91ff.; Bostrup,
Den israelitiske Sabbats Oprindelse og Karakter, pp. 50ff.; Bentzen, Den
israelitiske Sabbats Oprindelse og Historie, pp. 30ff., 50-51.

[3]Cf. Bentzen, Den israelitiske Sabbats Oprindelse og Historie,
pp. 74ff.

[4]Cf. the recent suggestion that the milieu of Dt. 5:12-15 is the
Babylonian captivity. Eduard Nielsen, The Ten Commandments in New Perspective: A Traditio-historical Approach, trans. by David J. Bourke,
SBT, Second Series, No. 7 (London: SCM Press Ltd., 1968), p. 40. See,
however, Peter R. Ackroyd, Exile and Restoration: A Study of Hebrew

history of the Sabbath institution, and perhaps some of the later ones

as well, reveal dependence on the Wellhausen structure of Israel's

religious history, but this structure is no longer acceptable, and can-

not be used for Sabbath studies.[1] Thirdly, the studies of the fourth

commandment[2] have tended to ignore other Sabbath laws found elsewhere,

but this is unfortunate, for as we shall see the regulations in the

fourth commandment are closely related to the other Sabbath laws.

Description of this investigation

It is in the light of the above situation that a new attempt is

undertaken to examine the structure and history of the various traditions

which contain Israel's theological contemplations on the Sabbath institu-

tions, as well as information about her Sabbath observance.

The subtitle of this study, "A Tradition-historical Investiga-

tion," indicates that the emphasis is primarily on the Old Testament

literature, and not on the Sabbath institution per se. Within this

---

Thought of the Sixth Century B. C. (Philadelphia: Westminster Press,
1968), pp. 35-36.

[1]Bentzen's high view of the Sabbath in the prophetic (pre-
exilic) period reveals such dependence. This becomes quite clear when
we read that the New Testament "restored" the exilic and postexilic
legalistic Sabbath to its earlier and purer form.

[2]Cf. Jenni, Die theologische Begründung. Although this study is
not limited to the Decalogue passages, it takes its bearing from them.
A recent excellent treatment is provided by A. R. Hulst, "Bemerkungen
zum Sabbatgebot," in Studia Biblica et Semitica: Theodoro Christiano
Vriezen Dedicata, ed. by W. C. van Unnik and A. S. van der Woude (Wagen-
ingen: H. Veenman & Zonen N.V., 1966), pp. 152-64. See also Henning
Graf Reventlow, Gebot und Predikt im Dekalog (Gerd Mohn: Gütersloher
Verlagshaus, 1962), pp. 45-62; Johann Jakob Stamm and Maurice E. Andrew,
The Ten Commandments in Recent Research, SBT, Second Series, No. 2
(London: SCM Press Ltd., 1967), pp. 90-91; Nielsen, The Ten Command-
ments, pp. 37-39, 88-89, 101-3, 112ff.

literature traditions will be isolated. These are "standard" or "customary" written or oral expressions dealing with the Sabbath or some
aspect thereof. Normally a tradition-historical study is thought to be
concerned with the preliterary stage of a body of literature,[1] but this
is too narrow a view for our purposes.

A tradition may be present in either oral or written form. It
will generally have been received by an individual or a community, which
means that it already has a history, and that it is located in a historical situation. It must, of course, also have a beginning, but that is
frequently hidden far behind the present form of the tradition and cannot be laid bare, though in other instances the process whereby a
tradition came into being can be detected, even if tentatively.
Normally the tradition is "passed on" or "transmitted," often without
much change, though it may also be distinctly modified to fit into a new
situation. Sometimes a tradition is severely modified and put to new
use in a new context, or it may even be completely dissolved, so that it
can only be detectable as disjointed elements of a new composition,
which then again may become traditional. It is the purpose of this
study to isolate and examine the Sabbath traditions, their form, content,
transmission, interpretation, and possible final dissolution. This is a
historical process, so we speak of tradition-history, and the history is
that of the community whose traditions are recorded in the Old Testament.

---

[1] Georg Fohrer, Introduction to the Old Testament, trans. by
David E. Green (Nashville: Abingdon Press, 1968), pp. 30, 113; Klaus
Koch, The Growth of the Biblical Tradition: The Form-Critical Method,
trans. by S. M. Cupitt (New York: Charles Scribner's Sons, 1969),
pp. 38ff., 57ff., 78ff.

Normally, traditions are categorized according to their literary form. We shall thus categorize them, but sometimes traditions cross the borders between such literary forms, as is the case with some Sabbath traditions; and we must, therefore, also categorize them according to basic themes, motifs, or content. Consequently, we have chosen six major categories into which the various traditions are fitted, and within which various literary forms are discussed. This is somewhat arbitrary, but serves to further the general overview of the study. The six categories are: (1) the Sabbath and the seventh day; (2) the Sabbath as social institution; (3) the Sabbath as cultic institution; (4) the Sabbath as law; (5) the creation Sabbath; (6) the Sabbath and the covenant. These six categories form chapters in section III of this study entitled, "Interpretation and Tradition."

In practice the Sabbath literature of the Old Testament does, of course, not fall into such a clear pattern as this structure might suggest. A good many Sabbath passages fit neither here nor there. Consequently, this study will not divide up the literature among these categories, each of which represents a particular traditional strand. Rather it will attempt to isolate specific passages which clearly represent "traditional" understandings or practices relative to the Sabbath. Such passages, generally found in the late literature, will be used to establish patterns of thought, to which other texts, perhaps in earlier literature, can be related.

This investigation of the Sabbath traditions is limited to the Old Testament literature. There will be no introductory analysis of the extra-Biblical literature relevant to the origin of the Sabbath. Such studies have already been made with great skill and erudition, and they will not be repeated here. Extra-Biblical literature will, however, be introduced at various points in the discussion, where it may help to illuminate not the Sabbath institution per se, but the Sabbath traditions couched in the Old Testament.

As a tradition-historical study this investigation will concentrate on the literature, not the institution. Consequently, the Sabbath literature will be examined with regard to any textual problems, literary characteristics, date and authorship, et cetera. This analysis will comprise section II of the study, entitled "The Literary Problem."

The final section (IV), entitled "Tradition and History," will attempt to bring some historical order into the material and conclusions of section III. Thus it will both serve as a summary to section III and also provide a conclusion to the study as a whole. It will first examine the traditional watershed in the history of the Old Testament Sabbath traditions, namely, the exile, and then proceed to discuss the traditions after and before this dividing point. A final summary will attempt to sketch the tradition-history of the Old Testament Sabbath.

It will be proposed that the Old Testament Sabbath literature consists far more of transmitted traditional material than created compositions. Some of these traditions were in existence very early, perhaps already in pre-Mosaic times, and remained virtually unchanged, or reappeared in slightly different form in later Old Testament literature. However, new traditions were also formed, particularly in the so-called creative period which has been located sometimes shortly before and during the exile. The early postexilic period also evidences

an awareness of these traditions concerning Sabbath observance, but
apparently they were not taken as seriously by the newly established
community as it is sometimes claimed.

II. THE LITERARY PROBLEM

The first task in a study of this kind is to describe the literature under observation. We now turn to this task. We shall evaluate the textual problems, note the context of the passages where necessary, discuss the literary types involved, and seek to determine authorship and date. We shall begin with the late Sabbath literature. In doing so we follow the general pattern of this study, namely, to begin our observations with the late and generally most extant Sabbath literature, and then to move back to the early and more scarce passages. This sequence also frees us from the monotony of following the familiar path from Genesis to Malachi or Chronicles.

A. Nehemiah

Neh. 9:14

Neh. 9:6-37 consists of a long penitential prayer which is commonly attributed to the Chronicler[1] or to a later redactor.[2] It may

---

[1]Martin Noth, Überlieferungsgeschichtliche Studien (Halle: Max Niemeyer Verlag, 1943), p. 148; Raymond A. Bowman, "Introduction and Exegesis to Ezra and Nehemiah," in The Interpreter's Bible, Vol. III, ed. by George A. Buttrick (New York: Abingdon Press, 1954), p. 746; Charles C. Torrey, The Composition and Historical Value of Ezra-Nehemiah (Giessen: J. Ricker'sche Buchhandlung, 1896), p. 50; Ulrich Kellermann, Nehemia: Quellen, Überlieferung, und Geschichte, BZAW, No. 102 (Berlin: Verlag Alfred Töpelmann, 1967), p. 35; Kurt Galling, Die Bücher der Chronik, Esra, Nehemia, ATD, Vol. XII (Göttingen: Vandenhoeck & Ruprecht, 1954), p. 239; Wilhelm Rudolph, Esra und Nehemia samt 3. Esra, HAT, Vol. XX (Tübingen: Verlag von J. C. B. Mohr [Paul Siebeck], 1949), p. 157; David N. Freedman, "The Chronicler's Purpose," CBQ, XXIII (1961), 436-42.

[2]Sigmund Mowinckel, Studien zu dem Buche Ezra-Nehemia, Vol. I:

21

have existed independently prior to its adoption into the present con-

text.[1] Perhaps it is of cultic provenance,[2] but more likely it is

simply a literary composition which utilizes various material from

Israel's historical traditions, e.g., the Pentateuch as a whole[3] and the

---

Die nachchronistische Redaktion des Buches. Die Listen, Skrifter utgitt
av det Norske Videnskaps-Akademi i Oslo, II Hist.-Filos. Klasse. Ny
Serie. No. 3 (Oslo: Universitetsforlaget, 1964), p. 56; Gustav Hölscher,
"Die Bücher Esra und Nehemia," in Die Heilige Schrift des Alten Testa-
ments, Vol. II, ed. by E. Kautzsch (Tübingen: Verlag J. C. B. Mohr
[Paul Siebeck], 1923), p. 544.

[1]According to Welch it was composed as a litany in north Israel
after the fall of Samaria, and before the return of the exiles in the
south. It is saturated with ideas characteristic of D, says Welch, and
there is a reference to the Assyrian power (vs. 32). Adam C. Welch,
"The Source of Nehemiah IX," ZAW, XLVII (1929), 130-37. Others have
related it to ancient pre-Ezra synagogue liturgies. See Julian Morgenstern, "The Chanukka Festival and the Calendar of Ancient Israel," HUCA,
XX (1947), 20-21; Leon J. Liebreich, "The Impact of Nehemiah 9:5:37 on
the Liturgy of the Synagogue," HUCA, XXXII (1961), 228. Unfortunately,
we have no synagogue liturgies from this period with which to compare
it, and there is scarcely any evidence that it existed as a pre-exilic
Israelite liturgy. On the contrary, the hymn seems to presuppose the
return from captivity (cf. Kellermann, Nehemia, pp. 35-36).

[2]Thus Rudolph, Esra und Nehemia, p. 157; Mowinckel, Studien, I,
58f.; Frieder Ahlemann, "Zur Esra-Quelle," ZAW, LIX (1942-43), 77-98;
Klaus Baltzer, Das Bundesformular, WMANT, No. 4 (2nd ed.; Neukirchen-
Vluyn: Neukirchener Verlag, 1964), p. 54.

[3]Cf. the "historical credos": Dt. 6:20-24; 36:5-9; Jos. 24:2-13;
I Sam. 12:6-11; Ps. 78; 105; 106; 135; Jer. 32:16-25. In 1938 Gerhard
von Rad suggested that the literary form of these credos is very old,
and that the earliest expressions of it (Dt. 6:20-24; 26:5-9) antecede
the Pentateuch as well as provide a germinal form of it. This study was
entitled Das formgeschichtliche Problem des Hexateuch, BWANT, fourth
series, No. 26 (Stuttgart: W. Kohlhammer Verlag, 1938). E. T. "The
Form-Critical Problem of the Hexateuch," in The Problem of the Hexateuch
and Other Essays, trans. by E. W. Trueman Dicken (New York: McGraw-Hill
Book Company, 1966), pp. 1-78. Despite its wide acceptance this thesis
of von Rad is now rejected by some scholars who consider the "historical
credos" to be late compositions based on a completed Pentateuch. For a
recent evaluation of this view, see J. Philip Hyatt, "Were There an
Ancient Historical Credo in Israel and an Independent Sinai Tradition?"
in Translating & Understanding the Old Testament. Essays in Honor of

Deuteronomistic history[1] seem to be well known by the composer of this chapter. Although it was customary for the Chronicler to include such prayers as well as speeches in his history,[2] the present one distinguishes itself from the normal historical surveys in Chronicles by emphasizing the distant past, and by neglecting to mention David and the Davidic dynasty.[3] It is, therefore, quite possible that the basic content of this prayer predates the work of the Chronicler, and it may well reflect the theological thinking in the time of Ezra, or even earlier. Perhaps it originated among the returned Levites who undoubtedly cherished the Deuteronomistic tradition even in postexilic times.[4] Verse 14, concerning the Sabbath, does not militate against such a dating.

Neh. 10:31, 33 (Heb. 10:32, 34)

Literary relationships have been proposed between this chapter

Herbert Gordon May, ed. by Harry Thomas Frank and William L. Reed (Nashville: Abingdon Press, 1970), pp. 152-70.

[1]Cf. the reference to the period of the judges (vss. 26-29). Note also the affirmation that there is not any break in the history of the relationship between God and his people (vs. 32), and that the present postexilic community is a continuation of the old tribal community. See the comments by Martin Noth, "The Laws in the Pentateuch: Their Assumption and Meaning," in The Laws in the Pentateuch and Other Studies, trans. by D. R. Ap-Thomas (Philadelphia: Fortress Press, 1966), pp. 81-83; von Rad, "The Form-Critical Problem of the Hexateuch," pp. 12-13.

[2]Cf. I Chr. 29:10-19; II Chr. 20:6-12; Ezra 9:6-15.

[3]Cf. Freedman, "The Chronicler's Purpose," p. 440.

[4]See Noth, "The Laws in the Pentateuch," p. 81; Kellermann, Nehemia, pp. 36-37; Gerhard von Rad, "The Levitical Sermon in I and II Chronicles," in The Problem of the Hexateuch, pp. 267-80.

and (1) the Ezra-Memoirs,[1] (2) the Nehemiah-Memoirs,[2] and (3) the work

of the Chronicler or a secondary chronicler serving as editor of the

---

[1]This proposal is now abandoned by most scholars. There is no gap in the Ezra source into which the chapter would suitably fit, and Ezra himself is conspicuously absent from Neh. 10. Thus Sigmund Mowinckel, Studien zu dem Buche Ezra-Nehemia, Vol. III: Die Ezrageschichte und das Gesetz Moses, Skrifter utgitt av det Norske Videnskaps-Akademi i Oslo, II. Hist.-Filos. Klasse. Ny Serie. No. 7 (Oslo: Universitetsforlaget, 1965), p. 143; Galling, Die Bücher der Chronik, p. 239. Exception to this view is taken by Alfred Jepsen, "Nehemia 10," ZAW, LXVI (1954), 101: "Es findet sich eine Urkunde, die zu dem werk Esras, wie es uns überliefert ist, gut zu passen scheint." It is possible that Neh. 8-9 represent the Chronicler's reworking of material from the Ezra-Memoirs. Cf. Otto Eissfeldt, The Old Testament: An Introduction, trans. by Peter R. Ackroyd (New York: Harper and Row, Publishers, 1965), p. 548. However, some scholars believe that this cannot be said about Neh. 10 which is unrelated to the preceding chapters. Thus Mowinckel, Studien, I, 53; Alfred Bertholet, Die Bücher Esra und Nehemia, KHC, Vol. XIX (Tübingen: Verlag von J. C. B. Mohr [Paul Siebeck], 1902), p. 76. Other scholars assume some kind of unity (not literary) between these chapters without considering them a part of the original Ezra-Memoirs. Noth, Überlieferungsgeschichtliche Studien, pp. 148-49; Torrey, The Composition, pp. 34, 50; Kellermann, Nehemia, p. 27; Rudolph, Esra und Nehemia, p. 157; Baltzer, Das Bundesformular, p. 51.

[2]Cf. Loring W. Batten, The Books of Ezra and Nehemiah, ICC, Vol. XII (New York: Charles Scribner's Sons, 1913), p. 373; Bertholet, Esra und Nehemia, p. 76; Artur Weiser, The Old Testament: Its Formation and Development, trans. by Dorthea M. Barton (New York: Association Press, 1961), p. 321; Rudolph, Esra und Nehemia, p. 173; Jacob M. Myers, Ezra, Nehemiah, AB, Vol. XIV (New York: Doubleday & Company, Inc., 1965), pp. 174-75. The argument is based on the proposal that the regulations in Neh. 10 correspond to the situation in Neh. 13, especially regarding the situation in the temple, mixed marriages, and the Sabbath. Militating against a literary relationship between the two chapters are the following points: (1) Neh. 10 does not have the style of the Nehemia-Denkschrift (Neh. 13), Mowinckel, Studien, III, 143-44; (2) Neh. 10 is full of concepts and words characteristic of the Chronicler, Kellermann, Nehemia, p. 41; (3) its emphasis on the cult is foreign to Neh. 13, Kellermann, Nehemia, p. 40; (4) the community's relationship to the people of the land and the Sabbath observance do not correspond in the two chapters, Jepsen, "Nehemia 10," pp. 101ff. Mowinckel concludes: "Es gibt es überhaupt keinen anderen Grund zu dem Versuch, Neh 10 mit EG oder mit N zu verbinden, als dass der nachchronistische Redaktor das Dokument hier in einem von ihm selbst gemachten sekundären Zusammenhang angebracht hat; d. h. es gibt keinen Grund." (Studien, III, 144).

whole Ezra-Nehemiah complex.[1] The third solution takes best account of the context and style of the chapter as a whole.[2] We therefore attribute it to the Chronicler or his associates who shaped the whole Ezra-Nehemiah narrative.

The historical relationships, however, are quite another matter. If we assume that the chapter is from the hand of the Chronicler, we cannot conclude that he spun it out of whole cloth. To answer the question of the historical situation of the chapter, we must first ask about its content and purpose. The suggestion that it originated among faithful Israelites in Judah prior to the return of the exiles has no textual evidence to support it and must be rejected.[3] There are three remaining proposals: It belongs (1) in the time of Nehemiah,[4] (2) in the time of

---

[1]Thus Mowinckel, Studien, III, 145; Kellermann, Nehemia, p. 41; Eissfeldt, Introduction, p. 549; Torrey, The Composition, p. 40; Noth, Überlieferungsgeschichtliche Studien, p. 148; cf. Rudolph, Esra und Nehemia, p. 173; Bowman, "Ezra and Nehemiah," p. 757. The date of the chapter's composition (Torrey) or adaptation from an old source (Bowman, Eissfeldt, Kellermann, Mowinckel, Rudolph) depends on the date given to the Chronicler or his associate, i.e., sometimes in the fourth century, B. C.

[2]Cf. the recent discussions in Jepsen, "Nehemia 10," pp. 97ff.; Kellermann, Nehemia, pp. 37ff.; Mowinckel, Studien, III, 142ff.

[3]Adam C. Welch, "The Share of N. Israel in the Restoration of the Temple Worship," ZAW, XLVIII (1930), 186. However, the chapter is unquestionably postexilic. The cultic regulations presuppose the second temple, and the identification of the "people of the land" with foreigners and disloyal Jews is characteristic of the time of Ezra and Nehemiah. Cf. Hubertus C. M. Vogt, Studie zur nachexilischen Gemeinde in Esra-Nehemia (Werl: Dietrich Coelde Verlag, 1966), p. 154.

[4]Bertholet, Esra und Nehemia, p. 76; Rudolph, Esra und Nehemia, p. 173. According to this view Neh. 10 contains the obligations placed on the people as a result of the digressions recorded in Neh. 13.

Ezra,[1] or (3) at some time after Ezra and Nehemiah.[2] The choice between these options is not easy. However, it does seem that there is no good reason for insisting that its milieu is later than that of Ezra and Nehemiah.[3] We will assume then that the historical situation reflected in this chapter is that of the latter part of the fifth century B.C. Originally it may have existed independently of the official Ezra and Nehemiah documents, but for all we know, verses 31 and 33 contain likely community obligations at this time.

Neh. 13:15-22

These verses belong to the Nehemiah-Memoirs,[4] a literary source which is characterized by several traits, the most important of which is

---

[1]Jepsen, "Nehemia 10," p. 101. "So gut also die Urkunde zu Ezra passt, so wenig im Grunde als Abschluss der Arbeit Nehemias." But while Neh. 10 fits the time of Ezra, and not that of Nehemiah, it also gives evidence of belonging before Nehemiah's time. From this Jepsen concludes that Ezra preceded Nehemiah historically, as also the Chronicler would have us believe (pp. 101-04).

[2]Cf. Mowinckel, Studien, III, 155; Kellermann, Nehemia, pp. 40-41. Though the Chronicler knew of the Ezra and Nehemiah sources, he radically restructured the material in the light of his own situation. The emphasis on the cult, total separation from the people of the land in marriage, and the strict Sabbath regulations indicate to Kellermann that the chapter looks back on Neh. 13 from a later time (the fourth century B.C.). Mowinckel suggests that the clear distinction between the community and the "people of the land" takes us to a time after Ezra, where Ezra is dated in the time of Artaxerxes II, or ca. 398/7 B.C. (Studien, III, 165).

[3]We cannot discuss the chronology of Ezra and Nehemiah here, but if we are to follow the likely traditional position that the two men were contemporaries, at least for a time, then the latter part of the fifth century B.C. would be the general period in question. The emphasis on the temple cult and the call for total separation from the people of the land (notably the Samaritans) are not impossible at this time.

[4]Kellermann, Nehemia, p. 48; Rudolph, Esra und Nehemia, p. 203; Bertholet, Esra und Nehemia, p. 90; Galling, Die Bücher der Chronik,

a recurrent call by the author for remembrance, viz., "Remember me, O my God, for good," or the like.[1] It is also generally agreed that the author of this source is Nehemiah himself,[2] or at least that it accurately reflects the character of this man and his work.[3] Consequently, we can locate the source in Jerusalem and date it towards the end of, or just after, the completion of Nehemiah's terms in office during the last quarter of the fifth century B.C.[4] Recent studies have revealed that the literary form of this source, although it is unique in the Old Testament, shows affinities with Near Eastern royal inscriptions,[5] and with

---

p. 253; Bowman, "Ezra and Nehemiah," p. 804; Gerhard von Rad, "Die Nehemia-Denkschrift," ZAW, LXXVI (1964), 187; Sigmund Mowinckel, Studien zu den Buche Ezra-Nehemia, Vol. II: Die Nehemia-Denkschrift, Skrifter utgitt av det Norske Videnskaps-Akademi i Oslo, II. Hist.-Filos. Klasse. Ny Serie. No. 1 (Oslo: Universitetsforlaget, 1964), p. 86; Noth, Überlieferungsgeschichtliche Studien, p. 131; Weiser, The Old Testament, p. 321; Fohrer, Introduction, p. 243; Eissfeldt, Introduction, p. 547.

[1]Neh. 5:19; 13:14, 22, 31; cf. Neh. 6:14; 13:29.

[2]An exception is Torrey who attributes Neh. 13 as a whole to the Chronicler (The Composition, pp. 48-49).

[3]Mowinckel suggests that Nehemiah, like most ancient rulers, was not a man of letters, and that a scribe wrote it in the total spirit of Nehemiah (Studien, II, 85-86).

[4]The first term lasted from 445/4-433 B.C. (20.-32. year of Artaxerxes [465-424 B.C.], Neh. 5:14). A second term, if it took place, must have begun prior to 424 B.C., since it too was initiated under Artaxerxes (Neh. 13:6). Kellermann has argued that Nehemiah held only one term in office in Jerusalem, since the situation in Neh. 13, of the so-called second term, fits much better in the beginning of the first term of Nehemiah's office (Nehemia, pp. 151-54). Cf. Mowinckel, Studien, III, 152-53.

[5]Cf. Sigmund Mowinckel, "Die vorderasiatischen Königs- und Fürsteninschriften," in Eucharisterion, H. Gunkel zum 60. Geburtstage, I, ed. by Hans Schmidt, FRLANT, No. 36 (Göttingen: Vandenhoeck & Ruprecht, 1923), pp. 278-322.

biographical inscriptions (often in tombs) of high Egyptian officials.[1]

It is suggested that such writings were deposited in sanctuaries, or placed in tombs, where they would be most accessible to the diety, or would benefit their authors the most. However, it would seem likely that Nehemiah's memoirs were designated for human readers as well. In any case, the document is characterized by an unashamed self-centeredness and absolute confidence in the worth of its author's endeavors which in our passage are directed towards the problem of Sabbath observance.

This leads us to a more difficult question, namely, to what extent verses 15-22 contain secondary material. It has become apparent in the light of recent studies that the strong arguments for secondary material in verse 15b are unfounded,[2] and attempts to discredit the

---

[1]Von Rad, "Die Nehemia-Denkschrift," p. 181. It is maintained here that Neh. 13 in particular has preserved the original form of such Denkschriften, whereas Neh. 1-7 tend to expand it into epic style.

[2]Cf. Mowinckel, Studien, II, 39-41; Hölscher, Esra und Nehemia, p. 560. The literary problems involve the use of ʾāᶜîd (I warned) which is considered too weak a verb as compared with the "authentic ʾārîbāh (I remonstrated) in vs. 17; the use of yôm haššabbāt (The Sabbath Day) rather than the "original" haššabbāt (the Sabbath); the fact that ʾāᶜîd has no object, as we would expect; the uncertainty about the meaning of ṣayid. It is quite correct that ᶜwd is a weaker word than ryb and is less dynamic. However, its quiet warning does call for serious considerations, cf. its use in Gen. 43:3; Ps. 50:7, 81:9; Neh. 9:26, 29, 34; 13:21; Ex. 19:21. It is translated "admonish," "protest," "bear witness," and "inculcate," (einschärfen), Ludwig Koehler and Walter Baumgartner, Lexicon in Veteris Testamenti Libros, 1958, p. 686; Wilhelm Gesenius and Frants Buhl, Handwörterbuch über das Alte Testament, 17th ed., 1949, p. 568. In this sense the verb is not inappropriate even to a man of Nehemiah's temperament. Moreover, it recurs in vs. 21 which is surely genuine. Yôm haššabbāt is not a secondary expression, for it occurs in the clearly authentic vss. 17 and 19. We must rather assume that it serves to place emphasis on the Sabbath as opposed to all other days. Cf. Kellermann, Nehemia, p. 52. The Syriac and Arabic versions insert an object (bām) for the verb (followed by Rudolph, Esra und

reference to the Tyrian tradesmen (vs. 16) are not convincing.[1] It has

also been accurately observed that the phrases "Judah and Jerusalem,"

Nehemia, p. 203; Bowman, "Ezra and Nehemiah," p. 812). However, the harder reading without the object is both terse and effective, and should not be emended. At any rate mikrām can be made the object for the verb. Ṣayid is a difficult word to translate. It is omitted in the Greek, Latin, and Ethiopic versions (cf. Bowman, "Ezra and Nehemiah," p. 812: "I bore witness against them that they should not sell"). Its basic meaning is "hunting," "game," and secondarily "provision," "food," according to Koehler and Baumgartner, Lexicon, p. 801. Mowinckel argues that "game" is more appropriate (Studien,II, 40), though this does not fit the context very easily. However, it is quite clear that Neh. 13:15 is concerned both with farm work and with trade on the Sabbath, and it is precisely this fact, more than lexicographical and syntactical problems, which causes offense in the mind of some scholars. Can we have authentic verses (15b-16) dealing with trade between vs. 15 and vs. 17 both of which are concerned with work in the fields? asks Mowinckel. He does not think so and assumes that the nobles (vs. 17) are blamed for allowing their fields to be worked and provisions to be brought in house on the Sabbath (Studien, II, 39-40). Consequently, hunting game, not trading food, would be a suitable parallel to the first noticed Sabbath profanation, namely, working in the fields. However, there is no good reason for the assumption that trading was in fact not part of the original issue, so that the translation "hunting," "game" in no way improves the passage.

[1]It has frequently been claimed that the reference to the men of Tyre (vs. 16) is secondary on the assumption that (1) Tyrian tradesmen did not operate in Nehemiah's time (Mowinckel, Studien, II, 41); (2) these foreigners have no place in Nehemiah's controversy (Batten, Ezra and Nehemiah, p. 298); (3) Neh. 13:16 is directly dependent on Neh. 10: 31 which is not from the Nehemiah source (Gustav Jahn, Die Bücher Esra (A und B) und Nehemja [Leiden: E. J. Brill, 1909], p. 171; cf. Galling, Die Bücher der Chronik, p. 253). However, their temporary or permanent presence in Judah (bāh may refer to Judah as well as to Jerusalem) is accepted as plausible by several exegetes. Thus Bertholet, Esra und Nehemia, p. 92; Myers, Ezra, Nehemiah, p. 210; Bowman, "Ezra and Nehemiah," pp. 812-13; Kellermann, Nehemia, p. 52. "Tyrische Handelsniederlassungen in den Grenzgebieten Judas sind für die Perserzeit durchaus denkbar." Additional information on the traders is gathered by Jacob M. Myers, "Some Considerations Bearing on the Date of Joel," ZAW, LXXIV (1962), 178-90. We conclude, therefore, that Tyrian tradesmen might well have operated in Judah at this time. Moreover, Neh. 13 is not dependent on Neh. 10; at least we have found no literary dependence. Finally, trading does in fact concern Nehemiah, and so do the traders, whatever their nationality, for his actions are directed against those who carry goods through the gates, and only indirectly against the

and "in this city," and verses 17-18 as a whole appear to be influenced by the Deuteronomistic or perhaps the Chronicler's style.[1] However, these verses fit very well in the context, and it is quite possible that Nehemiah here, as elsewhere, slips into the style of the Deuteronomistic-Levitical circles.[2] The most seriously questioned part of the whole pericope is verse 22a, and it may indeed be secondary, though not necessarily.[3] Finally, verse 19 presents some difficulties, especially with regard to the verb ṣālᵃlû,[4] but there is no reason to consider it

_____

prospective recipients of the wares. It is the working farmers, not the Tyrian tradesmen, who escape his strictures.

[1]Cf. Torrey, The Composition, pp. 48-49; Jahn, Die Bücher Esra, p. 172; et al.

[2]"Nehemia spricht also hier wie in 1:5ff. nicht seine eigene Sprache" (Kellermann, Nehemia, p. 53).

[3]It is generally assigned to the Chronicler who wanted to find a role for the Levites. Thus Batten, Ezra and Nehemiah, p. 297; Mowinckel, Studien, II, 41. Rudolph considers it original with Nehemiah (Esra und Nehemia, pp. 207-8). It is a question, however, if the Chronicler would have created such a secular work for the Levites, whereas Nehemiah might not have had any scruples about doing so. Besides Levites, but not laymen, could be sanctified for Sabbath work. Thus Bowman, "Ezra and Nehemiah," p. 814; Myers, Ezra, Nehemiah, p. 216.

[4]Various explanations have been given of this difficult word. (1) The LXX reads katéstisan which may mean "set up" and apply to the doors of the gate. (2) Another suggestion associates ṣālᵃlû with "darkness," perhaps related to the Accadian ṣillu meaning "shadow," "shaded place." See The Assyrian Dictionary (Chicago: The Oriental Institute, 1956-), Vol. ṣ, pp. 189ff. The meaning would then be, "when it became dark in the gate," or "when the shadows became long in the gate," the gate being here an elaborate, elongated structure, not just a door. Cf. Bertholet, Esra und Nehemia, p. 92; Rudolph, Esra und Nehemia, p. 203. (3) The verb may also be associated with the Accadian ṣalālu which means "lie asleep," "fall asleep," "inactive." It is used about cities and places of transport, like a port. The following illustrations of its use are noted in The Assyrian Dictionary, Vol. s, p. 69, par. 2. URU-GN . . . ēnaḫma iṣ-lal (the city of Calah fell in ruins and lies deserted); ṣa-lil nēbiru ṣa-lil kāru mārē mallāhi kališunu ṣal-lu (asleep is the ferry, asleep the pier, all the sailors are fast asleep).

secondary (thus Mowinckel). Its meaning is fairly clear; it refers to the time of Nehemiah's precautionary activities at the gates just prior to the onset of the Sabbath.

B. Jeremiah and Lamentations

Jer. 17:19-27

The textual problems in this passage are not directly related to the references to the Sabbath and will not be discussed here. However, the question of the provenance of this single Sabbath passage in Jeremiah merits some attention. Generally speaking, the passage is attributed to a secondary hand.[1] It is argued that its style is Deuteronomic, and that its concern with cultic regulations (cessation of work

Cf. Jahn, Die Bücher Esra, p. 172; Bowman, "Ezra and Nehemiah," p. 813; Myers, Ezra, Nehemiah, p. 210. All of these understand the gates to be quiet or empty at the onset of the Sabbath. Thus also the Vulgate (quievissent). The meaning would be that Nehemiah closed the doors in the gates, when these were quiet and empty at the end of the day before the Sabbath.

[1] Sigmund Mowinckel, Zur Komposition des Buches Jeremia (Kristiania [Oslo]: Jacob Dybwad, 1914), p. 49; Bernhard Duhm, Das Buch Jeremia, KHC, Vol. XI (Tübingen: Verlag von J. C. B. Mohr [Paul Siebeck], 1901), pp. 149-50; Paul Voltz, Studien zum Text des Jeremia (Leipzig: J. C. Hinrichs'sche Buchhandlung, 1920), pp. 151-52; Adam C. Welch, The Book of Jeremiah (London: National Adult School Union, 1928), p. 47; Artur Weiser, Das Buch Jeremia, Kapitel 1-25:13, ATD, Vol. XX (5th ed.; Göttingen: Vandenheock & Ruprecht, 1966), p. 149; Herbert G. May, "Towards an Objective Approach to the Book of Jeremiah: The Biographer," JBL, LXI (1942), 150-51; Carl H. Cornill, Das Buch Jeremia (Leipzig: Chr. Herm. Tauchnitz, 1905), p. 219; Jean Steinmann, Le prophète Jérémie: Sa vie, son ouvre et son temp (Paris: Les Éditions du Cerf, 1952), p. 301; John W. Miller, Das Verhältnis Jeremias und Hesekiels sprachlich und theologisch untersucht (Assen: Van Gorcum & Comp., 1955), p. 53; Wilhelm Rudolph, Jeremia, HAT, Vol. XII (2nd ed.; Tübingen: Verlag von J. C. B. Mohr [Paul Siebeck], 1958), p. 109, J. Philip Hyatt, "Introduction and Exegesis to Jeremiah," in The Interpreter's Bible, Vol. V, ed. by George A. Buttrick (New York: Abingdon Press, 1956), pp. 958-59.

and perhaps trade on the Sabbath) are contrary to the spirit of Jeremiah and belong at a later time, e.g., the time of Ezra and Nehemiah (Neh. 13: 15-22). However, recent studies have questioned this radical insistence on unauthenticity, arguing that Deuteronomic traits and style do not mititate against the view that the passage is from the time and environment of Jeremiah.[1] It has further been suggested that its language is not postexilic,[2] that the content of the prose sermons generally speaking does not falsify the ideas of Jeremiah,[3] and that consequently a

---

[1]Deuteronomic characteristics (repetitions, usage of certain words, expressions, viewpoints, and style) are in fact to be expected at the time covered by the activities of Jeremiah, whether he began his career in 626/7 B.C., as it is generally assumed, or in 609 B.C. (cf. J. Philip Hyatt, "The Beginning of Jeremiah's Prophecy," ZAW, LXXVIII [1966], 204-14). We must assume that Jeremiah was acquainted with the first edition of Deuteronomy in some way. It has been suggested by John Bright that if Jeremiah in a moment of less poetic rapture should have resorted to prose, perhaps in a sermon, he might well have used Deuteronomic prose, as preachers must customarily have done at this time ("The Date of the Prose Sermons of Jeremiah," JBL, LXX [1951], 15-35). That Jer. 17:19-27 is Deuteronomic in character cannot be doubted, but "Deuteronomic" does not necessarily make the passage late and unauthentic.

[2]The close association of this passage with postexilic literature, notably Nehemiah, Deutero-Isaiah, Trito-Isaiah, and Zechariah (May, Cornill, Voltz, Duhm, Welch, et al., above, n. 1, p. 31), has been rejected by Bright, "The Date of the Prose Sermons of Jeremiah." He demonstrates that the language of Jeremiah's prose sermons, including Jer. 17:19-27, is in fact not typical of postexilic literature, or even of D^2 (the postexilic redaction of Deuteronomy). This means that the Deuteronomic influences in Jer. 17:19-27 belong better in Jeremiah's own time or shortly thereafter, than in a much later period.

[3]Bright rejects the idea that the Deuteronomistic editor of the prose sermons in any way misrepresents or produces major distortions of the authentic Jeremiah ("The Date of the Prose Sermons of Jeremiah," pp. 28-29). This position he has more recently maintained with some caution. Cf. John Bright, Jeremiah, AB, Vol. XXI (New York: Doubleday & Company, Inc., 1965), p. lxxii. Some of the Deuteronomic sermons, viz., the temple sermon (Jer. 7) oppose traditional Deuteronomic theories. Moreover, the similarities between Jer. 7 and Jer. 17:19-27 are remarkable enough for us not to assume that two very different

kernel of our passage may derive from Jeremiah himself.[1]

If the Deuteronomic character does not necessarily make the passage unauthentic in its entirety, we must ask if not the so-called strict, external, or legalistic emphasis on the Sabbath makes it impossible to attribute any of it to Jeremiah.[2] To examine this question carefully would be impossible in this context, but a few observations may help clarify the issue. (1) The crucial question for a critical evaluation of the origin of this passage is not whether Jeremiah could have said it, but whether there is any evidence that it could only have been said in postexilic times, e.g., in the time of Nehemiah. No such evidence is present. (2) The demands for Sabbath observance are in fact not so very strict, for they only require that people do not carry burdens, wares, or tools past the gates, and out of their houses, i.e., that they do not work. But they are apparently free to do anything else inside or outside their houses and the city.[3] (3) The real offense in

---

traditions were responsible for these two sermons. Bright therefore concludes that the Deuteronomic sermons fairly accurately reflect the ideas of Jeremiah.

[1]Cf. Rudolph, Jeremia, p. 109; Steinmann, Jérémie, p. 301; Weiser, Jeremia, p. 149; John Bright, Jeremiah, p. 120; Elmer A. Leslie, Jeremiah: Chronologically Arranged, Translated, and Interpreted (Nashville: Abingdon Press, 1954), p. 316; A. Aeschimann, Le prophète Jérémie (Paris: Delachauz & Niestle, 1959), p. 121; W. Emery Barnes, "Prophecy and the Sabbath: A Note on the Teaching of Jeremiah," JThS, XXIX (1928), 386-90; Albert Condamin, Le livre de Jérémie (Paris: Librairie Lecoffre, 1936), p. 150; et al. The last two studies attribute the Sabbath passage in its present form to Jeremiah.

[2]It is generally assumed by modern scholarship that the prophet's only concern was, in the words of Condamin (Jérémie, p. 149), "les bonnes disposition du coeur," and that the author of the present Sabbath passage "loves the cult in detail" (Hyatt, "Jeremiah," p. 958).

[3]Prohibitions against work on the Sabbath were known among the

this passage is that so much is made to depend on this single regulation, namely, the king's well-being (vs. 25), the survival of the city (vs. 27), its prosperity (vs. 26), and the very lives of its inhabitants (vs. 21).[1] In the light of all this, what can be said about the origin of this passage?

The most satisfactory solution to this question will recognize the strong Deuteronomic traits in the passage. This fact, together with a consideration of its content, should not, however, lead us to propose a late, postexilic date for it. We can be quite certain that the passage should not be dated later than the middle of the sixth century B.C. Should these verses be associated with Jeremiah in any way? It is possible that we are dealing with words and ideas of the prophet, as they were understood or misunderstood by his disciples. To seek the ipsissima verba of the prophet by textual surgery would in the nature of the case be futile. However, although the passage may be a sheer fabrication by one of Jeremiah's disciples, its early date suggests that its content may not be in total disagreement with the ideas of the prophet. And so it seems possible, even if this cannot be demonstrated, that this passage originated in some form or another with Jeremiah.

---

older prophets (Am. 8:5). They are, of course, also present in the Decalogue (Ex. 20:8-11; Dt. 5:12-15), and in Ex. 23:12; 34:21. Note also Jeremiah's own concern with the law (Jer. 7:5f., 8-9; 22:13-19).

[1]Bᵉnapšôtêkem (for the sake of your lives) could also be translated "at the risk/peril of your lives" (cf. II Sam. 23:17). See Cornill, Jeremia, p. 219.

Lam. 2:6

The first verse in this strophe is textually complicated, though
the general meaning is clear. Yahweh has extended his destructive force
to the very temple, the place of festivals and of cultic personnel. The
second verse which is equally terse may be accurately translated:
Yahweh has caused festival and Sabbath to be forgotten in Zion.[1]

There is general agreement among scholars today that Lam. 2, in
which this strophe occurs, must have been written shortly after 587 B.C.,
while the actual destruction of Jerusalem was vividly remembered by the
author.[2]

---

[1]Sikkah is the pi⁽el form which has a causative meaning (Koehler
and Baumgartner, Lexicon, p. 969). The qal active form is more common
of course, but Theodore H. Robinson's suggested emendation in Biblia
Hebraica, 3rd. (sakah for sikkah, with the addition of ꜣet ꜣašer ⁽asah)
on the basis of LXX does not improve the verse, nor make any more sense.
That Yahweh has caused these festivals to be forgotten is adequate
explanation for the termination of their celebration. Cf. Brevard S.
Childs, Memory and Tradition in Israel, SBT, No. 37 (London: SCM Press
Ltd., 1962), pp. 31-44.

[2]The tradition that Jeremiah is the author of Lamentations,
traced to LXX and the Targum, is now rejected by most scholars on internal evidence, but it is generally agreed that at least chs. 2, 4, and 5
come from the time immediately following the destruction of Jerusalem
(587/6 B.C.) and were written by an eyewitness. Cf. Eissfeldt, Introduction, p. 503; Fohrer, Introduction, p. 298; Weiser, The Old
Testament, p. 306; Wilhelm Rudolph, Das Buch Ruth, Das Hohe Lied, Die
Klagelieder, KAT, Vol. XVII (Gerd Mohn: Gütersloher Verlagshaus, 1963),
p. 193; Artur Weiser, "Klagelieder," in Helmer Ringgren, Artur Weiser,
and Walther Zimmerli, Spruche, Prediger, Das Hohe Lied, Klagelieder, Das
Buch Ester, ATD, Vol. XVI (2nd ed.; Göttingen: Vandenhoeck & Ruprecht,
1967), p. 301; Max Haller, Die fünf Megilloth, HAT, Vol. XVIII (Tübingen:
Verlag von J. C. B. Mohr [Paul Siebeck], 1940), p. 93; Theophile J. Meek,
"Introduction and Exegesis to Lamentations," in The Interpreter's Bible,
Vol. VI, ed. by George A. Buttrick (New York: Abingdon Press, 1956),
p. 5; Norman K. Gottwald, Studies in the Book of Lamentations, SBT, No.
14 (London: SCM Press Ltd., 1954), p. 21; Hans-Joachim Kraus,
Klagelieder [Threni], BK, Vol. XX (Neukirchen-Vluyn: Neukirchener Verlag, 1956), p. 11. Kraus dates all five chapters immediately after the
587/6 B.C. catastrophe.

C. III Isaiah

Is. 56:1-8

This passage introduces the so-called Trito-Isaiah which, in distinction from Deutero-Isaiah, originated in Jerusalem after the exile.[1] It is concerned primarily with the position of foreigners and eunuchs in the community, and repeatedly insists that one thing which must be done by every member of the community is "to keep the Sabbath from profaning it" (vss. 2, 4, 6). When should these verses be dated?[2]

(1) The prominence of the Sabbath suggests to most interpreters a post-exilic date, and a late one at that,[3] partly because of the general

---

[1]It is generally agreed that Is. 56-66 consist of prophetic oracles belonging to a prophet or a circle of prophets identified as Trito-Isaiah. Exceptions to this view are taken by conservative scholars who attribute Is. 1-66 to Isaiah of Jerusalem, and by scholars who characterize Is. 40-66 as Deutero-Isaianic. Cf. Charles C. Torrey, The Second Isaiah (New York: Charles Scribner's Sons, 1928). Meesters maintains that the individual(s) responsible for Is. 40-66, including the Sabbath passages, were commentators on genuine Isaiah traditions and produced documents similar to 1QpHab. of the Qumran community. He concludes that Is. 56:1-8; 58:13 contain a kernel of Isaianic material, and that Is. 66:23 is an authentic Isaiah oracle (Op zoek naar de oorsprong van de Sabbat, n. 1, p. 28, pp. 148-51).

[2]Attempts to separate vss. 1-2 from vss. 3-8 are frustrated by the similar function of the Sabbath in vss. 2, 4, 6. See, however, Claus Westermann, Das Buch Jesaja: Kapitel 40-66, ATD, Vol. XIX (Göttingen: Vandenhoeck & Ruprecht, 1966), pp. 248-49. This suggests that at least vss. 2-8 belong to the pericope. Whether or not vs. 1 belongs also depends on whether or not righteousness and salvation precede the requirements of the law in the mind of the author. Cf. James Muilenburg, "Introduction and Exegesis to Isaiah 40-66," in The Interpreter's Bible, Vol. V, ed. by George A. Buttrick (New York: Abingdon Press, 1956), p. 653; Ludwig Glahn, Der Prophet der Heimkehr: Jesaja 40-66 (Copenhagen: Levin & Munksgaard, 1934), p. 37. There is no a priori reason for denying that Is. 56 may have shared this high view of salvation and righteousness with Deutero-Isaiah.

[3]It is normally dated sometimes in the fifth century B.C. Cf. Fohrer, Introduction, p. 385; Eissfeldt, Introduction, p. 443; Weiser,

assumption that the Sabbath became a unique institution in postexilic times,[1] and partly because Deutero-Isaiah, who spoke during the exile, makes no mention of it.[2] (2) The main concern of this passage is with foreigners and eunuchs, individuals who would normally be excluded from the community (Dt. 23:1-7). Since it is difficult to imagine a discussion of the acceptance of such individuals into the community at the time of Ezra and Nehemiah during the second half of the fifth century, it is necessary to think of the early fifth century,[3] or even the late sixth century B.C.[4] as providing the most suitable milieu for these verses. The late sixth century B.C. would, in fact, provide a very likely occasion for Is. 56:1-8. Among the exiles contemplating return were undoubtedly many eunuchs and foreigners who were attached to the

The Old Testament, p. 207; Torrey, The Second Isaiah, p. 439; Westermann, Das Buch Jesaja, p. 244.

[1]Westermann argues that the Sabbath served in postexilic times as a criterion of orthodoxy, and that Is. 56:3-8 reflects this. "Der Sabbat der im Exil zum Bekenntniszeichen geworden war, bekommt nach dem Exil darüber hinaus die Bedeutung eines entscheidenden Kriteriums für die Rechtgläubigkeit." Westermann, Das Buch Jessaja, p. 248. It is not at all clear on which side of 539 B.C. Is. 56:1-8 is placed by this distinction. That is especially true about vss. 1-2 which are more Deutero-Isaianic than vss. 3-8 (Bernhard Duhm, Das Buch Jesaja Übersetz und erklärt, HK, Pt. III, Vol. I [4th ed.; Göttingen: Vandenhoeck & Ruprecht, 1922], p. 419).

[2]Such an argument is of little value, but it is an accurate observation that the mood in these verses (cult, law, Sabbath, sacrifices, temple, and prayer) is different from what we find in Deutero-Isaiah. Cf. Muilenburg, "Isaiah 40-66," p. 653; Westermann, Das Buch Jesaja, p. 248. However, it is unnecessary to judge these verses a later addition simply because the Sabbath is mentioned. Cf. Torrey, The Second Isaiah, p. 439; Duhm, Das Buch Jesaja, p. 419.

[3]See above, n. 1.

[4]Cf. Muilenburg, "Isaiah 40-66," pp. 653-54; Glahn, Der Prophet der Heimkehr, pp. 30-31.

community by marriage, or perhaps as a result of the general displace-
ment of persons during the war. It is only natural that these persons
would be concerned about their role in the restored community. This
concern would be especially acute during the very early decades of the
returning process, and Is. 56:1-8 would provide an answer to the questions of these persons.

The reading in 1QIsa[a] reveals a marked difference in the word
order of verse 6, but the general sense of the verse is not changed
thereby as far as the Sabbath is concerned.

Is. 58:13

Is. 58:13-14 have suffered the same fate as Is. 56:1-8. These
verses have been judged a secondary addition by many commentators.[1] An
analysis of Is. 58 as a whole is likely to reveal, however, that verses
13-14 are an integral part of the chapter which would be left like a
torso upon their exclusion.[2] Without engaging in such an analysis which
would take us beyond the concerns of this study, two observations will
illustrate this point. (1) The concern in Is. 58 with true worship
(fast) is climaxed by the reference to the Sabbath, the very important
religious institution in exilic and postexilic times.[3] (2) There is no

---

[1]Cf. Eissfeldt, Introduction, p. 443; Karl Marti, Das Buch
Jesaja, KHC, Vol. X (Tübingen: Verlag von J. C. B. Mohr [Paul Siebeck],
1900), p. 373; Westermann, Das Buch Jesaja, p. 271; Duhm, Das Buch
Jesaja, p. 440.

[2]Muilenburg, "Isaiah 40-66," p. 677.

[3]Muilenburg compares the climaxing role of the Sabbath in
Is. 58:13 with the one which it occupies in the creation account (Gen.
2:1-3). "Isaiah 40-66," p. 677.

conflict between the so-called social concern of verses 1-12 and the
cultic interest in verses 13-14, for the genuine observance of the Sabbath is precisely to refrain from "seeking one's own pleasure" (cf.
vs. 3), i.e., the call to Sabbath observance does not stand in opposi-
tion to the call for a genuine fast.[1] For these reasons there is no
need to locate verses 13-14 in the fifth century B.C., or even later.
Muilenburg is probably quite right when he compares them to Deutero-
Isaiah and Zechariah and dates them 538-520 B.C.[2]

Is. 66:23

This verse is particularly difficult to date, for it describes
the place of Sabbath and new moon worship in the new creation of the
visionary prophet (cf. Zech. 14). However, there is general agreement,
with but few exceptions,[3] that verses 17-24 of this chapter are secondary to the main body of Is. 56-66, and that these verses are rather
late.[4] However, it is futile to speculate about the precise point after

---

[1]It is unfortunate that Westermann, in his otherwise insightful
commentary, has so completely misunderstood the function of Is. 58:13-14,
when he writes: "Der Ton liegt dort [vss. 3f] auf dem Mitmenschlichen,
. . während v.13 allein vom Entheiligen des heiligen Tages spricht."
Das Buch Jesaja, p. 271. See Muilenburg, "Isaiah 40-66," p. 414.

[2]"Isaiah 40-66," p. 677. These verses are thus from Trito-
Isaiah, meaning basically "Isaianic" material that is later than
Deutero-Isaiah.

[3]Conservative scholars naturally attribute Is. 66 to Isaiah of
Jerusalem. Meesters has argued that this particular verse derives from
Isaiah because it associates Sabbath and new moon like Is. 1:13 (Op zoek
naar de oorsprong van de Sabbat, p. 150).

[4]Cf. Duhm, Das Buch Jesaja, p. 489; Fohrer, Introduction,
p. 388; Marti, Das Buch Jesaja, p. 414; Muilenburg, "Isaiah 40-66,"
p. 769; Westermann, Das Buch Jesaja, p. 244; et al.

the beginning of the fifth century B.C., when a Jerusalem visionary
prophet might have been capable of such a description.[1] The construction middê-ḥōdeš beḥodšô, middê-šabbāt bešabbattô with the 3rd. pers.
sg. suffix has led to the speculation that ḥōdeš and šabbāt may mean
month and week respectively,[2] but although such a reading does make
sense here, it is doubtful that Sabbath and new moon should be used in
that way in this single place. The phrase simply means: "Every new
moon and every Sabbath," or "from new moon to new moon and from Sabbath
to Sabbath."[3]

D. Ezekiel

Ezek. 20:12-13, 16, 20-21, 24

The question of the literary relationships of Ezekiel's Sabbath
material is particularly frustrating, partly because of the endless
debates over primary and secondary material in the book,[4] and partly

---

[1]The harsh description of Gehenna in Is. 66:23 has led to a date
as late as the second century B.C., but this is certainly not required.

[2]Duhm reads: "Jeden Monat an seinem Neumond und jede Woche an
ihrem Sabbat. . . ." (Das Buch Jesaja, p. 389). Cf. Marti, Das Buch
Jesaja, p. 414.

[3]Cf. I Sam. 6:16; Zech. 14:16.

[4]This debate cannot be entered upon here. However, the sharp
distinction which older scholars made between the material the prophet
himself preserved for posterity (ipsissima verba), and the remaining
secondary material from the redactor is no longer upheld. For this view
see especially Gustav Hölscher, Hesekiel der Dichter und das Buch, BZAW,
No. 39 (Giessen: Verlag von Alfred Töpelmann, 1924). Recent scholarship rather views the book as a collection of material, derived mostly
from the prophet, often expanded by his followers, but with relatively
little purely secondary material. Cf. Eissfeldt, Introduction, pp. 380-
ff.; Fohrer, Introduction, pp. 410ff.; H. H. Rowley, "The Book of
Ezekiel in Modern Study," BJRL, XXXVI (1953-54), 146-90. Also found in
Men of God: Studies in Old Testament History and Prophecy (London:

because of the very sketchy treatment of the Sabbath itself. Thus
Walther Eichrodt has declared the most prominent references to the Sabbath (Ezek. 20) secondary, because they occur too prominently and
consistently in this chapter to be genuine Ezekielian.[1] He suggests
that a priestly editor inserted these Sabbath references to indicate
that to him the universal Sabbath institution, inaugurated at Sinai, is
the most basic ingredient of Israel's covenant. However, this view
flounders on the fact that the Sabbath does not occupy such a unique
position in this chapter, in distinction from its other appearances in
Ezekiel. What then is the provenance of these references to the

---

Thomas Nelson and Sons Ltd., 1963), pp. 169-210; Curt Kuhl, "Zum Stand
der Hesekiel-Forschung," ThR, XXIV (1956-57), 1-53.

[1]"Der Sabbat bei Hesekiel: Ein Beitrag zur Nachgeschichte des
Prophetentextes," in Lex Tua Varitas: Festschrift für Hubert Junker,
ed. by H. Gross and F. Mussner (Trier: Paulinus-Verlag, 1961), pp. 65-
74. This view is reiterated in Eichrodt's commentary Der Prophet
Hesekiel: Kapitel 19-48, ATD, Vol. XXII, Pt. 2 (Göttingen: Vandenhoeck
& Ruprecht, 1966). He argues that the Sabbath does not appear in
Ezekiel where we would expect it, viz., Ezek. 20:27-29; 18:6ff.; 26:
6ff.; 33:25ff., and especially where God's requirements for his people
are enumerated. Secondly, he maintains that where it does appear elsewhere in the book, its role is less significant than in ch. 20. This is
the case with Ezek. 22:26, where the offense against the Sabbath is only
one example of the general disregard for the distinction between clean
and unclean, holy and profane. However, the first of these is an argument from silence, and the second is not very convincing. Ezek. 22:26
contains a double accusation separated by an explanatory parenthesis as
follows: Her priests have violated my law and profaned my holy things
(they have not distinguished between holy and profane, nor taught the
distinction between clean and unclean), and they have turned their eyes
from my Sabbaths, and I am profaned in their midst. The Sabbath appears
in parallel to the holy things and the Torah, and the point is that
because of the inability on the part of the priests to distinguish
between holy and profane, the Sabbath, the Torah, the holy equipment in
the temple, and God himself have been profaned. The Sabbath is not
simply an illustration of the general inability among the priests to
distinguish the holy from the profane.

Sabbath? Are they the work of a priestly writer (Eichrodt), or some such late hand,[1] or are they, and the chapter as a whole or in part, from the prophet Ezekiel whose work began <u>ca</u>. 593/2 B.C. and continued till after 585 B.C.?[2] Although this question cannot easily be answered, three observations may help to clarify it. (1) The similarity between Ezek. 20:1-32 and other reviews of Israel's history, and between the Sabbath material here and in Ex. 31:13 can best be explained by assuming that the prophet did not copy his information from other literature, but shared the traditions of Israel's historians and priests.[3] (2) The central issue in Ezekiel's treatment of the Sabbath is, in distinction from

---

[1]Cf. Hölscher, <u>Hesekiel</u>, p. 110; George A. Cook, <u>The Book of Ezekiel</u>, ICC, Vol. XXI (Edinburgh: T. & T. Clark, 1951), p. 213. It is rightly observed that Ezek. 20:12 demonstrates marked similarities to Ex. 31:13. Note the expressions, "a sign between me and you/them," and "that I, the LORD, sanctify you/them." However, the fact that despite the similarities the material is used differently in the two places suggests that it was not copied from one place into the other (Alfred Bertholet and Kurt Galling, <u>Hesekiel</u>, HAT, Vol. XIII (Tübingen: Verlag von J. C. B. Mohr [Paul Siebeck], 1936), p. 70). Rather the material was used completely at the writer's discretion. See Walther Zimmerli, <u>Ezechiel</u>, BK, Vol. XIII (Neukirchen-Vluyn: Neukirchener Verlag, 1969), p. 447.

[2]Bertholet and Galling, <u>Hesekiel</u>, pp. 70-71; Eissfeldt, <u>Introduction</u>, p. 376; Georg Fohrer, <u>Die Hauptprobleme des Buches Ezechiel</u>, BZAW, No. 72 (Berlin: Verlag Alfred Töpelmann, 1952), p. 83; Zimmerli, <u>Ezechiel</u>, p. 440; "The Word of God in the Book of Ezekiel," JThC, IV (1967), 5; Henning Graf Reventlow, <u>Wächter über Israel: Ezechiel und seine Tradition</u>, BZAW, No. 82 (Berlin: Verlag Alfred Töpelmann, 1962), pp. 76, 83.

[3]We cannot follow Hölscher who attempts by analyzing style in Ezekiel to extract genuine and secondary parts of the book. The attempt of Bertholet and Galling to accomplish the same goal by determining literary dependencies is equally futile. The prophet was free to adopt material directly (cf. Ex. 31:13ff.) and to make use of a literary genre (cf. Ps. 106; Neh. 9:6ff.), as well as to employ these freely and creatively. In short, the relationship of Ezek. 20 and Ex. 31 is most plausibly explained by the prophet's acquaintance with priestly and

Ex. 31:13ff., that the Sabbath[1] as a covenant sign should be holy (vss. 12, 20) but has been profaned (vss. 13, 16, 21, 24). In this sense the Sabbath references fit well into Ezek. 20 and the book as a whole. (3) The tension between holy and profane appears in the other Sabbath references in Ezekiel as well, and in the book as a whole. The Sabbath texts in Ezek. 20 are, therefore, not contrary to the spirit of Ezekiel (Eichrodt), but, it may be asked, are they not so frequent in and so fundamental to this chapter that they must be secondary? Not clearly so, for the repetitions of the reference to the Sabbath in this chapter are only due to the particular literary genre adopted by the prophet here, namely, the historical review in reverse, i.e., that which enumerates, not the repeated acts of divine salvation, but the repeated acts of human degradation.[2] Finally, the Sabbath was clearly of some importance to Ezekiel's view of the community, as its projected role in the restored community demonstrates (Ezek. 46:1-6).[3] In other words, there is no incongruence between the Sabbath references in Ezek. 20 and in the rest of the book.

---

legal traditions. Cf. Zimmerli, Ezechiel, p. 447; Fohrer, Die Hauptprobleme, pp. 151-52.

[1]Except for Ezek. 46:1, 4, 12, Sabbath is in the plural in this book.

[2]Cf. Zimmerli, "The Word of God in the Book of Ezekiel," pp. 5ff. In distinction from Ps. 106 and Neh. 9 the present historical review is marked by a tight structure, e.g., the rebellions are always of the same nature, and God's deliverance is brought about in the same manner after each outburst of sin.

[3]Note the elaborate ceremonies and the increased sacrifices (vs. 4).

Ezek. 22:8, 26; 23:38

These passages, especially Ezek. 22:26, 23:38, are similar to some Sabbath laws in H,[1] and the question of literary relationships thus arises again. Closer examination shows, however, that the similarities are overshadowed by some differences, notably with reference to the verbs. In H we have šmr (keep) and yr> (fear, reverence), but in Ezekiel we have ḥll (profane), bzh (despise), and ṭm> (polute, defile). Moreover, in H the verses in question are phrased as laws concerning the Sabbath and sanctuary, whereas in Ezekiel they contain accusations directed against the general lack of respect for the sanctuary, holy items, and the Sabbath. There can thus be no question of literary dependence, let alone copying, from one body of literature to the other. Rather the similarities between the passages in H and in Ezekiel can best be explained by assuming that Ezekiel shared the traditions responsible for the legal pronouncements in H.

The verbs of Ezek. 22:8 are in 2nd. pers. sg. fem. and refer to Jerusalem,[2] in distinction from the 3rd. pers. pl. verbs in the context. Moreover, the cultic overtones of this verse stand in contrast to the preceding and succeeding ethical accusations. For these reasons the verse has repeatedly been dismissed as secondary.[3] However, the

---

[1]Cf. Lev. 19:30, 26:2, "You shall keep my Sabbaths and reverence my sanctuary: I am the Lord."

[2]LXX has the verbs in 3rd. pers. pl. Cf. Bertholet and Galling, Hesekiel, p. 78.

[3]Hölscher, Hesekiel, p. 117; Georg Fohrer and Kurt Galling, Ezechiel, HAT, Vol. XIII (Tübingen: Verlag von J. C. B. Mohr [Paul Siebeck], 1955), pp. 127-28; Volkmar Herntrich, Ezechielprobleme, BZAW,

distinction between cultic and moral offenses may not have been apparent to the minds of Ezekiel and his contemporaries, and since the point made here regarding the Sabbath follows that of Ezek. 20, it is certainly not out of place in Ezekiel.[1]

Ezek. 22:26 appears in a context which is considered secondary by most interpreters,[2] although the theme of the verse (distinction between the holy and the common) and the remark about the Sabbath (they have disregarded my Sabbaths) are in no way foreign to Ezekiel.[3]

The intensifying bayyôm hahû² (in the same day) in Ezek. 23:38 does not militate against the genuineness of the verse, but the whole section, verses 36-49, is difficult, and appears to be redactional.[4] In any case, verse 38 does not contribute anything further to the Sabbath material in Ezekiel.

Ezek. 44:24; 45:17

Of the remaining passages (Ezek. 44:24; 45:17; 46:1-4, 12) the first gives little difficulty and matching insight. Ezek. 44:24 appears

---

No. 61 (Giessen: Verlag von Alfred Töpelmann, 1932), p. 107; Eichrodt, Hesekiel, p. 203; cf. Cook, Ezekiel, p. 241.

[1]Consequently, its genuineness is also affirmed. Cf. Zimmerli, Ezechiel, pp. 509-10.

[2]Cf. Eichrodt, Hesekiel, p. 209; Hölscher, Hesekiel, p. 120; Fohrer, Die Hauptprobleme, pp. 99-100; Herntrich, Ezechielprobleme, p. 107.

[3]Cf. Zimmerli, Ezechiel, p. 525.

[4]Thus Cook, Ezekiel, p. 256; Herntrich, Ezechielprobleme, p. 108; Eichrodt, Hesekiel, p. 222; Bertholet and Galling, Hesekiel, p. 85; Zimmerli, Ezechiel, p. 540; Isaac G. Matthews, Ezekiel (Philadelphia: American Baptist Publication Society, 1939), p. 85.

in a context which provides a break in the chapter from a stylistic
point of view, and according to some interpreters may be secondary.[1]

Ezek. 45:17 assigns the duty of providing the Sabbath offerings
to the prince. Zimmerli prefers the variant reading ûbᵉkol for bᵉkol
("and in all the appointed feasts . . ."), where the waw is a coordina-
tive conjunction (and).[2] However, whether this is correct, i.e.,
whether there were appointed feasts in addition to those already mentioned, or whether the Sabbath was one of these appointed feasts, i.e.,
the waw is of the explicative kind (even, that is), no new light is
thrown on the festal characterization of the Sabbath institution, for
Ezek. 45:13ff. is concerned primarily with sacrifices, not with the
nature of the feast days. The verse is more often than not attributed
to a secondary hand.[3]

Ezek. 46:1-4, 12

This Ezekielian passage[4] describes the roles of the prince[5] and
the people of the land (ᶜam-hāᵓāreṣ). The prince represents the

---

[1]Cf. Hölscher, Hesekiel, p. 198; Eichrodt, Hesekiel, p. 397;
Zimmerli, Ezechiel, p. 1133; Helmut Gese, Der Verfassungsentwurf des
Ezechiel, Kap. 40-48: Traditionsgeschichtlich Untersucht (Tübingen:
J. C. B. Mohr [Paul Siebeck], 1957), p. 61.

[2]Following forty-one MSS Edd Vrs.

[3]Cf. Eichrodt, Hesekiel, p. 405; Zimmerli, Ezechiel, p. 1153.

[4]Some scholars consider it secondary, viz. Bertholet and Galling,
Hesekiel, p. 162; Eichrodt, Hesekiel, p. 408; Zimmerli, Ezechiel, p. 1169.

[5]Cf. Erling Hammershaimb, "Ezekiel's View of the Monarchy," in
Some Aspects of Old Testament Prophecy from Isaiah to Malachi (Århus:
Rosenkilde og Bagger, 1966), pp. 51-62. Ezekiel stood on the borderline
between the old king ideology and the postexilic priestly community.
The prince holds the role of the old priest-king.

community in cultic matters, and the "people of the land" is the lay
community.[1] This fact has prompted an exilic dating of the passage, at
a time before the people of the land became identified with Israel's
enemies, and the prince became replaced by the priest as the cultic
leader of the community.[2] The discrepancy between the number of sacri-
ficial animals mentioned in verse 4 and in Num 28:9-10 may be
accidental, but it is possible that the six lambs and the one ram in
Ezek. 46:4 correspond to the six working days and the seventh-day Sabbath, and do not reflect actual practices.[3] We cannot associate the
passage with the priestly laws in any certain way. At the same time it
is possible that traditional practices and thoughts about the Sabbath
are reflected here, viz., the expression yᵉmê hammaᶜseh (working days).[4]
It is rendered "profane days" by the Targum, and although this rendering
(profane as opposed to holy) is really close to the other Ezekielian
Sabbath material, the reading in the M.T. should be maintained. Even
here where the cultic significance of the Sabbath is exploited, its

---

[1]The "people of the land" refers to the whole body of citizens.
See Roland de Vaux, Ancient Israel, Vol. I: Social Institutions (New
York: McGraw-Hill Book Company, 1965), p. 71; Ernst Würthwein, Der
ᶜAmm-haᶻarez im Alten Testment, BWANT, No. 69 (Stuttgart: W. Kohlhammer
Verlag, 1936), p. 49. After the exile, however, the people of the land,
often named "peoples of the land" (cf. Ezra and Nehemiah), came to refer
to non-Jewish, or faithless Jewish inhabitants of Judah. See Vogt,
Studie zur nachexilischen Gemeinde, p. 154; de Vaux, Ancient Israel, I,
72.

[2]Cf. Gese, Der Verfassungsentwurf, pp. 110ff.; Hammershaimb,
"Ezekiel's View of the Monarchy," pp. 61-62.

[3]Fohrer and Galling, Ezechiel, p. 254.

[4]This expression is unique in the Old Testament, though the idea
behind it is not. Cf. Zimmerli, Ezechiel, p. 1167.

traditional characterization as a day without work cannot be forgotten.

E. Kings and Chronicles

II Kg. 4:23

This curious little remark in the Elisha cycle implies that when
the account was formed it was customary to visit a prophet on a Sabbath
and on a new moon, but not at other times. To date this account, which
presumably originated in north Israel, is virtually impossible.[1] In the
first place, it is generally assumed that the Elisha material (II Kg. 2-
13) originally was made up of independent accounts relating various
incidents in the prophet's life.[2] These accounts, of which II Kg. 4:18-
37 is one, were undoubtedly preserved by the followers (disciples) of
the prophet.[3] It is safe to assume that many such accounts, no doubt
more than are preserved in the Books of Kings, would be in circulation
shortly after the prophet's death, i.e., in the first part of the eighth
century B.C., perhaps earlier, although there is, of course, no proof of
this. It is noteworthy, however, that the association of Sabbath and
new moon is repeated in Is. 1:13; Am. 8:5; Hos. 2:11, all oracles from
eighth century prophets.

---

[1]According to W. O. E. Oesterley and Theodore H. Robinson it is
the passage which mentions the Sabbath for the first time (Hebrew
Religion: Its Origin and Development [2nd rev. ed.: London: Macmillan
Company, 1937], p. 135).

[2]Cf. Eissfeldt, Introduction, pp. 294-95; Fohrer, Introduction,
pp. 233-34.

[3]In a number of accounts Elisha appears with a group of disciples, the sons of the prophet (II Kg. 2:1-18, 4:38-41, 42-44; 6:1-7).
These individuals and perhaps other beneficiaries of the prophet's
activities would anxiously guard his memory and preserve the record of
his life.

It has been observed repeatedly that the Elisha cycle bears
marked resemblance to the Elijah cycle in I Kg. 17-II Kg. 10. This certainly is true about the narrative of the Shunammite woman (II Kg. 4:8-
37, 8:1-6, cf. I Kg. 17:17-24). Consequently, some kind of relationship
between them has been proposed.[1] However, it is possible that the similarities are in fact of a secondary nature, and were caused by the
recognition among the prophets' disciples that their masters indeed
stood in a master-disciple relationship. Consequently, their activities
of a similar nature would tend to be harmonized.[2] If this is correct, a
story dealing with the restoration of a boy's life should be attributed
to both the Elisha and Elijah cycles. In the passage under observation
we are told that this event did not happen on a Sabbath or a new moon.

---

[1]Either that the Elisha narratives depend on the Elijah material
(I. Benzinger, Die Bücher der Könige, KHC, Vol. IX (Tübingen: Verlag
von J. C. B. Mohr [Paul Siebeck], 1899), p. 129; Rudolf Kilian, "Die
Totenerweckungen Elias und Elisas - eine Motivwanderung?" BZ, NF.X
[1966], 35-36), or vice versa (Georg Fohrer, Elia, AThANT, No. 53 [2nd
ed.; Zürich: Zwingli Verlag, 1968], pp. 35-36). However, it is not
easy to decide which is primary (Weiser, The Old Testament, p. 62).
Perhaps the two cycles existed independently to begin with. See John
Gray, I & II Kings: A Commentary (Philadelphia: Westminster Press,
1963), p. 417; Odil H. Steck, Überlieferung und Zeitgeschichte in den
Elia-Erzählungen, WMANT, No. 26 (Neukirchen-Vluyn: Neukirchener Verlag,
1960), p. 10.

[2]Kilian ("Die Totenerweckungen," p. 47) has compared the two
accounts and has observed the following seven points of similarity between them: (1) The child is dead or shows signs of being dead; (2) the
mother reproaches the prophet; (3) the child is placed in the prophet's
private quarters; (4) the prophet is alone with the child; (5) he prays
to Yahweh; (6) he places himself on the dead; (7) the child is revived
and returned to his mother. The reproach (2) is a natural reaction of
the mother who would ask, Why this catastrophe under the very nose of
the man of God? However, the remaining parallels all refer to the
prophet's activities in order to secure revivification. They may be
explained as "transference of themes" (Weiser, The Old Testament, p. 62)
by disciples of the prophets who would secure both for the master prophet
and for his disciple (Elisha) the proper procedure of revivification.

Consequently, we need not assume a late date for this incident in the Elisha cycle, namely, a date sufficiently far removed from the time of the prophet that the revivification theme could be safely transferred from the Elijah cycle.

II Kg. 11:4-12; II Chr. 23:1-11

All the detailed problems associated with the account of the overthrow of Athaliah cannot claim attention here, but a few observations may help bring the crucial verses into view.

This account appears both in II Kg. 11 and in II Chr. 23, but there is no doubt that the version in II Kg. is primary, for the Chronicler's account evidences the peculiar interest of its writer, on the one hand, and reflects traits characteristic of the older narrative in Kings, on the other. The Chronicler has adjusted an old account to his own orientation.[1]

Whether the original account in Kings is itself composite has been debated,[2] but the more important question for the present

---

[1]See Jacob M. Myers, II Chronicles, AB, Vol. XIII (New York: Doubleday & Company, Inc., 1965), p. 131; Eissfeldt, Introduction, p. 538; I. Benzinger, Die Bücher der Chronik, KHC, Vol. X (Tübingen: Verlag von J. C. B. Mohr [Paul Siebeck], 1901), p. 112. The Chronicler's great interest in the Davidic line is reflected in vs. 3 (cf. II Kg. 11: 4). He also reveals his characteristic concern with the purity of the temple (vs. 6). But more important is his interest in the Levites. The soldiers (perhaps the royal bodyguard of foreigners) which appear in the account of Kings have been replaced by priests and Levites in the Chronicler's account (II Chr. 23:4-7). Nevertheless, a part of the military mood is preserved, viz., the coming off and going on duty, the guarding of the gates and entrances, the act of protecting the king, the distribution of weapons, et cetera.

[2]The question has been raised, whether we have here two accounts of the revolt, one (vss. 1-17) involving the palace and the temple personnel, and the other (vss. 18-20) involving the entire people. Cf.

discussion concerns the provenance of that part of the story which refers to the Sabbath. From the rather precise description of the events and their timing, and the slight confusion about the actual procedure, one gets the distinct impression that we are dealing with an account which was transmitted into the present narrative at a time when the military maneuvers at the temple on the Sabbath were no longer practiced. It appears that the brief account in the sources could not recall to the editor's mind the exact procedure, or if he did understand it, he recognized the difficulties in the story and offered some elaborations for the benefit of his readers.[1] It is likely that the event was recorded in the official archives of Judah, undoubtedly shortly after it took place.[2]

Eissfeldt, Introduction, pp. 297-98; Gustav Hölscher, "Das Buch der Könige: Seine Quellen und seine Redaktion," in Eucharisterion, H. Gunkel zum 60. Geburtstage, I, ed. by Hans Schmidt, FRLANT, No. 36 (Göttingen: Vandenhoeck & Ruprecht, 1923), pp. 158-213. For a contrary opinion see Wilhelm Rudolph, "Die Einheitlichkeit der Erzählung vom Sturz der Atalja (II Kön 11)," in Festschrift Alfred Bertholet zum 80 Geburtstag, ed. by Walter Baumgartner, et al. (Tübingen: J. C. B. Mohr [Paul Siebeck], 1950), pp. 473-78. The arguments of Rudolph for the basic unity of the chapter seem most persuasive. He correctly argues, among other things, that a surprise revolt involving all the people is impossible, and secondly, that the queen is not killed twice in the chapter (vs. 16 and vs. 20). Vs. 20 rather records the fact of her death.

[1]It is possible that II Kg. 11:6 is an attempt to clarify matters. Cf. Rudolph, "Die Einheitlichkeit," pp. 474-78. Other scholars consider the verse a gloss. Edward L. Curtis and Albert A. Madsen, The Books of Chronicles, ICC, Vol. XI (New York: Charles Scribner's Sons, 1910), p. 426; Benzinger, Könige, p. 157.

[2]Cf. Fohrer, Introduction, p. 232; Eissfeldt, Introduction, pp. 297-98; Samuel R. Driver, An Introduction to the Literature of the Old Testament, Meridian Books (New York: World Publishing Company, 1956), p. 196; Julius Wellhausen, Die Composition des Hexateuchs und der historischen Bücher des Alten Testaments (2nd ed.; Berlin: Druck und Verlag von Georg Reimer, 1889), p. 293.

What actually did take place that Sabbath is difficult to determine from II Kg. 11:4-7,[1] but the execution of Jehoiada's command (vs. 9) reveals that his objective was to retain both the guards going off duty (bā᾽ê) and those coming on duty (yōṣᵊê) on the Sabbath in the temple premises, so as to ensure the safety of the king.

This narrative holds two implications regarding the Sabbath. (1) The Sabbath was the time for changing the guard, or at least guards were changed on this day. (2) There is evidence that the temple was crowded with people on this day.

<u>II Kg. 16:18</u>

This most difficult reference to the Sabbath need not detain us for long, for it contributes little to our subject. The difficulties are mainly textual,[2] and center in the word translated "covered way," but whose meaning is unknown.[3] However, the context and all the

---

[1]The more common explanation is that the two companies of soldiers normally on duty at the palace compound and the one company on duty at the temple changed duties on the Sabbath. In this instance, however, all three companies were retained at the temple. Cf. Benzinger, König, pp. 156-58; Curtis and Madsen, <u>Chronicles</u>, p. 426; H. H. Rowley, <u>Worship in Ancient Israel: Its Form and Meaning</u> (Philadelphia: Fortress Press, 1967), p. 90; Norman H. Snaith, "Introduction and Exegesis to 1-2 Kings," in <u>The Interpreter's Bible</u>, Vol. III, ed. by George A. Buttrick (New York: Abingdon Press, 1954), p. 246.

[2]Hēsēb (he turned aside) is difficult, and hēsir (he removed) is a common conjectured emendation. This would require the reading mibbêt (from the house) rather than bêt (in or of the house). But this again is a conjecture. Cf. Gray, <u>I & II Kings</u>, p. 576. LXX and the Syriac version read bᵊbêt-᾽adōnāy (in the house of the Lord), vs. 18a. This is perhaps a correct interpretation (cf. vs. 18b). Thus Gray, <u>I & II Kings</u>, p. 576; Snaith, "1-2 Kings," p. 278; Meesters, <u>Op zook naar de oorsprong van de Sabbat</u>, p. 146.

[3]The Hebrew word is myysk (qere: mûsak). It is a hapax legomenon and its meaning is unknown (Benzinger, <u>Könige</u>, p. 172).

suggested meanings of the word indicate that it involved some structure
constructed of valuable material.[1] It was probably located in the
temple, or between the temple and the palace, and it was used by the
king on the Sabbath. This information, we may assume, was available to
the historian in the official annals of Judah.[2]

I Chr. 9:32

Recent studies have discredited the formerly held third century
B.C. dating of the Chronicler,[3] and have placed him in the first part of
the fourth century B.C. and even earlier.[4] I Chr. 1-9 have commonly

---

However, it is usually understood as a building structure: R.S.V.
translates "the covered way"; LXX reads tòn themélion tîs kathédras (the
foundation of the seat); the reading of the Targum (tiqqûsā>) is translated "rampart," "embankment," or "wall" by Morris Jastrow, A Dictionary
of the Targumin, the Talmud Babli and Yerushalmi, and the Midrashic
Literature, I (New York: Title Publishing Company, 1943), p. 534.
Several additional proposals have been made. Gray derives the word from
the verb skk (put up a barrier), cf. Job 3:23; 38:8. The barrier would
be a gate opened for the king on the Sabbath, as described in Ezek. 46:
1-4 (I & II Kings, pp. 575-76). Snaith ("1-2 Kings," p. 277) combines
the previously mentioned proposals by translating "The covering of the
seat," but he gives no reason for doing so. Finally, Meesters proposes
that the idea of a seat in LXX would suggest "koninklijke loge," a type
of structure which would protect the king against rain, sun, and wind.
It could be called a Sabbatskoepel (Sabbath pavilion). (Op zoek naar de
oorsprong van de Sabbat, p. 146).

[1]The king's robbery of the temple valuables would help to pay
his tribute to Assyria.

[2]Cf. Noth, Überlieferungsgeschichtliche Studien, p. 76.

[3]Cf. Curtis and Madsen, Chronicles, p. 6; Torrey, The Composition, pp. 52ff. More recently Noth, Überlieferungsgeschichtliche
Studien, p. 199; Galling, Die Bücher der Chronik, p. 14; Fohrer, Introduction, p. 239.

[4]See especially William F. Albright, "The Date and Personality
of the Chronicler," JBL, XXXIX (1920), 104-24. Albright demonstrates
that the latest historical situations of the Chronicler's work are to be
dated about the turn of the fifth century B.C., and that its language,

been considered secondary chapters,[1] or at least to have been radically
expanded with the addition of secondary material. Chapter 9, or certainly part of it, would be one such addition.[2] We cannot be quite
certain about the origin of this chapter, but it is very possible that
some of the lists here are based on old ones found in the archives which
the returning community preserved. I Chr. 9 also shows some affinity to
Neh. 9,[3] and it is possible that here we have an account of the ideal or
actual role of the Levites in the temple in the early fourth century
B.C. It has also been suggested that this function assigned to the

particularly the Aramaic sections, corresponds with the language used in
the latter part of the fifth century B.C. The Elephantine letters are
particularly important for these considerations. Cf. Eissfeldt, Introduction, p. 540; Jacob M. Myers, I Chronicles, AB, Vol. XXII (New York:
Doubleday & Company, Inc., 1965), p. lxxxix; Wilhelm Rudolph, "Problems
of the Books of Chronicles," VT, IV (1954), 402. An even earlier date
has been suggested by Freedman ("The Chronicler's Purpose," p. 441). He
proposes a time shortly after the completion of the temple (ca. 515 B.C.)
as the time when the question of the Davidic line was most burning. At
such a time the Chronicler might have begun his history of Israel, which
is strongly oriented towards David and the Davidic succession. Cf. Adam
C. Welch, The Work of the Chronicler (London: Oxford University Press,
1939), pp. 149ff.

[1]Cf. Freedman, "The Chronicler's Purpose," p. 441; Myers, I
Chronicles, p. xli; Galling, Die Bücher der Chronik, p. 10; Snaith,
"1-2 Kings," p. 349. Other scholars have argued that I Chr. 1-9 belong
intrinsically in the Chronicler's work, because these chapters help the
Chronicler by way of preparatory statements to focus on the Davidic
dynasty. This position has been restated recently by Rudolph, "Problems
of the Books of Chronicles," p. 404.

[2]Cf. Eissfeldt, Introduction, p. 540; Fohrer, Introduction, p.
244; Benzinger, Die Bücher der Chronik, p. 35; Wilhelm Rudolph,
Chronikbücher, HAT, Vol. XXI (Tübingen: Verlag von J. C. B. Mohr [Paul
Siebeck], 1955), pp. 83-84.

[3]Cf. Rudolph, Chronikbücher, pp. 83-84. A more cautious position is adopted by Myers, I Chronicles, pp. 67ff.

Kohathites[1] by Chronicles dates back to very ancient times.[2]

I Chr. 23:30-31

I Chr. 23-27 presents particular literary and structural difficulties, and is, in the words of one commentator, "so confused that in
certain cases it defies, in my judgment, every effort to bring it into
order."[3] There is general agreement that it is a secondary addition,
and that it is not a unified one,[4] but the precise relationship of it,
including I Chr. 9:24-32, to the Chronicler is not at all clear.[5] It
appears that contemporary conditions are discussed in these verses, but
we do not know if they were contemporary with the Chronicler, or if we
are dealing with an earlier Sabbath liturgy which is now assigned to
Levitical singers. It is noteworthy that the old association of Sabbath
and new moon is preserved here, but these verses are certainly not older
than the fourth century B.C.

---

[1]LXX reads: Baniah, the Kohathite, of their brothers. . . .

[2]Cf. I Sam. 21:4. See Bentzen, Den israelitiske Sabbats
Oprindelse og Historie, p. 34. See below, pp. 78-79.

[3]Welch, The Work of the Chronicler, p. 81

[4]Most commentators follow now Noth on this point (Überlieferungsgeschichtliche Studien, pp. 112ff.). Cf. also Eichrodt, Introduction, p. 540; Fohrer, Introduction, p. 244.

[5]Noth (Überlieferungsgeschichtliche Studien, pp. 114-15) is
certain that the chapters as a whole contain regulations of the late
postexilic period, and secondary to the Chronicler's narrative.
Rudolph, on the other hand, assumes that I Chr. 23:25-32 is earlier than
the Chronicler's work, because of the smaller role played by the Levites
as compared to that played by the priests (Chronikbücher, p. 158).

II Chr. 2:4 (Heb. 2:3)

This verse appears in the Chronicler's account of the construction of the Solomonic temple.[1] That account repeats its parallel in
I Kg. 5-7, but not in detail, and it also makes some points of its own,
e.g., our passage (I Chr. 2:4-6) which is absent in Kings.[2]

II Chr. 8:13; 31:3

In the first passage the Chronicler expands on the parallel
account in Kings (I Kg. 9:25). There the king (Solomon) is described as
offering offerings on the altar three times a year, presumably at the
occasion of the three major festivals. The Chronicler, on the other
hand, understands the royal offerings as cultic requirements placed upon
the king by the "commandment of Moses," and includes within these
requirements the daily, weekly (Sabbath), and monthly (new moon) sacrifices (cf. Num. 28-29).

In the second passage we learn that King Hezekiah also provided
offerings at these same occasions, according to the "law of Yahweh." It
was not required in this law (presumably Num. 28-29) that the king
should provide the sacrifices for the offerings.[3] Rather, the law
referred only to the prescribed types of sacrifices for the daily,

---

[1]There is little question that II Chr. 1-9 (the Solomonic
history) is from the Chronicler himself. Cf. Noth, Überlieferungsgeschichtliche Studien, pp. 116-17. For a contrary opinion, see W. A. L.
Elmslie, "Introduction and Exegesis to 1-2 Chronicles," in The Interpreter's Bible, Vol. III, ed. by George A. Buttrick (New York: Abingdon
Press, 1954), p. 445.

[2]See below, p. 144.

[3]Cf. Rudolph, Chronikbücher, p. 306.

weekly, and monthly feast days, as well as for the annual festivals. It is very likely, however, that the king, or prince (Ezek. 45:17), could not escape the performance of such an expensive service,[1] and it is certainly the Chronicler's idea that he should not do so.

II Chr. 36:21

Having left the chronological framework of the Deuteronomistic historian behind, the Chronicler[2] now carries his account through the exile with the assistance of Jer. 25:11-14; 29:10,[3] Lev. 26:34-35, 43. There is good reason to support the view that the seventy year theme of Jeremiah,[4] and the motif of the seventh year[5] have been combined here.[6]

---

[1]Cf. Ibid.; Curtis and Madsen, Chronicles, pp. 478-79.

[2]According to Elmslie ("1-2 Chronicles," p. 547) it is a later addition to the work of the Chronicler.

[3]Rudolph (Chronikbücher, p. 336) has proposed that vs. 21a refers back to vs. 20, and that vs. 21b can, therefore, not be a quotation from Jeremiah.

[4]For the significance of the seventy year period see William Foxwell Albright, From Stone Age to Christianity: Monotheism and the Historical Process, Anchor Books (2nd ed.; New York: Doubleday & Company, 1957), pp. 18-19. Albright argues that the seventy year period is not to be taken literally, but as a symbolic period indicating a temporary destruction of a city, perhaps as a result of a divine punishment. See also the summary and conclusion regarding the seventy year period by Reikele Borger, "An Additional Remark on P. R. Ackroyd, JNES, XVII, 23-27," JNES, XVIII (1959), 74. A more extended analysis is provided by Otto Plöger, "Siebzig Jahre," in Festschrift Friedrich Baumgärtel zum 70. Geburtstag 14. Januar 1958, ed. by Leohard Rost (Erlangen: Universitätsbund, 1959), pp. 124-30.

[5]Cf. Rudolph, Chronikbücher, pp. 337-38; Benzinger, Die Bücher der Chronik, p. 135; Curtis and Madsen, Chronicles, pp. 524-25.

[6]See below, pp. 213-21, for a discussion of the Sabbath for the land.

F. Isaiah, Hosea, and Amos

Is. 1:13

This verse occurs in a series of prophetic tôrāh (vss. 10-17),
is undoubtedly from the prophet Isaiah of Jerusalem,[1] and could be
assigned to any time of the prophet's life, as is the case with Is. 1
generally.[2] The crucial passage reads as follows: ḥōdeš wᵉšabbāt qᵉrōʾ
miqrāʾ / lōʾ-ʾûkal ʾāwen waᶜaṣārāh. The association of Sabbath and new
moon is well known,[3] but the next expression (qᵉrōʾmiqrāʾ) is unusual
and has raised some questions. (1) The more frequent expression (miqrāʾ
qōdeš) does not appear in this verse;[4] (2) It does not have the expected
conjunction (waw) which some translators feel obliged to insert anyway.[5]
Consequently, the whole line has been dismissed as a late interpolation
into the text.[6] Hans Wildberger, however, has rightly questioned this

---

[1]Cf. Eissfeldt, Introduction, p. 443; Fohrer, Introduction, p.
336; Weiser, The Old Testament, p. 187; Hans Wildberger, Jesaja, BK,
Vol. X (Neukirchen-Vluyn: Neukirchener Verlag, 1965), p. 37.

[2]It has been suggested rather convincingly that Is. 1 contains a
collection of material from Isaiah, assembled so as to reflect the main
themes of his message. In this way, Is. 1 is a true introduction to the
book. Cf. Georg Fohrer, "Jesaja 1 als Zusammenfassung der Verkündigung
Jesajas," ZAW, LXXIV (1962), 253.

[3]Cf. II Kg. 4:23; Am. 8:5; Hos. 2:11, Is. 66:23; Ezek. 46:1, 3.

[4]Of the twenty-two occurrences of miqrāʾ all but four appear
with qōdeš (in P). Cf. Julian Morgenstern, "Two Compound Technical
Terms in Biblical Hebrew," JBL, XLIII (1924), 314; Ernst Kutsch,
"קרא," ZAW, LXV (1953), 247-53.

[5]Thus R.S.V. "New moon and sabbath and the calling of assem-
blies--I cannot endure iniquity and solemn assembly."

[6]Thus Karl Marti, Das Buch Jesaja, KHC, Vol. X (Tübingen: Ver-
lag J. C. B. Mohr [Paul Siebeck], 1900), p. 12; Friedrich Schwally,
"Miscellen," ZAW, XI (1891), 257; Morgenstern, "Two Compound Technical
Terms in Biblical Hebrew," p. 316.

procedure,[1] and has proposed that miqrā² here should be understood in the light of the frequently used expression miqrā² qōdeš, meaning simply a feast day, but not an assembly.[2] This would mean firstly that qᵉrō ² miqrā² does not stand in conjunction with, but in apposition to, new moon and Sabbath, and secondly that nothing much can be concluded about Sabbath and new moon assemblies or congregations from this passage.[3]

In the second stich, lō²-²ûkal would generally be followed by an infinitive, but the terse nature of the expression may have forced it out.[4] LXX reads nisteían (fast) for ²āwen (evil), but the defense of this reading by modern interpreters[5] reflects their projected prophetic

---

[1] Jesaja, p. 34. "Aber schon metrisch sind die beiden Wörter nicht zu entbehren, und das מקרא eine Abkürzung von קדש מקרא sei, das erst nachexilisch ist, leuchtet nicht ein."

[2] Ibid. See also the studies by Kutsch, "מקרא," pp. 247-53 and Morgenstern, "Two Compound Technical Terms in Biblical Hebrew," pp. 311-320. Both studies abandon the common translation of miqrā², namely, "assembly." Cf. Gesenius and Buhl, Handwörterbuch, p. 457; Koehler and Baumgartner, Lexicon, p. 562. Rather, it is argued, miqrā² must be associated with the very common expression miqrā² qōdeš (Ex. 12:16; Lev. 23:3, 7, 8, 21, 24, 27, 35, 36; Num. 28:18, 26; 29:1, 7, 12). But whereas Morgenstern considers it a late (postexilic) expression, and translates it, on the basis of etymological considerations, as "proclamation of a taboo," Kutsch shows more convincingly that in all occurrences, except three (Num. 10:2; Is. 4:5; Neh. 8:8) miqrā² qōdeš and miqrā² clearly mean "festival," "feast day," but not assembly.

[3] We cannot conclude, however, that "new moon and sabbath" and miqrā² are identical, but that all three words refer to feast days. Cf. Kutsch, "מקרא," p. 249. "So steht מקרא קרא nicht as gleichwertige dritte Grösse neben חדש und שבת. Auch wird beides nicht miteinander gleichgesetz; denn מקרא unfasst mehr als nur Neumond und Sabbat, wie Lev. 23 zeigt."

[4] Cf. Marti, Das Buch Jesaja, p. 12.

[5] Cf. Otto Kaiser, Der Prophet Jesaja: Kapitel 1-12, ATD, Vol. XVII (Göttingen: Vandenhoeck & Ruprecht, 1963), p. 9; "Ich ertrage nicht Fasten und Arbeitsruhe."

antagonism towards the cult. Rather, since ᶜaṣārāh should probably be translated "feast day" also,[1] one must see the words ꜣawen wa ᶜaṣārāh as the prophet's ironical combination of two mutually exclusive ideas, namely, evil (whether magic power or moral evil) and the festival, therefore lōꜣ-ꜣûkal.[2] The whole passage could then be translated: New moon and Sabbath--the proclaiming of festival--I cannot endure iniquity and feast day.

Hos. 2:11 (Heb. 2:13)

This verse appears in a well defined section (Hos. 2) in which Hosea expounds the theme of Yahweh as the first man and Israel as his

---

[1]See Meesters, Op zoek naar de oorsprong van de Sabbat, p. 147; Wildberger, Jesaja, p. 43; Ernst Kutsch, "Die Wurzel ‎עצר im Hebräischen," VT, II (1952), 57-69. The precise meaning of ᶜaṣārāh is not easy to determine. The root meaning is generally associated with "suppression," "restraint," "abstinence," "holding back," "refraining from," or the like, and it is used about ordinary activities, e.g., work. See Koehler and Baumgartner, Lexicon, p. 729; Gesenius and Buhl, Handwörterbuch, p. 612; Kutsch, "Die Wurzel ‎עצר im Hebräischen," pp. 57, 65. Theodor H. Gaster has suggested that the root ᶜṣr from which ᶜaṣārāh is derived means "restraint" and refers to a lent or a period of taboo (Thespis, Anchor Books [New ed.; New York: Doubleday & Company, Inc., 1961], p. 30). This motif is certainly present in the translation of LXX (nisteian kai ꜣargian), if the fast is preparatory for the festival. Cf. Marti, Das Buch Jesaja, p. 12; George B. Gray, The Book of Isaiah: I-XXXIV, ICC, Vol. XVIII (Edinburgh: T. & T. Clark, 1912), p. 22. However, since there is general agreement that the root has to do with refraining from activities (work), and since the word applies to feast days (Lev. 23:36; Num. 29:35; Dt. 16:8), Kutsch's reconstruction of its meaning is more plausible: Arbeitsruhe > Feier (Feiertag) > Festversammlung. ᶜaṣārāh then has a double meaning: (1) desistere ab opere; (2) celebrare. "Wie ‎עצרה ist auch ‎עצרה der 'Feiertag,'" (Kutsch, "Die Wurzel ‎עצר im Hebräischen," p. 66).

[2]Such a use of paradox is common in this chapter, e.g., appearing before Yahweh while trampling his courts (vs. 12); spreading forth hands full of blood (vs. 15).

faithless wife.[1] Wolff has proposed that it belongs in the early part
of Hosea's activities (ca. 750 B.C.), at a time when internal or external disturbances did not yet occupy his mind.[2] This is a plausible
date, and it agrees with the position of verse 11 in the book as a
whole.

The ḥag, ḥōdeš, šabbāt, and môʿēd[3] are an enumeration of the
joys of Israel, but we learn nothing about the way in which these
occasions were celebrated. The repeated 3rd. pers. fem. sg. suffix
emphasizes the point of the context, namely, that these festivals are
Israel's, and that Yahweh has no stake in them. We should probably follow LXX in translating the festivals in the plural, taking them as
collective nouns.[4] Šabbāt and ḥōdeš are then the repeated weekly and
monthly feast days, ḥag probably refers to the three major yearly
festivals,[5] whereas môʿēd is used to indicate all the seasons of
festivity, including the above five.

---

[1]Hans Walter Wolff, Dodekapropheton 1: Hoshea, BK, Vol. XIV
(2nd ed.; Neukirchen-Vluyn: Neukirchener Verlag, 1965), p. 39. Wolff
calls it a kerygmatische Einheit.

[2]Ibid.

[3]Attempts to discount wᵉkōl môʿadāh as a gloss are not successful. Cf. Karl Marti, Das Dodekapropheton, KHC, Vol. XIII (Tübingen:
Verlag von J. C. B. Mohr [Paul Siebeck], 1904), p. 26. Môʿēd is rather
a designation for all the appointed festivals in Israel.

[4]This is generally done in translations, cf. R.S.V.

[5]Rudolph accepts the collective reading of the nouns, but argues
that since vs. 12 implies that only one agricultural year is involved,
ḥag must, in order to be collective, refer to the three main festivals,
and not just the fall harvest festival. Wilhelm Rudolph, Hoshea, KAT,
Vol. XIII, Pt. 1 (Gerd Mohn: Gütersloher Verlagshaus, 1966), p. 71.
Cf. Wolff, Dodekapropheton 1: Hoshea, p. 46.

Am. 8:5

These words from the eighth century north Israelite prophet Amos
are not really concerned with the Sabbath, but with the oppression of
the poor. This fact, however, does not make what is here said about the
Sabbath less telling. To sell bread to the hungry and needy is one
thing, to do so dishonestly by tinkering with the measure and weight is
quite another, and to contemplate such practices with anticipation on
the Sabbath is very disturbing indeed. The implication seems to be that
general trade or commerce was not approved of on the Sabbath, although
we cannot conclude that strict inactivity was called for.[1] Whether the
Sabbath was regarded as a special privilege extended to the employed
class, whose cause Amos was defending, does not follow either,[2] but it
does seem to be implied that merely to wait for the conclusion of the
Sabbath is not acceptable to the prophet, at least not if he who waits
is also contemplating evil.

G. The Pentateuch

Priestly Texts

The Priestly literature is now generally dated in the fifth or
even the sixth century B.C.[3] However, it is also apparent that we find

---

[1]Marti, Dodekapropheton, p. 216.

[2]Cf. R. S. Cripps, A Critical and Exegetical Commentary on the
Book of Amos (London: S.P.C.K., 1955), p. 315.

[3]It is usually placed before the Chronicler who was acquainted
with the whole Pentateuch in its present form, but after D and the sixth
century prophets, i.e., in the middle of the fifth century or in the
very end of the sixth century B.C. Cf. Martin Noth, Überlieferungsgeschichte des Pentateuch (Stuttgart: W. Kohlhammer Verlag, 1948), pp.
259ff.; Eissfeldt, Introduction, p. 207; Weiser, The Old Testament, pp.

in this body of literature both legal and cultic material as well as

historical and theological themes which antedate its composition.[1] We

will now examine the Sabbath texts which are found in what is called the

Priestly source.

Gen. 2:1-4a

Textually this passage gives little difficulty.[2] It forms the

conclusion of the priestly creation account, and thus it belongs in the

---

138-39. Other scholars date it in the late Persian period. Cf. J. G.
Vink, "The date and Origin of the Priestly Code in the Old Testament,"
in Oudtestamentlische Studiëen, Vol. XV, ed. by P. A. H. De Boer
(Leiden: E. J. Brill, 1969), pp. 2-144. Some attempts have been made
to date it during the exile or just before the fall of Jerusalem in the
late seventh century. Arvid S. Kapelrud, "The Date of the Priestly
Code," ASTI, III (1964), 58-64; Elias Auerbach, "Die babylonische
Datierung im Pentateuch und das Alter des Priesterkodex," VT, II (1951),
334-42; Johannes Hempel, "Priesterkodex," Paulys Realencyclopädie der
Classischen Altertumswissenschaft, Neue Bearbeitung, Vol. XXII, Pt. 2
(Stuttgart: Alfred Druckenmüller Verlag, 1954), cols. 1965-66. Finally
it has been proposed that the Priestly literature developed during an
extended period of time beginning early in Israel's history. Cf. E. A.
Speiser, Genesis, AB, Vol. I (New York: Doubleday & Company, Inc.,
1964), p. xxvi.

[1]This is certainly true with regard to the Sabbath passages, as
we shall see below, and unquestionably also with regard to many cultic
regulations, and probably some narrative material as well, e.g., the
creation account. Cf. Cuthbert A. Simpson, "Introduction and Exegesis
to Genesis," in The Interpreter's Bible, Vol. I, ed. by George A.
Buttrick (New York: Abingdon Press, 1952), p. 450; Ackroyd, Exile and
Restoration, pp. 35-36.

[2]LXX, Syriac, and Samaritan Pentateuch all read "sixth day" (vs.
2), but the harder reading in M.T. is to be preferred. The emendation
in the versions reflect the rigoristic emphasis on abstinence from work
on the Sabbath in later Judaism, as we meet it in Rabbinic and Essene
thought. The original reading has been explained in four different
ways: (1) The writer of Gen. 2:1-4 actually suggests that some aspect
of creation was performed and concluded on the seventh day, e.g., the
rest day. Cf. Heinrich Holzinger, Genesis, KHC, Vol. I (Tübingen: Verlag von J. C. B. Mohr [Paul Siebeck], 1898), p. 15. This view is now
generally rejected, for it is not likely that Israel would think of God
as completing his work on the Sabbath, particularly at the time of the

64

priestly history, at least in its final form. It has long been proposed

that Israel's contact with Mesopotamian myths during the exile gave rise

to this particular way of telling the creation story.[1] The concluding

exile. Cf. Speiser, Genesis, p. 7; Claus Westermann, Genesis, BK, Vol.
I (Neukirchen-Vluyn: Neukirchener Verlag, 1966--), p. 233. (2) The
numeral should have been "sixth" as in the versions. We have already
said that this is the emended, not the original reading. (3) The verb
should be understood as a pluperfect, i.e., on the seventh day God had
completed his work. Cf. Umberto Cassuto, A Commentary on the Book of
Genesis. Pt. I: From Adam to Noah, Genesis I-VI 8, trans. by I. Abrahams (Jerusalem: Magnes Press, Hebrew University, 1961), pp. 61-62;
Westermann, Genesis, p. 233; Werner H. Schmidt, Die Schöpfungsgeschichte
der Priesterschrift: Zur Überlieferungsgeschichte von Genesis I1-II4a
und II4b-III24, WMANT, No. 17 (2nd ed.; Neukirchen-Vluyn: Neukirchener
Verlag, 1967), p. 156. (4) The verb carries some other shade of meaning. Thus Speiser, Genesis, p. 5: "God brought to a close the work
. . .."; Alexander Heidel, The Babylonian Genesis: The Story of Creation,
Phoenix Books (2nd ed.; Chicago: University of Chicago Press, 1951), p.
127: "God declared His work finished." The evidence, especially as
presented by Cassuto, seems to favor the third proposal.
        The expression laᶜªsôt (vs. 3b) makes the sentence sound
pleonastic, but there is not sufficient reason for emending the text.
The infinitive verb with the prefixed l is used here to describe attend-
ing circumstance. See Wilhelm Gesenius and Emil Kautzsch, Hebrew
Grammar, trans. by A. E. Cowley (2nd ed.; Oxford: Clarendon Press,
1910), par. 114,o; Koehler and Baumgartner, Lexicon, p. 465, par. 25d.
Perhaps we have here the author's recollection of a dual creation
account, by divine act and by divine word.

        [1]It is curious, of course, why a nationalistic writer like P,
who either was in captivity or had just returned from it, should be so
enthralled by the myths of his captors as to incorporate them in his own
nationalistic and religious history. Gunkel foresaw that problem, when
he wrote: "Es spricht also alles dafür, dass wir Gen 1 nicht anders
betrachtet durfen, wie PC überhaupt, nämlich als die jüdische Bearbeitung altisraelitisch Tradition." (Schöpfung und Chaos, p. 136). He
subsequently proposed that the knowledge of Babylonian myth, which
supposedly must have been available to the original composer of Gen. 1:
1-2,4a, entered Israel in pre-exilic and preprophetic times and was
merely revived in postexilic Judaism (Schöpfung und Chaos, pp. 169-70).
If the priestly author operated shortly after, or even during, the
exile, as it is now often assumed, the above mentioned considerations
would lead us to propose that the so-called Babylonian myths in the
priestly creation account were domesticated by the Israelite theologians
before the work by P, for it would indeed be strange, if religious and
nationalistic patriots such as P should resort to the bizarre creation

reference to the seventh day of rest would, according to this view, correspond with the exilic and postexilic emphasis on the Sabbath institution in Israel.[1]

The priestly creation narrative shows unevenness in two ways. (1) It relates a series of divine creative acts, but announces parallel with these that creation was accomplished by a series of divine words. (2) The eight parts of creation are then fitted into a six-seven day scheme.[2] A simplistic solution to this unevenness might propose that an old account with eight or ten creative acts was supplemented with a later creation by the divine word,[3] and finally submitted to the six-seven day

themes celebrated by their captors in order to compose their own creation account.

[1]According to Gunkel the introduction of the Sabbath at this point is an "ätiologischer Mythus" which answers the question: Why is the Sabbath, i.e., the seventh day, the sacred feast day? Hermann Gunkel, Genesis Übersetz und erklärt, HK, Pt. I, Vol. I (5th ed.; Göttingen: Vandenhoeck & Ruprecht, 1922), p. 115. Cf. Simpson, "Genesis," p. 489. This is improbable, as we shall see, firstly because the Sabbath was not such an innovation in exilic and postexilic times that an etiological myth would be required to explain it, and secondly because Gen. 2:1-3 depends on the Sabbath institution, and not vice versa. Moreover, Gen. 2:1-3 lack the literary characteristics of an etiological story. For a recent re-evaluation of the etiological narrative in the Old Testament, see Burke O. Long, The Problem of Etiological Narrative in the Old Testament, BZAW, No. 108 (Berlin: Verlag Alfred Töpelmann, 1968).

[2]The literary structure of the creation chapter cannot detain us here. Two recent examinations of it with analyses of the recent literature are found in Schmidt, Die Schöpfungsgeschichte, pp. 9-22, 49-73, 160ff.; Westermann, Genesis, pp. 113ff.

[3]We must no longer assume, however, that creation by the divine word is a very late phenomenon in ancient Near Eastern creation literature. Cf. "The Theology of Memphis," in James B. Pritchard, ed., Ancient Near Eastern Texts Relating to the Old Testament (2nd ed.; Princeton: Princeton University Press, 1955), pp. 4-6. Hereafter referred to as ANET. See especially Klaus Koch, "Wort und Einheit des

scheme.[1] The present form of Gen. 2:1-3 definitely belongs to the last stage of such a process, but the question still remains, whether it also contains some traditional material.[2] This is quite likely in regard to verse 1,[3] but verses 2-3 form a closely knit unit, from which no section can be immediately extracted as traditional.[4] Schmidt has rightly observed concerning the traditional material: "Der vorgegebene Stoff wurde nicht einfach ungehindert aufgenommen, sondern selbst kritisch überarbeitet."[5] From a literary point of view our passage is, therefore, a unity, and the question of a prior existing tradition must be

---

Schöpfergottes in Memphis und Jerusalem: Zur Einzigartigkeit Israels," ZThK, LXII (1965), 251-93.

[1]This last process is generally attributed to the priestly writer. Cf. Schmidt, Die Schöpfungsgeschichte, pp. 160ff.; Westermann, Genesis, pp. 123-26. Exception to this view is taken only by conservative scholars. Cf. Cassuto, Book of Genesis, pp. 71-72.

[2]The divine otiositas motif may have been present in the tradition, and may have been responsible for attaching the week with its seventh day of rest to the creation account. See below, pp. 174-203. Schmidt, Die Schöpfungsgeschichte, p. 161; Westermann, Genesis, p. 231.

[3]Cf. Westermann, Genesis, p. 231; Schmidt, Die Schöpfungsgeschichte, p. 155; Leonhard Rost, "Der Schöpfungsbericht der Priesterschrift," CuW, X (1934), 172-78.

[4]Cf. Schmidt, Die Schöpfungsgeschichte, p. 155; Westermann, Genesis, p. 231. There is a certain rhythm about the verses, almost poetic in character with some liturgical qualities. Note especially vss. 2a, 2b, 3a, each of which has seven words, divided into two parts the first of which concludes with "the seventh day."
  Vs. 2a: waykal ꜣelōhîm bayyôm haššebîꜥî melaꜣketô ꜣašer ꜥāsāh
  Vs. 2b: wayyišbōt bayyôm haššebîꜥî mikkol-melaꜣketô ꜣašer ꜥāsāh
  Vs. 3a: waybārek ꜣelōhîm ꜣet-yôm haššebîꜥî wayqadēs ꜣōtô
These lines appear to rise to a crecendo in vs. 3a with the words blessed and sanctified. Vs. 3b is a bit longer, almost pleonastic, and serves as an anticlimax to the structure as a whole.

[5]Schmidt, Die Schöpfungsgeschichte, p. 160.

discussed within the larger framework of the creation account and the week.[1]

Ex. 16:4-5, 22-30

Ex. 16 shows unusual unevenness and poses extraordinary difficulties for the literary analyst.[2] Of the two sections which are related to the Sabbath question, verses 4-5, 22-30, the first holds least difficulties. It clearly is an intrusion into the narrative about the congregation's request for flesh and bread (vss. 2-3, 6ff.). In it God answers the request simply with a promise of bread from heaven, in contrast to verses 6ff., the proper sequence, which promises both flesh (in the evening) and bread (in the morning). The context of these two verses is attributed to P, but verses 4-5, which are considered to be part of an older narrative, are generally assigned to JE,[3] or at least

---

[1]See below, pp. 174-203.

[2]There are repetitions, e.g., vss. 28-30 repeat what has already been reported earlier, and vss. 4-5 anticipate the surprising weekly pattern for the appearance of the manna, as told in vss. 21-22. But even more frustrating is the disjointed JE material scattered in this chapter which is basically priestly in character.

[3]Thus Wellhausen, Die Composition des Hexateuchs, p. 81; Driver, Introduction, p. 30. Other scholars attribute it to E and a Deuteronomistic addition (vs. 4b). Cf. Gustav Hölscher, Geschichtsschreibung in Israel: Untersuchungen zum Jahvisten und Elohisten (Lund: C. W. K. Gleerup, 1952), pp. 308-9. Still others attribute it to J with or without Deuteronomistic additions. Cf. Bruno Baentsch, Exodus-Leviticus, HK, Pt. I, Vol. II,1 (Göttingen: Vandenhoeck & Ruprecht, 1903), pp. 147-48; Wilhelm Rudolph, Der "Elohist" von Exodus bis Josua, BZAW, No. 68 (Berlin: Verlag von Alfred Töpelmann, 1938), pp. 34-5; Georg Beer and Kurt Galling, Exodus, HAT, Vol. III (Tübingen: Verlag von J. C. B. Mohr [Paul Siebeck], 1939), p. 91; Martin Noth, Exodus: A Commentary, trans. by J. S. Bowden (Philadelphia: Westminster Press, 1962), p. 132; Fohrer, Introduction, p. 161.

to an old account of the manna.[1]

The second section (vss. 23-30) contains a mixture of priestly material, especially in verses 22-26,[2] older material, notably but not exclusively in verses 27 (28)-30,[3] and several elements which appear to be simply additions, viz., verse 28. In the light of this composition of the chapter, we can best explain its construction by assuming that

_____

[1] According to Noth (Überlieferungsgsschichte des Pentateuch, p. 14) this passage belonged originally in Num. 11, and its present position is due solely to the priestly writer of Ex. 16. However, not all of Ex. 16:4-5 appear in Num. 11, so that secondary material must have been added. In addition to possible secondary Deuteronomistic additions in vs. 4, it has been proposed that all of vs. 5, dealing with the double portion of manna on the sixth day, is secondary and under the influence of vss. 22ff. Cf. J. Coert Rylaarsdam, "Introduction and Exegesis to Exodus," in The Interpreter's Bible, Vol. I, ed. by George A. Buttrick (New York: Abingdon Press, 1952), p. 950; Rudolph, Der "Elohist," p. 275. However, in the light of our present knowledge of the antiquity of the Sabbath institution (unquestionably premonarchical), there is no reason to question that J (or any old narrative strand) would make mention of it. We have no evidence that such a statement could not have been made, when the old narrative was prepared.

[2] The following expressions are characteristic of P: "all the leaders" (vs. 22), "the congregation" (vs. 22), "this is what the Lord has commanded" (vs. 23), "a day of solemn rest" (vs. 23).

[3] There is no agreement as to what verses belong here. Noth (Exodus, p. 132) includes vss. 28-31, vs. 28 being a Deuteronomistic gloss, however. Other scholars include vss. 27-30. Thus Beer and Galling, Exodus, p. 91; Gerhard von Rad, Die Priesterschrift im Hexateuch literarisch untersucht und theologisch gewerted, BWANT, No. 65 (Stuttgart-Berlin: Verlag W. Kohlhammer, 1934), pp. 27-30. Baentsch (Exodus-Leviticus, p. 155) will include only vs. 29, vss. 28, 30 being considered redactional. It is very doubtful, however, if literary analysis can really succeed in extracting the old material here, because it is infiltrated into P and not added mechanically. Thus vs. 22a reflects vs. 5; vs. 23b reflects Num. 11:8 (older than P); vss. 26, 29 seem to know the old Sabbath laws (Ex. 23:12; 34:21); vss. 27, 29 also reflect vss. 4-5. There is thus reason to believe that we have remnants of old material throughout the chapter. Cf. the conclusions of the recent analysis by Bruce J. Malina, The Palestinian Manna Tradition: The Manna Tradition in the Palestinian Targums and its Relationship to the New Testament Writings (Leiden: E. J. Brill, 1968), pp. 1-41.

its writer (P) incorporated a number of traditions from the older manna account, added explanations characteristic of P to them,[1] and expanded the Sabbath motif of the old manna story.[2] In a later section we shall attempt to isolate passages which may contain traditional material.

Ex. 31:12-17

Yahweh's speech to Moses on the mountain (Ex. 24-31) concludes with this reference to the Sabbath which, along with the whole speech, is usually attributed to the priestly historian.[3] Moreover, it is generally assumed that it was intended to emphasize the fact that the construction of the tabernacle must not interfere with the observance of the Sabbath.[4]

There are, however, serious breaks in this passage, and its unity is not easily maintained.[5] It has been proposed that it was

---

[1]E.g., vss. 22a, 23, 24, 25, 26b.

[2]While the old account appears merely to have narrated the sequence of the manna provision with an appeal for the people to recognize it, the later expansion has shifted the emphasis from the gift of the manna to the requirements for the Sabbath, e.g., the expressions, "tomorrow is a solemn rest"; "Sabbath to the Lord."

[3]Cf. Fohrer, Introduction, p. 180; Eissfeldt, Introduction, p. 189; von Rad, Die Priesterschrift, pp. 63ff.; Beer and Galling, Exodus, pp. 151-52; Rylaarsdam, "Exodus," p. 1061; Klaus Koch, Die Priesterschrift von Exodus 25 bis Leviticus 16: Eine überlieferungsgeschichtliche und literarkritische Untersuchung, FRLANT, No. 71 (Göttingen: Vandenhoeck & Ruprecht, 1959), pp. 37-38.

[4]This is the most obvious conclusion to be drawn from the context, cf. Noth, Exodus, pp. 240-41; Meesters, Op zoek naar de oorsprong van de Sabbat, p. 124.

[5]Vs. 13a and vs. 14a resemble each other closely. Vs. 14a and vs. 15b both require the death penalty for working on the Sabbath. Additional repetitions are found in vss. 16a, 17a. Moreover, in

composed from two different sources,[1] or that an original statement was expanded with secondary additions.[2] To the first proposal it may be objected that two or more consecutive sources cannot be differentiated,[3] and to the second proposal it may be said that even the additions (perhaps the section in 3rd pers., vss. 15-17) contain traditional elements. A more adequate explanation of the disunity in this passage is accomplished by assuming the existence of a number of early and late traditions, most of them legal, which, except for obvious additions and modifications (vss. 14a, 16b), have been preserved in their basic character and form. This fact can account for the wooden nature of the pericope, as well as its inability to be closely related to its context, assuming that it was so intended.[4] What we have then are rather fixed

vss. 12-14 Yahweh appears in 1st pers. and Israel in 2nd pers. pl., whereas in vss. 15-17 Yahweh and Israel are both addressed in 3rd pers.

[1]Cf. von Rad, Die Priesterschrift, pp. 63-64. p^A: vss. 12, 13b, 14; p^B: vss. 13a, 15-17.

[2]After noting the similarities between this passage, Ezekiel (Ezek. 20, 22, 23, 44, 45, 46), and H (Lev. 19, 23, 26), Baentsch proposes that it consists of a kernel from H or Ezekiel, and that this was subsequently reworked by a priestly writer (Exodus-Leviticus, pp. 266-68).

[3]The source theory for P, especially as developed by von Rad, is generally being discredited. Cf. Paul Humbert, "Die literarische Zweiheit der Priester-Codex in der Genesis (Kritische Untersuchungen der These von von Rad)," ZAW, LVIII (1940-41), 30-57; Weiser, The Old Testament, pp. 137-38. As for Ex. 31:12-17, the two "sources" demonstrate both similarities and dissimilarities, but no continuing sources can be detected here, or in P as a whole.

[4]It is remarkable that a Sabbath command presumably intended to ensure the observation of this day during the construction of the tabernacle should employ so many different commandments and statements about the Sabbath without once making reference to the context of the passage. The reason might be that the traditions of the priestly writer gave him no freedom in formulating the Sabbath laws for the tabernacle craftsmen.

traditional ways of speaking of the Sabbath. These may have had different origins, but they were available to the priestly writer who strung
them together without much alteration. We will examine these traditions
in the following section.

Ex. 35:2-3

The priestly account of the construction of the sanctuary is
introduced by a brief Sabbath command corresponding to Ex. 31:15. It
bears the traits of the priestly writer,[1] but may have as its basis a
traditional Sabbath law.[2] The prohibition against making fires on the
Sabbath (vs. 3) may also be a late (priestly) literary product,[3] but it
has intrigued many interpreters as a possible primitive Sabbath regulation, a suggestion which shall be pursued later.[4]

It is generally assumed that the Sabbath command appears at the
beginning of Moses' speech regarding the new sanctuary building project
to ensure that even these building activities would not take place on

---

In other words, the Sabbath laws existed in rather fixed form for the
writer of this passage.

[1]Cf. the introduction (vs. 1), and the expressions: "Sabbath of
solemn rest"; "holy Sabbath . . . to the Lord"; "in all your habitations."

[2]The theme: six days you shall work, but the seventh day you
shall rest, is very old (Ex. 23:12; 34:21). See below, pp. 161-65.

[3]Thus Noth, Exodus, p. 275; Baentsch, Exodus-Leviticus, p. 288.

[4]Von Rad (Die Priesterschrift, p. 64), noting that vs. 3 is not
part of God's speech to Moses in Ex. 31:12-17, doubts that the verse is
original in its present position. Two additional passages (Ex. 16:23;
Num. 15:32-6) give specific Sabbath commands, and both have to do with
making fires, probably for the purpose of cooking. It is quite possible,
therefore, that the prohibition against fire making, whatever the reason
for it may be, is an old one. See below, pp. 136-38, 153.

the holy day.[1] However, the passage is not integrated into the account of the building activities, except perhaps for verse 3.[2] Verse 2, on the other hand, is similar not only to Ex. 31:15, but equally much to the priestly Sabbath laws in Lev. 19, 23 (see below). Its presence here may, therefore, not be governed by the context, but it may just reflect the general preoccupation of the priestly literature with the Sabbath. If so, we may think of an impulsive recitation at important junctions of standard Sabbath laws as the raison d'etre for this verse.[3] Neverthe-less, the occurrence of Sabbath laws in connection with the speeches of Yahweh and Moses regarding the construction of the tabernacle is worth our attention, and it is quite possible that we should associate these laws with their context.

Lev. 16:31

Lev. 16 appears within the priestly narrative (Pg) and contains old ritual regulations for the day of atonement.[4] The verse in question

---

[1]Cf. Baentsch, Exodus-Leviticus, p. 288; Beer and Galling, Exodus, p. 67; Rylaarsdam, "Exodus," p. 1082; Meesters, Op zoek naar de oorsprong van de Sabbat, p. 126.

[2]It is possible that the prohibition against making fires makes specific reference to the work of the artisans who were to prepare the metals for the construction. Cf. Rylaarsdam, "Exodus," p. 1082. Beer and Galling emend the text to read: "Nicht sollt ihr ein Feuer anzünden zu allen von euch geplanten Werken am siebenten Tag" (Exodus, p. 164).

[3]Sabbath laws appear at the end of Yahweh's speech (Ex. 31:12-17), at the beginning of Moses' speech (Ex. 35:2-3), at the beginning of the list of festivals (Lev. 23:3), and at the beginning of the curses and blessing with which H concludes (Lev. 26:2).

[4]It is generally thought that there was in existence a basic P narrative to which legal material and other expansions were added subse-quently. Lev. 16 is one such addition which has an identity and a

interprets this important day of the great fall festival as a šabbat
šabbātôn. It is possible that this interpretation of the day of atonement is pre-exilic,[1] but, although the Sabbath of rest is an old
institution, it is not likely, for verses 29-34 look particularly like
an interpretative expansion of the description of the day of atonement
in the previous part of the chapter.[2]

Lev. 19:3, 30

Recent research in the Holiness Code (H),[3] Lev. 16-26, has led
to the recognition of at least three types of material in these

---

[1] literary history all of its own. Cf. Martin Noth, Leviticus: A
Commentary, trans. by J. E. Anderson (Philadelphia: Westminster Press,
1965), pp. 117-26; Karl Elliger, Leviticus, HAT, Vol. IV (Tübingen:
J. C. B. Mohr [Paul Siebeck], 1966), pp. 9ff. It is, however, often
very difficult to separate satisfactorily the narrative from the laws,
and we must probably assume that both historical and cultic legal
material have always been indigenous to P. It is true, however, that
isolated blocks of legal material, viz., H, appear in P, but they are in
no way secondary in date to their context. We should thus understand P
as a literary composite consisting of legal, cultic, and narrative
material from various periods.

[1] Cf. Paul Heinisch, Das Buch Leviticus, HS, Pt. I, Vol. 3 (Bonn:
Peter Hanstein Verlagsbuchhandlung, 1935), pp. 79-80.

[2] Cf. Noth, Leviticus, p. 126; Elliger, Leviticus, pp. 207-9
(dated ca. 400 B.C.).

[3] Cf. the following recent studies: Walter Kornfeld, Studien zum
Heiligkeitsgesetz (Lev. 17-26) (Vienna: Herder Verlag, 1952); A. Quast,
"Analyse des Sündenbewusstseins Israel nach dem Heiligkeitsgesetz" (un-
published dr. theol. dissertation, University of Göttingen, 1957);
Henning Graf Reventlow, Das Heiligkeitsgesetz formgeschichtlich
untersucht, WMANT, No. 6 (Neukirchen-Vluyn: Neukirchener Verlag, 1961);
Rudolph Kilian, Literarkritische und formgeschichtliche Untersuchung des
Heiligkeitsgesetzes (Bonn: Peter Hanstein's Verlag GMBH, 1963);
Christian Feucht, Untersuchungen zum Heiligkeitsgesetz (Berlin: Evange-
lische Verlagsanstalt, 1964).

chapters.[1] (1) Phrases and expressions which are typical of the general

context of Leviticus, i.e., from P. (2) Several collections of laws,

some of which show great antiquity. (3) Elaborations or expansions of

the laws, perhaps through preaching on them.[2] This material fell

together at an early time (certainly pre-exilic for the most part), and

it was subsequently adopted into the so-called P source.

As for the position of Lev. 19:3, 30 within the threefold

structure outlined above, opinions differ. We will, therefore, make a

few observations about the layer in which these laws would best fit.

(1) It has been demonstrated that Lev. 19 contains series of apodeictic

laws.[3] These terse pronouncements regarding agriculture, moral behavior,

---

[1]This is probably an oversimplification, but a workable one for
our purposes. A position which aims at a very fine stratification of
the material in H is held by Elliger, Leviticus, pp. 14-20. His view,
that the Vorlage went through four redactions (Ph^1, Ph^2, Ph^3, Ph^4), and
that these account for only the main stages of the development of H,
must be supported by a meticulous examination of the text, a task for
which my eye is not sharp enough, and even then his conclusions are not
quite convincing.

[2]Cf. Gerhard von Rad, Studies in Deuteronomy, trans. by D. Stalker, SBT, No. 9 (London: SCM Press, Ltd., 1953), pp. 25-36; Reventlow,
Das Heiligkeitsgesetz, pp. 162ff. It is not easy to determine which
circles were responsible for surrounding these old laws with later homiletic expansions. Reventlow has proposed in his study (Das
Heiligkeitsgesetz, pp. 126ff.) that the liturgy of covenantal festivals
has through the centuries produced H: "Das Heiligkeitsgesetz ist ein
Gottesdienstliches Dokument." However, his study fails to establish any
covenant terminology or forms in H. Another recent study concludes what
von Rad might have concluded long ago, namely, that H stands in the
Deuteronomic tradition, and that it dates from the exile. Winfried
Thiel, "Erwägungen zum Alter des Heiligkeitsgesetzes," ZAW, LXXXI (1969),
40-73. The lack of a formal covenant structure in the chapters and the
nature of the content, some of which is designed for the clergy, seem to
indicate that we are dealing with laws and hortatory additions for the
instruction of priest and layman alike, but not with remnants of
covenant liturgies.

[3]Von Rad, Studies in Deuteronomy, pp. 25-36; Kilian,

mixing of different kinds of material, sexual relations, et cetera, no doubt reach far back into antiquity, but the Sabbath laws hardly belong here. (2) Verses 3, 30 are generally regarded as early by those scholars who look for decalogues, similar to the one in Ex. 20; Dt. 5, in this chapter.[1] However, we cannot be certain that the pattern of a decalogue is present at all. In fact, it is both questionable and unnecessary to look for one.[2] If so, the Sabbath laws must make it on their own.

Both of them read, "and you shall keep my Sabbaths"; but whereas the former is preceded by a reference to the fifth commandment, the latter is followed by a call to "reverence my sanctuary." The verbs are identical in the two verses, and the one used about the Sabbath (šmr) is typical both of the Deuteronomistic and priestly literature. The plural

---

Untersuchung des Heiligkeitsgesetzes, pp. 57-63.

[1]Cf. Julian Morgenstern, "The Decalogue of the Holiness Code," HUCA, XXVI (1955), 1-27. This decalogue was, according to Morgenstern, used for the dedication of the second temple. Also Sigmund Mowinckel, "Zur Geschichte der Dekaloge," ZAW, LV (1937), 218-35. Mowinckel proposes to have found two decalogues in this chapter, A (vss. 3-12a) with the verbs in plural, and B (vss. 13a-18a) with the verbs in singular. The H decalogue (Lev. 19) is dated between the cultic "decalogue" (Ex. 34:11ff.) and the ethical decalogue (Ex. 20; Dt. 5). The criterion for this stratification is the degree to which the cultic and ritual laws have undergone a socio-ethical metamorphosis. Reventlow has correctly objected to these simple value judgments (Das Heiligkeitsgesetz, pp. 65, 67-8). Recently Elliger has found a dodecalogue with verbs in the singular and a decalogue with verbs in plural, but vss. 3, 30 do not belong in either (Leviticus, p. 254).

[2]The fact that the legal material in Lev. 19 is interspersed with hortatory comments makes it necessary to edit out the old laws and collect ten of them to reconstruct a decalogue. Since such attempts have failed to produce a collection containing laws fairly similar to the laws in the traditional Decalogue, it is much better to abandon altogether the decalogue idea in Lev. 19.

(Sabbaths) occurs apart from H particularly in Ezekiel, i.e., in the later literature. Finally, the terse "you shall keep my Sabbaths" presumes that everyone knew what was meant by this regulation. There is thus some reason for assuming that we have in the laws a late restatement of traditional Sabbath laws, at a time after the formulation of the Decalogue, but probably before the exile.[1]

Lev. 23:3

It is generally assumed that verses 2-3 are a secondary exilic addition to this chapter which is itself a literary composite.[2] The existence of two superscriptions (vs. 2 and vs. 4) strongly supports this assumption.[3] However, there are reasons to suppose that the verse is not, therefore, a late and free composition. It does contain characteristics of the late literature, and it is fitted into the context of

---

[1]Kilian has proposed that vs. 30, which is independent of vs. 3 because of the different contexts of the two laws, is pre-exilic (Untersuchung des Heiligkeitsgesetzes, p. 53). The Sabbath, he argues, occupied a unique and independent role not shared by the sanctuary during the exile. See however Ezek. 23:38. Elliger (Leviticus, pp. 245ff.) suggests that the laws (vss. 3-4), which are taken from the Decalogue, served Ph[1] to associate this chapter with the Sinai legal corpus, whereas vs. 30 was an earlier addition to his Vorlage. In any case, the unique association of Sabbath and sanctuary (vs. 30) and of Sabbath and reverence for parents (vs. 3) indicate very forcefully that the Sabbath laws are part of the traditions behind this chapter. Cf. Kilian, Untersuchung des Heiligkeitsgesetzes, pp. 63-64.

[2]The main elements are the older agricultural three-part festival calendar (vss. 9-22, 39-43) and the later priestly two-part calendar (vss. 1-8, 23-38). Cf. Reventlow, Das Heiligkeitsgesetz, pp. 103ff.; Kilian, Untersuchung des Heiligkeitsgesetzes, pp. 102ff.; Noth, Leviticus, pp. 165-68.

[3]In addition, it is pointed out that the Sabbath as a weekly feast day does not naturally belong in a festival calendar which recounts yearly festivals.

the festal calendar by means of expressions such as "holy convocation,"
"a Sabbath of solemn rest," "you shall do no work," "to Yahweh. Nevertheless, one theme stands out as a traditional one: "Six days shall
work be done; but on the seventh day is a Sabbath of solemn rest." We
have already met it in Ex. 31:25; 35:2, and it also appears in the
fourth commandment of the Decalogue and in the old laws in Ex. 23:12;
34:21. The next phrase, "you shall do no work" (kol-mᵉlā>kāh lō>
taᶜᵃsû) occurs in identical form, except in reverse word order, in the
fourth commandment (Ex. 20:9, Dt. 5:14). However, it is also a common
phrase in Lev. 23, and not much can be concluded from it.[1] It is a safe
conclusion, therefore, that verse 3 is a secondary addition in this
chapter, and that it is purposefully fitted into the context of the
festal calendar, but that a traditional Sabbath law lies behind it in
its present form.

Lev. 23:11, 15, 16

The Sabbath is referred to in verses 11, 15, 16 in connection
with the timing of certain cultic activities and festivals. The verses
appear in what is generally considered the older part of the chapter,[2]
but apart from attributing it to H, no further discussion will be necessary at this point. For a discussion of the problematic expression "the
morrow after the Sabbath," see below, p. 109.

---

[1] Vss. 8, 21, 25, 36.

[2] See, however, Elliger, Leviticus, p. 311.

Lev. 23:32

A close relationship exists between this verse and Lev. 16:31 which is also dealing with the day of atonement.[1] It is possible that Lev. 16:31 depends on Lev. 23:32 and was perhaps added at the occasion of H's incorporation into the literature of P.[2] At any rate, the verse itself looks like an expansion on the regulations regarding the day of atonement by means of the Sabbath theme. The expressions šabbat šabbātôn and tišbᵉtû šabbattᵉkem (cf. Lev. 25:2, 26:34) point to a late date, with no ancient material lurking behind our present text.

Lev. 23:38

Lev. 23:38 forms the conclusion of the festival calendar. It excludes the Sabbath from the festivals, but not from the religious life of the community. Perhaps the remark "besides the sabbaths" is related to the insertion of the Sabbath command in verse 3.[3]

Lev. 24:8

The regulations concerning the lamps and the showbread (vss. 1-9) are attributed to the priestly writer,[4] not as a free

---

[1] The wording is partly identical in the two verses: "It shall be to you a sabbath of solemn rest, and you shall afflict yourselves."

[2] Cf. Elliger, Leviticus, p. 207; Kilian, Untersuchung des Heiligkeitsgesetzes, p. 108; Noth, Leviticus, pp. 173-74. The relationship between the verses could certainly be reversed (thus Kilian), but since Lev. 23:26-32 contain no reference to the rites of Lev. 16, it is assumed that the characterization of the day of atonement as a Sabbath (involving affliction and abstention from work) must be primary in Lev. 23, but it is quite uncertain.

[3] Cf. Meesters, Op zoek naar de oorsprong van de Sabbat, p. 135.

[4] Noth, Leviticus, p. 177; Kilian, Untersuchung des

invention,[1] but as a free reworking of traditions which are part of the wilderness theme in P.[2] However, although there is good reason to believe that the institution of sacred bread is ancient,[3] we have no early confirmation about the particular Sabbath ritual involving the exchange of fresh bread. We cannot trace early traditions behind this text, as far as the Sabbath is concerned.

Lev. 25:1-7

The regulations concerning the sabbatical year appear as a well defined unit in this chapter[4] and are attributed to the Holiness Code

---

Heiligkeitsgesetzes, p. 111; Thiel, "Heiligkeitsgesetzes," p. 60; cf. Elliger, Leviticus, pp. 324ff.

[1]Thus Wellhausen, Die Composition des Hexateuchs, p. 165. "In Kap. 24 ist V. 1-9 zweifelsohne eine Novelle zu Q [P]."

[2]See the studies by Koch, Die Priesterschrift von Exodus 25 bis Leviticus 16; Rolf Rendtorff, Die Gesetze in der Priesterschrift: Eine gattungsgeschichtliche Untersuchung, FRLANT, N.F., No. 44 (Göttingen: Vandenhoeck & Ruprecht, 1954). Cf. Reventlow, Das Heiligkeitsgesetz, pp. 117-18. It is difficult if not impossible, however, to extract old elements of the wilderness theme in this reworking, for though the passage is consciously describing the wilderness sanctuary, it never asks historically and scientifically what that sanctuary was really like. In the words of Reventlow: "Tempel und Wüstenheiligtum werden als eine 'mystische' Einheit betrachtet." If this is correct, the historical question is practically forbidding.

[3]See above, p. 55.

[4]Cf. Elliger, Leviticus, pp. 338ff. The relationship of it to the much longer section (vss. 8-17) concerning the jubilee year is not at all clear. According to one theory the latter is an idealistic theory developed "on paper" in the exile by means of an analogy with the festival of weeks. Cf. Wellhausen, Die Composition des Hexateuch, p. 169; Baentsch, Exodus-Leviticus, p. 424; Kilian, Untersuchung des Heiligkeitsgesetzes, p. 146; Thiel, "Heiligkeitsgesetzes," p. 61. Reventlow has attempted to show the failure of this view by demonstrating that both the sabbatical year and the year of jubilee belong to the Vorlage of the chapter (Das Heiligkeitsgesetz, p. 139).

with little or no priestly redaction.[1] The main content expressed in
verses 3-7 by means of short commands in 2nd. pers. sg. is, therefore,
no doubt quite old.[2]

Our primary concern in this study is not, however, with the
antiquity of the regulation of the sabbatical year, nor with the institution per se, but rather with the influence of the Sabbath, including
the Sabbath terminology, on it, and vice versa. We shall examine this
question below.

Lev. 26:2, 34-35, 43

Lev. 26:2 is identical with Lev. 19:30 and may very well be a
repetition of it. Verses 34-35, 43 elaborate upon the regulations for
the sabbatical year by promising a Sabbath to the land in return for
those sabbatical years it had not received.[3] These verses also appear
in the conclusion of H, and since they provide an explanation for the

---

[1]Vss. 1-2 are generally attributed to a secondary hand, as well
as such expressions as "the land shall keep a Sabbath," "a Sabbath of
solemn rest." It is worth noting that none of the other references to
the sabbatical year in the Pentateuch outside H (Ex. 21:2-6; 23:10-11;
Dt. 15:12-18) use the words šabbāt or šabbātôn to describe this year.

[2]According to Reventlow (Das Heiligkeitsgesetz, p. 133) it dates
back to the eighth century B.C., but this is not generally accepted. It
is interesting, however, that of the various regulations for the sabbatical year Lev. 25:1-7 is most similar to the ones found in Ex. 23:10-11,
i.e., in B.

[3]According to R.S.V. the land will enjoy its Sabbaths. One
meaning of the verb rṣh is "enjoy," "find pleasure in" (Greek eudokísei).
An alternative translation is based on the second meaning of the verb,
namely, "pay off," or in hiphᶜil "make good." Cf. Koehler and Baumgartner, Lexicon, 906; Elliger, Leviticus, p. 363; Siegmund Fraenkel,
"Zur Wurzel רצה," ZAW, XIX (1899), 181. The idea of having restored or
made good fits the context very well, i.e., the land will now receive
what was formerly denied it.

destruction of the land, they are assigned to the time of the exile.[1]
The change from 2nd. pers. pl. to 3rd. pers. pl. in verse 40 has suggested to some scholars an unevenness in the last part of the chapter,[2]
but the similarity of the language in verses 34-35 and verse 43 leads us
to believe that the verses are not altogether independent of each other.

Num. 15:32-36

The etiological legal narrative[3] is designed to settle a dispute
by referring to the rulings instituted by Israel's authoritative ancestors. The present narrative is generally assigned to and bears the
marks of P,[4] or even a later hand.[5] Nevertheless, we shall no doubt
look for an old tradition behind these verses, especially so in the

---

[1]Cf. Elliger, Leviticus, pp. 371-72; Baentsch, Exodus-Leviticus,
p. 431; Wellhausen, Die Composition des Hexateuchs, p. 173; Kilian,
Untersuchung des Heiligkeitsgesetzes, p. 152; Feucht, Heiligkeitsgesetz,
p. 171; Noth, Leviticus, p. 201. Reventlow (Das Heiligkeitsgesetz, p.
160) takes exception to this concensus opinion, when he understands
vss. 34-35 to present the possible future fate of the community, and
vss. 40-46 to reveal the final outcome of the theological reflection on
the blessing and curse theme in Lev. 26, all on the basis of pre-exilic
covenant theology, i.e., the verses are pre-exilic.

[2]Cf. Elliger, Leviticus, p. 369.

[3]Cf. Lev. 24:10-23; Ex. 12:26-27; 13:14-15. It may be compared
to the Islamic hadit, whereby customs and laws are traced to the actions
or decisions of worthy ancestors. Eissfeldt, Introduction, pp. 31-32.

[4]Eissfeldt, Introduction, p. 205; Fohrer, Introduction, p. 180.

[5]This is done on the basis of the Midrashic character of the
regulation, and particularly because of the verb prš (vs. 34) which in
the sense of "make clear" is late Hebrew. Koehler and Baumgartner,
Lexicon, p. 782-83; Gesenius and Buhl, Handwörterbuch, p. 663. Cf.
George B. Gray, Numbers, ICC, Vol. IV (New York: Charles Scribner's
Sons, 1903), p. 182.

light of other related prohibitions which appear to be ancient.[1]

Num. 28:9-10

The specification regarding Sabbath sacrifices is generally not regarded as coming from pre-exilic times.[2] In exilic and postexilic times, on the other hand, we do find information indicating that such laws were effective, i.e., that the Sabbath sacrifices were regulated.[3] This does not mean that the Sabbath was not a cultic feast day before the exile,[4] but no law or practice specifying the amount or nature of the Sabbath sacrifices is known in pre-exilic literature. It may be, of course, that this regulation in P is based on older practices, a question to which we will return below.

---

[1]Cf. Ex. 16:23; 35:3. The practice of deriving contemporary legal practices from the ruling of important ancestors was not just a literary device, but a practical one. The rulings of the ancestors were indeed remembered. We may thus suppose that the story of the woodgatherer existed in the memory of the priestly circles, and served to emphasize the seriousness of working on the Sabbath, even though the task was innocent. The gathering of sticks implies making a fire (I Kg. 17:12), presumably for the purpose of cooking or perhaps the preparation of tools. Cf. J. Weingreen, "The Case of the Woodgatherer (Numbers XV 32-36)," VT, XVI (1966), 361-64; Anthony Phillips, "The Case of the Woodgatherer Reconsidered," VT, XIX (1969), 125-38.

[2]Cf. John Marsh, "Introduction and Exegesis to Numbers," in The Interpreter's Bible, Vol. II, ed. by George A. Buttrick (New York: Abingdon Press, 1953), pp. 174-75; Gray, Numbers, p. 410; Meesters, Op zoek naar de oorsprong van de Sabbat, p. 141. The general thrust of the argument is that Num. 28 is too meticulously composed to provide a credible account of pre-exilic affairs. Notable are the precise times for sacrifice, the precise quantities of sacrifice, and in addition to these, the lack of participation in the sacrifices by the worshippers, as was customarily done in older times.

[3]Cf. II Chr. 8:13; 31:3; Neh. 10:33; Josephus, Ant. III, 10.

[4]Allusions may be given in Is. 1:13; Hos. 2:11. Cf. Gray, Numbers, p. 410; Martin Noth, Das vierte Buch Mose: Numeri, ATD, Vol. VII (Göttingen: Vandenhoeck & Ruprecht, 1966), p. 192.

The Decalogue and Other Codes

Ex. 20:8-11; Dt. 5:12-15

The Sabbath commandment in the Decalogue shows marked variations in its two recensions. We shall first discuss these and then turn to the question of the "original" command.

Ex. 20:8 begins with zākôr (remember) while Dt. 5:12 has šāmôr (keep, observe). The search for the original verb has not yet succeeded, but since šāmôr is characteristic of Deuteronomy, it has been attributed to the author of D. Still, we cannot be certain that zākôr in Ex. 20:8 preceded it.[1] This first word, however, has little significance for the interpretation of the commandment as a whole.[2] Dt. 5:12 adds "as the LORD your God commanded you." This is clearly a Deuteronomic insertion

---

[1]Some scholars hold that šāmôr coming from D is older than zākôr from the hand of P. Cf. Ludwig Köhler, "Der Dekalog," ThR, N.F. I (1929), 180; Hulst, "Bemerkungen zum Sabbatgebot," pp. 158-59. Others, noting that šāmôr is typical of D, argue that zākôr is original. Cf. Nielsen, The Ten Commandments, p. 38; Werner Keszler, "Die literarische, historische und theologische Problematik des Dekalogs," VT, VII (1957), pp. 9-10; Norbert Lohfink, "Zur Dekalogfassung von Dt. 5," BZ, N.F. IX (1965), pp. 22-23. Perhaps the original verb cannot be determined with any certainty. Cf. Stamm and Andrew, The Ten Commandments, pp. 14-15.

[2]Henning Graf Reventlow, Gebot und Predigt im Dekalog (Gerd Mohn: Gütersloher Verlagshaus, 1962), p. 45; Noth, Exodus, p. 164; Meesters, Op zoek naar de oorsprong van de Sabbat, p. 101; Willy Schottroff, "Gedenken" im Alten Orient und im Alten Testament: Die Wurzel zākar im Semitischen Sprachkreis, WMANT, No. 15 (Neukirchen-Vluyn: Neukirchener Verlag, 1964), p. 155. For a contrary opinion see Childs, Memory and Tradition, p. 55. In Childs's view zākôr is original, but it was replaced by šāmôr in D, when at a later time "remember" had developed from being a purely psychological term (be aware of, recognize) into being a theological expression for Israel's relationship to God's saving acts in history. With this change zākôr could no longer be used about the festivals, for Israel was not to remember festivals, but to observe them in order to remember. It is a question, however, if "remember" did not continue to be used in its purely psychological sense even after D (cf. Lev. 26:42; Neh. 13:14, 22; Jon. 2:7).

84

which appears elsewhere in the book, viz., Dt. 5:16; 20:17. It is
missing in Ex. 20:8, the parallel verse, as well as in the Nash papyrus.
The next addition is the typically Deuteronomic expansion, "your ox and
your ass and all. . . ." It too merits little attention. The final
addition appears in Dt. 5:14b as follows, "that your manservant and your
maidservant may rest as well as you." It is rather important, for it is
related to the Deuteronomic reason for the Sabbath which is different
from that given in Ex. 20:11. This leaves the two variant reasons for
the Sabbath observance (Ex. 20:11, Dt. 5:15). The first one is clearly
related to Gen. 2:1-3 and Ex. 31:17; and it is, therefore, attributed to
P, who may also be responsible for parts of verses 8-10. The second
reason is Deuteronomic in character (cf. Dt. 15:15; 16:12; 24:18, 22),
and so it is attributed to the circles responsible for Deuteronomy.

The fourth commandment in the present Decalogue is unquestionably a composite law consisting of early segments and later expansions.
It has, therefore, long been a pressing problem to identify the oldest
and original part of the commandment. This has been a particularly
meaningful task in recent decades, when it has been generally assumed
that the ten commandments in some form or other reach back to Mosaic
times.[1]

---

[1]Julius Wellhausen and his students assigned the Decalogue to
the time of the prophets, or even later. For a comprehensive bibliography see Rowley, "Moses and the Decalogue," nn. 2-4, p. 1. However, a
number of important studies in the early part of this century beginning
with Hugo Gressmann's Mose und seine Zeit (Göttingen, 1913) have
changed this late dating. Cf. Hans Schmidt, "Mose und der Dekalog," in
Eucharisterion: H. Gunkel zum 60. Geburtstage, I, ed. by Hans Schmidt,
FRLANT, No. 36 (Göttingen: Vandenhoeck & Ruprecht, 1923), pp. 78-119;
Sigmund Mowinckel, Le Décalogue (Paris: Librairie Félix Alcan, 1927);
Albrecht Alt, "Die Ursprünge des israelitischen Rechts," (1934), E.T.

Several criteria have been employed in extracting the original
commandments, including the fourth.[1] (1) Since expansions are generally
suffixed, they could be eliminated by extracting only the first brief
prohibition in each commandment. The short laws (VI-VIII) would then
provide some kind of pattern for the original commandments, except in
the case of IV and V which contain positive commandments. Following
this criterion, the original Sabbath commandment would read, "Remember
(observe) the sabbath day, (to keep it holy)."[2] (2) Following a

---

"The Origins of Israelite Law," in Essays on Old Testament History and
Religion, trans. by R. A. Wilson, Anchor Books (New York: Doubleday &
Company, Inc., 1968), pp. 103-71. The results of these and other studies
have established a very broad agreement among scholars, both critical
and conservative, that a basic Decalogue without the later expansions
should be dated in Mosaic times. This conclusion is based on considerations of the content of the code and the form of the individual laws
within it. The literature is too numerous to be discussed here, but
reference can be made to the excellent bibliographies by Rowley, "Moses
and the Decalogue," pp. 1-2; Johann Jakob Stamm, "Dreissig Jahre
Dekalogforschung," ThR, N.F. XXVII (1961), 189-239, 281-305; Stamm and
Andrew, The Ten Commandments, pp. 22ff.

[1]It is generally accepted that the fourth commandment was part
of the original Decalogue. An exception to this view was taken by
Schmidt, "Mose und der Dekalog," pp. 105ff. Here the original Decalogue
is reconstructed without the fourth and fifth commandments on the ground
that the Sabbath institution is a late development in the history of
ancient Israel, but this view is no longer tenable.

[2]This is the near classical expression of the original fourth
commandment. Cf. Kittel, Geschichte des Volkes Israel, pp. 383-84;
Mowinckel, La Décalogue, pp. 4-5; Adolphe Lods, Histoire de la littéra-
ture hebraïque et juive (Paris: Payot, 1950), pp. 338-39; Stamm,
"Dreissig Jahre Dekalogforschung," p. 201; J. Philip Hyatt, "Moses and
the Ethical Decalogue," Encounter, XXVI (1965), 202. "To keep it holy"
may be secondary, for the oldest Sabbath was primarily a day of rest.
Cf. Georg Fohrer, "Das sogenannte apodiktisch formulierte Recht und der
Dekalog," KuD, XI (1965), 64 (n. 51); for a contrary opinion see Alfred
Jepsen, "Beiträge zur Auslegung und Geschichte des Dekalogs," ZAW,
LXXIX (1967), 293.

suggestion by Sellin and Alt,[1] certain scholars seek greater uniformity in the original laws of the Decalogue. This is achieved by introducing all the laws with a negative command (lō˒ plus the imperfect), and by structuring them according to a certain rhythm (four stresses).[2] The Sabbath law has been reconstructed according to this criterion as follows: "Thou shalt not do any work on the sabbath (day)."[3] Though this reconstruction produces a uniform poetic sounding law code, it is very hypothetical. The commandment lō˒ ta⁽ᵃseh mᵉlā˒kāh bᵉyôm haššabbāt does indeed contain words characteristic of the Sabbath laws (cf. Ex. 31:15; 35:2-3; Lev. 23:3, et cetera), and part of the sentence appears in Ex. 20:9 and Dt. 5:13. However, in all these laws the prohibition against work follows the reference to the six-seven day scheme. It is, therefore, questionable that precisely this prohibition should be isolated as the original commandment, and made to serve without its normal context. (3) It is much more likely that any attempt to create uniformity in the code should be avoided. Not all the laws must begin with lō˒ followed by the imperfect, and a uniform rhythm need not be

---

[1]Alt, "The Origins of Israelite Law," p. 152; Ernst Sellin, Geschichte des israelitisch-jüdischen Volkes, I (Leipzig: Quelle & Meyer, 1924), p. 84.

[2]Cf. Karlheins H. Rabast, Das apodiktische Recht im Deuteronomium und im Heiligkeitsgesetz (Berlin-Hermsdorf: Heimatdienstverlag, 1948), pp. 35-38. Rabast, who was Alt's pupil, arrived at a dodecalogue. He is followed quite closely by Nielsen, The Ten Commandments, pp. 84-86. Here, however, the number ten is preserved. Both studies lengthen the three short commandments (VI-VIII) by adding objects for the verbs so as to preserve the rhythm.

[3]Nielsen, The Ten Commandments, pp. 88-89, adds bᵉyôm and reads "on the Sabbath day," because it and not simply "on the Sabbath" is attested before Nehemiah.

maintained.[1] If, therefore, uniformity in the opening words and in rhythm are required to have a true series of laws, we must assume that the Decalogue originally was composed of two or three such short series.[2]

We must thus not seek conformity with the short prohibitions in the Decalogue when attempting to uncover the oldest form of the fourth commandment. If this is correct, there is really no reason for suspecting a positive command like "Remember the Sabbath day, to keep it holy." Its formulation corresponds, except for the verb, with the one in Dt. 5:12. We have, of course, no other clearly early illustration of it;[3] and, consequently, its antiquity depends solely on its presence in the Decalogue, which in its oldest form goes back to Mosaic times.[4]

---

[1]It is now recognized that more than one form belongs within the apodeictic type laws as found in the Decalogue. Cf. Erhard Gerstenberger, Wesen und Herkunft des "apodiktischen Rechts," WMANT, No. 20 (Neukirchen-Vluyn: Neukirchener Verlag, 1965), pp. 23ff.; Fohrer, "Das sogenannte apodiktisch formulierte Recht," pp. 49-74; Jepsen, "Beiträge zur Auslegung," pp. 298f.; Walther Eichrodt, "The Law and the Gospel," Interpretation, XI (1957), 27. The reconstructions of Rabast and Nielsen, though carefully thought out, are good illustrations of form-critical tyranny. Here the preoccupation with the "pure form" has done actual injustice to the text.

[2]According to Fohrer ("Das sogenannte apodiktisch formulierte Recht," p. 62) "Es gibt keine Möglichkeit die 10 Sätze des Dekalogs in eine gleichförmige Fassung zu bringen." He further proposes that three different types of apodeictic law lie behind the oldest Decalogue: (1) Five prohibitions (I, II, III, IX, X) in 2nd pers. imperf. with lōʾ, each with three stresses; (2) three prohibitions (VI, VII, VIII) in 2nd pers. imperf. with lōʾ, each having two stresses; (3) two commands (IV, V), each with three stresses.

[3]"Remember the sabbath day" occurs nowhere else, and the two passages which bear some resemblance (Num. 15:40; Ps. 103:18) are both dated in postexilic times. The Deuteronomic version ("Observe the sabbath day") shares the verb šmr with several other Sabbath laws, e.g., Ex. 31:13, 14, 16; Lev. 19:3, 30; Ezek. 44:24.

[4]The literary history of the Decalogue is complex and cannot be examined here. It is generally assigned to the E narrative (in

The next phrases in the commandment continue: "Six days you shall labor, and do all your work; but the seventh day is a sabbath to the LORD your God; in it you shall not do any work. . . ." These would presumably be a subsequent elaboration of the original law. It is remarkable, however, that precisely this formulation of the Sabbath regulation is preserved in other early Sabbath laws, viz., Ex. 23:12; 34:21. For this reason, and since the above phrases appear identically in Ex. 20:9-10 and in Dt. 5:13-14, it has been suggested by Rowley that they form the original fourth commandment.[1] Although this proposal further complicates the form of the original Decalogue, it merits our attention, for we are here dealing with a very old Sabbath motif. The expansion of this theme, the enumeration of those to whom it applies, is

distinction from the so-called J decalogue in Ex. 34), but it is not an E composition. We should probably assume that it existed in its original form as the Sinai-Horeb covenant code par excellence prior to E. Perhaps it was preserved and functioned as such in the covenant cult (Mowinckel, Alt, et al.) or in the tribal ethos (Gerstenberger), or in both.

[1]"Moses and the Decalogue," pp. 30-31. The suggested original law is: "Six days shalt thou labour and do all thy work; but the seventh day is a Sabbath unto the Lord thy God." For a further examination of this type of law, see below, pp. 161-65. Jepsen ("Beiträge zur Auslegung," pp. 285ff.) has suggested that the basic form of the commandment is double, consisting of a Gottesrede and a Prophetenrede. To the first belongs the command to remember the Sabbath day, and to the second the regulation regarding the six days and the seventh day. A further attempt to show that Ex. 20:9-10 is not a later expansion of Ex. 20:8 has been made by John D. W. Watts, "Infinitive Absolute as Imperative and the Interpretation of Exodus 20:8," ZAW, LXXIV (1962), 141-45. Watts says that the infinitive absolute can never substitute for a finite construction, but should be translated as a gerundive. Ex. 20:8-9 should then be translated: "Remembering the Sabbath day to hallow it, six days you shall labor and do all your work. But the seventh day is a Sabbath to Yahweh, your God." See however, Gesenius and Kautzsch, Hebrew Grammer, pp. 345-46; Hans Bauer and Pontus Leander, Historische Grammatik der hebräischen Sprache des Alten Testamentes (Hildesheim: Georg Olms Verlagsbuchhandlung, 1962), pp. 277-78.

not part of the commandment proper, but is a later expansion, a kind of midrash.

Ex. 34:21; 23:12

The first of these verses is generally attributed to the J narrative,[1] and although it has been considered one of the laws in a Yahwistic decalogue (Ex. 34:11-26),[2] it is unlikely that the laws in this chapter ever composed a code similar to the Decalogue.[3] As a part of the J narrative we may also assume that these laws were functioning in premonarchical times,[4] while, on the other hand, their agricultural

---

[1]Cf. Otto Eissfeldt, Hexateuch-Synopse (Leipzig: J. H. Hinrichs'sche Buchhandlung, 1922), p. 158; Fohrer, Introduction, p. 148; Rowley, "Moses and the Decalogue," p. 10; Murray L. Newman, Jr., The People of the Covenant: A Study of Israel from Moses to the Monarchy (Nashville: Abingdon Press, 1962), pp. 39ff.; Julian Morgenstern, "The Oldest Document of the Hexateuch," HUCA, IV (1927), 1-138. This last study assigns it to the pre-Yahwistic source K.

[2]This was first suggested in 1773 by Goethe in an essay entitled: "Zwo wichtige bisher unerörtete Fragen." Here the question, "Was stund auf den Tafeln des Bunds?" was answered with a treatment of Ex. 34:14-26. See Otto Eissfeldt, "Goethes Beurteilung des Kultischen Dekalogs von Ex. 34 im lichte der Pentateuchkritik," ZThK, LXIII (1966), 135-44.

[3]There appear to be twelve rather than ten laws, and only three of them find a parallel in Ex. 20. Cf. Hans-Joachim Kraus, Worship in Israel: A Cultic History of the Old Testament, trans. by G. Buswell (Richmond, Va.: John Knox Press, 1966), p. 29. Several scholars have claimed that the so-called cultic decalogue is only a secondary collection of laws gleaned from the Book of the Covenant (B), Ex. 20:23-24. Cf. Robert H. Pfeiffer, "The Oldest Decalogue," JBL, XLIII (1924), 294-310; Rudolph, Der "Elohist," p. 59; Alt, "The Origins of Israelite Law," p. 151, n. 95. For a review of the enormous literature on this subject, see Rowley, "Moses and the Decalogue," pp. 7-9.

[4]Morgenstern suggests that the laws are characteristic of an agriculturally oriented society ("The Oldest Document," p. 63). Cf. Alfred Jepsen, Untersuchungen zum Bundesbuch, BWANT, No. 41 (Stuttgart: Verlag von W. Kohlhammer, 1927), pp. 95, 98-99.

orientation would give them a _terminus post quem_ at the conquest,[1] but of this we cannot be absolutely certain.[2]

The second passage (Ex. 23:12) appears in the concluding part of the Book of the Covenant (Ex. 21-23). This law code consists of a variety of legal material dealing with both social and cultic matters.[3] Since the section containing the Sabbath law (Ex. 23:10-19) is somewhat similar to Ex. 34:11-26, some attempts have been made to construct a decalogue from it, but without generally accepted results.[4] There is general agreement, however, that the code should be dated later than the conquest, for it reflects the existence of a complex settled society. It is undoubtedly also earlier than D,[5] and since it has no reference at all to the monarchy, it is generally placed in the period of the

---

[1]Cf. Walter Beyerlin, Origins and History of the Oldest Sinaitic Traditions, trans. by S. Rudman (Oxford: Basil Blackwell, 1961), p. 85; Jepsen, Untersuchungen zum Bundesbuch, p. 95.

[2]Recent observations to the effect that the preconquest Israelites were not wandering nomads, but semisettled ass nomads living on the fringes of the desert, perhaps in the Negeb area, make it possible for agriculturally oriented laws to have arisen in preconquest days. Cf. John Bright, A History of Israel (Philadelphia: Westminster Press, 1959), pp. 72-73; Newman, The People of the Covenant, pp. 72ff.; H. H. Rowley, From Joseph to Joshua: Biblical Traditions in the Light of Archaeology (London: Oxford University Press, 1950), pp. 157ff. See now also the discussion by William Foxwell Albright, Yahweh and the Gods of Canaan: A Historical Analysis of Two Contrasting Faiths (New York: Doubleday & Company, Inc., 1968), pp. 64-73.

[3]Cf. Jepsen, Untersuchungen zum Bundesbuch; Julian Morgenstern, "The Book of the Covenant," HUCA, V (1928), 1-151; Henri Cazelles, Études sur le code de l'alliance (Paris: Letouzey et Ané, 1946).

[4]Cf. Pfeiffer, "The Oldest Decalogue," p. 308; Baentsch, Exodus-Leviticus, pp. 185-86; Jepsen, Untersuchungen zum Bundesbuch, p. 108.

[5]This judgment is based on the fact that the Deuteronomic law shows a more progressive stage in the development of Israelite law. Cf. Noth, Exodus, p. 175.

pre-monarchical settlement.[1]

The formal similarities between the two laws are striking, and it is only natural to expect some kind of relationship between them, especially since both are attributed to the same general period. Perhaps both are dependent on a common tradition.[2] Another sign of a relationship may be traced in Ex. 23:12 whose socio-humanitarian explanation of the Sabbath regulation resembles the one found in Dt. 5: 14b. Presumably the latter depends on the former.[3] We may conclude then that these two Sabbath laws, which are actually regulations for the six-seven working day schedule, are among the oldest in the Old Testament literature.

We can now sum up the results of the literary analysis of the Sabbath texts with a few general observations. The textual difficulties in the Sabbath passages are nowhere of a serious nature and do not pose any major problem for our investigation. Another general observation is

---

[1]For the dating of the Book of the Covenant see Jepsen, Untersuchungen zum Bundesbuch, pp. 97ff.; Fohrer, Introduction, pp. 136-37. In its present position this law code is actually an intrusion into the E narrative, but form-critical studies have shown that the laws within it antedate E, and as a whole they show great antiquity. See especially, Alt, "The Origins of Israelite Law," pp. 112ff.

[2]Thus Jepsen, Untersuchungen zum Bundesbuch, pp. 94ff.; Kittel, Geschichte des Volkes Israel, p. 315. This question of relationships should not be confused with the question of the relationship between J and B. These are two bodies of literature with quite different functions, and both of them were apparently incorporating already existent laws, deriving them perhaps from a common source. See above, n. 4, pp. 87-88.

[3]It is, of course, possible that Ex. 23:12 is an old Sabbath law (six days you shall work, but on the seventh day you shall rest) which has been expanded by a Deuteronomic addition. However, the expansion in Dt. 5:14b-15 is more extensive and presumably later.

that most of the Sabbath passages are in the nature of law. This is
true not only of those in the Pentateuch, but in a sense also of those
in the late prophetic literature, viz., Jer. 17:19-27; Is. 56:1-8; 58:
13; 66:23, and most of the passages in Ezekiel. The texts which
describe Sabbath activities in the early prophets and in Kings are noteworthy because of the incidental nature of their appearance. Finally,
as to the question of authorship and date, we find Sabbath passages
throughout the Old Testament literature, from the earliest parts to the
latest. This testifies to the vitality of the Sabbath institution. At
the same time, we observe that most references to the Sabbath are
strangely monotonous and unimaginative. We shall discuss them carefully
below, but it is worth remarking here that approximately the same thing
must be said about the Sabbath many times and during so long a period of
literary history. We have attempted a date for most passages, but as we
shall see in the following, the dates assigned to the Sabbath passages
belong in many instances only to the end-stage of their history. Formal
analysis will suggest that the Sabbath material frequently antedates its
literary formulation.

III.   INTERPRETATION AND TRADITION

When we raise the question of the tradition-history of the Sabbath in the Old Testament literature, we cannot help touching upon the
question of the origin of the Sabbath, for the traditions we are to
explore must have a beginning within or outside the Old Testament, and
that beginning may not be far removed from the beginning of the Sabbath
institution itself. Now, we have accepted the conclusion that the
question of the origin of the Sabbath cannot be satisfactorily answered
from a study of extra-Biblical literature, but that the starting point
for an examination of the Old Testament Sabbath must be the Old Testament itself. It is from within this body of literature that the
question of the beginning of the Sabbath traditions, and ultimately of
the origin of the institution itself, must be raised.

However, the quest into the origin of the Sabbath has not been
fruitless, for it has provided numerous illustrations of what Biblical
students may call the most characteristic features of the Old Testament
Sabbath. We must, of course, be very careful in drawing causal
relationships between these illustrations and the features of the Sabbath which they illustrate; and we can generally not be certain that a
similar feature means an original feature. Nevertheless, the study of
the origin of the Sabbath has revealed some original or fundamental
characteristics of the Sabbath; and it is with these that the next three
chapters will be concerned. First we shall discuss the Sabbath as the
seventh day, then the Sabbath as a social institution, and thirdly the

Sabbath as a cultic institution. It is in the examination of the traditions relative to these aspects of the Sabbath that we expect to touch upon the question of the origin of the Sabbath, without attempting to provide another hypothetical answer. In other words, we think that here we are dealing with some of the earliest Sabbath traditions which nevertheless had a long history. In the following three chapters we shall continue our examination of the Sabbath traditions, giving special attention to the ways in which the Sabbath entered Israel's religious understanding. First we will examine the creation Sabbath, then the Sabbath as law, and lastly the Sabbath as a sign of the covenant.

A. The Sabbath and the Seventh Day

The problem

To say that the Old Testament Sabbath is the seventh day is a tautology to most people, and yet a number of studies have questioned just this identification. We shall first mention these and then turn to an examination of the Biblical material relevant to the subject.

The association of Sabbath and new moon in the Old Testament,[1] and the discovery of some Babylonian texts which identify the Accadian word šabattu with the day of the full moon,[2] have led many scholars to

---

[1]II Kg. 4:23; I Chr. 23:31; II Chr. 2:3; 8:13; 21:3; Neh. 10:33; Is. 1:13; 66:23; Ezek. 45:17; 46:3; Hos. 2:11; Am. 8:5. It is nowhere implied that both Sabbath and new moon occurred only once a month, i.e., their association need not have been caused by their common frequency. Cf. Budde, "Antwort auf Johannes Meinholds 'Zur Frage,'" pp. 135-48; Meesters, Op zoek naar de oorsprong van de Sabbat, pp. 33-34.

[2]Two types of information are marshalled in support of this view. (1) The Accadian word šabattu/šapattu is used to indicate the fifteenth day of the month, the midmonth, or the day of the full moon. (For the b/p variation see Benno Landsberger, Der kultische Kalender der

believe that the Sabbath was originally a monthly and not a weekly day, namely, the day of the full moon.[1]

Babylonier und Assyrer [Leipzig: J. C. Hinrichs'sche Buchhandlung, 1915], p. 133; Kraeling, "The Present Status of the Sabbath Question," p. 221; Zimmern, "Sabbath," p. 200; Friedrich Delitzsch, Babel und Bibel [5th ed.; Leipzig: J. C. Hinrichs'sche Buchhandlung, 1905], pp. 62-5. This study will adopt the view that the two words are identical). For this identification of the word šabattu, cf. Pinches, "Sapattu," pp. 51-56 (plate); Enūma eliš, V, 18 in Pritchard, ed., ANET, p. 68; Arthur Ungnad, Babylonische Briefe aus der Zeit der Hammurapi-Dynastie (Leipzig: J. C. Hinrichs'sche Buchhandlung, 1914), pp. 216-17 (letter 246, 28); W. G. Lambert and A. R. Millard, Atra-Hasīs: The Babylonian Story of the Flood (Oxford: Clarendon Press, 1969), pp. 56-57 (I, 206, 221). Cf. Landsberger, Der Kultische Kalender, pp. 110ff.; Stephen Langdon, Babylonian Menologies and the Semitic Calendars (London: Oxford University Press, 1935), pp. 90-91; Zimmern, "Sabbath," pp. 199-202. (2) In an inscription first published by Rowlinson in 1891 a verb šabâtu is identified with another verb gamâru, meaning "finish," "complete." If this verb is related to the noun šabattu, then the association of šabattu and the day of the full moon would be further established. The relevant texts are noted in The Assyrian Dictionary, Vol. G, pp. 25, 28. They appear in the lexical series Anum VIII, 59; IX, 1ff: ša-ba-tu=ga-ma-ru; [š] a-pa-tu, ga-ma-ru, pu-ru-su-u=da-a-nu.
From these and similar usages of šabattu (cf. Kemal Balkan, "The Old Assyrian Week," in Studies in Honor of Benno Landsberger on his Seventy-Fifth Birthday April 21, 1965, ed. by H. Güterbock and Th. Jacobsen [Chicago: University of Chicago Press, 1965], pp. 164, 170) it is concluded that the Babylonian šabattu is the day of the full moon. The discrepancy between the fifteenth day and the day of the full moon may be more apparent than real. Pinches' text reads ū-ḫuia-kam=šapatti (fifteenth day=šapatti), but the word, meaning full moon, appears in Enūma eliš, and here its meaning is determined by two seven day periods (cf. the Atra-Hasīs epic [see above] which reads, the 1., 7., and šapatti day of the month). The šabattu is the day of the mid-lunar month, or the day of the full moon. The number fifteen would be arrived at, if one divided the approximately thirty days long month by two, and the number fourteen would appear, if one measured two moon quarters, each approximately seven days long. If the šabattu was determined by observing the full moon, it might fall on the thirteenth to the sixteenth day. See, however, Walter Harrelson, From Fertility Cult to Worship (New York: Doubleday & Company, Inc., 1969), p. 28.

[1]The identification of Sabbath and new moon in early (pre-exilic) Israel has been defended particularly by Johannes Meinhold. See above, n. 1, p. 4. Many other scholars have adopted his position. Cf. Gustav Hölscher, Geschichte der israelitischen und jüdischen Religion (Giessen: Verlag von Alfred Töpelmann, 1922), p. 80; Georg Beer, Schabbath: Der Mischnatractat "Sabbat" (Tübingen: J. C. B. Mohr [Paul

Other scholars, particularly some decades ago, associated the
Sabbath with the lunar phases.[1] Since the month is approximately, but

---

Siebeck], 1908), pp. 11ff.; Samuel H. Hooke, The Origins of Early
Semitic Ritual (London: Oxford University Press, 1938), pp. 58-59;
Morris Jastrow, "On הַשַּׁבָּת מִמָּחֳרָת (The Day after the Sabbath)," AJSL,
XXX (1913-14), 101ff.; Adolphe Lods, Israel: From its Beginning to the
Middle of Eighth Century, trans. by S. H. Hooke (New York: Alfred A.
Knopf, 1932), p. 438; Mahler, "Der Sabbat," pp. 47ff.; Handbuch, pp.
49ff.; Karl Marti, Geschichte der israelitischen Religion (5th ed.;
Strassburg: Friedrich Bull Verlagsbuchhandlung, 1907), p. 52; Theophile
J. Meek, "The Sabbath in the Old Testament: Its Origin and Development,"
JBL, XXXVIII (1914), 201-12; Mowinckel, Le Décalogue, p. 90; Oesterly
and Robinson, Hebrew Religion, pp. 135-36; Robert H. Pfeiffer, Religion
in the Old Testament: The History of a Spiritual Triumph (New York:
Harper & Brothers, 1961), pp. 92-93; Otto Procksch, Theologie des Alten
Testaments (Gütersloh: C. Bertelsmann Verlag, 1950), p. 544; Tur-Sinai,
"Sabbat und Woche," p. 21; et al. Norman H. Snaith has developed an
interesting variation of this theory by identifying Sabbath and new
moon. The Jewish New Year Festival: Its Origin and Development (London:
Society for Promoting Christian Knowledge, 1947) pp. 103ff.

[1]The publication of the Babylonian menologies (cf. Langdon,
Babylonian Menologies, pp. 73ff.; see above, n. 3, p. 2) has revealed
the existence of certain regularly occurring evil days (ûmê lemnûti), on
which it was ill advised for the king, the physician, and the prophet to
perform certain prescribed acts. The existence of the ûmê lemnûti is
old, but the seventh century B.C. Assyrian calendars restricted their
number to five, the 7., 14., 19., 21., 28. day of the month. On these
days particular care should be taken not to stir the anger of the gods.
They are never called šabattu, but three factors have suggested a connection between them and the Old Testament Sabbath. (1) In the
Assyrian reform calendar (seventh century B.C.) they occur approximately
every seventh day. The 19. day may be the 49. day, i.e., the third
"Sabbath" in the next month. (2) The days are characterized by restrictions on certain types of activity, although it is uncertain if there
was a general diminishing of activities on these days. Cf. C. H. W.
Johns, Assyrian Deeds and Documents, Vol. II (London: George Bell and
Sons, 1901), pp. 40-41; "The Babylonian Sabbath," ExT, XVII (1905-6),
566-67. (3) The šabattu is identified in Babylonian texts as ûm nûḫ
libbi (a day of the resting of the heart). Cf. CT, XVIII, 23, 1. 17 (K
4397) for an example of this identification which appears in a number of
texts. The above mentioned identification does not make the šabattu
into a day of rest, as the early discoverers of the texts thought, but
into a day of pacification when the heart of the gods is appeased or at
rest. (See above, n. 1, p. 2). If a connection could be maintained
between the šabattu day of appeasement and the ûmê lemnûti, on the one
hand, and between the šabattu and the šabbāt, on the other hand, then a
good case could be made for associating the Sabbath originally with

not exactly, twenty-eight days long,[1] the Sabbath would not occur every
seventh day consistently throughout the year according to this position.

Some ancient Israelite festivals lasted seven days,[2] and one of
them was celebrated after a period of seven times seven days.[3] It has
been proposed that the Sabbath was originally associated with these
occasions in particular, rather than with a seven-day week running
throughout the year.[4]

Finally, it has been proposed that the weekly Sabbath once
occurred at intervals other than the traditional seven-day one, e.g., at
five-, six-, or ten-day intervals.[5]

---

these ûmê lemnûti, and ultimately with the phases of the moon. It has
also been proposed that the original Sabbath was derived from the lunar
phases without the assistance of the Babylonian menologies. See above,
nn. 1-2, p. 6; cf. Kornfeld, "Der Sabbath im Alten Testament," p. 21.

[1]A lunation lasts 29 days, 12 hours, 44 minutes, and 3 seconds,
i.e., the lunar months would have been alternately 29 and 30 days.

[2]The feast of unleavened bread and the feast of booths.

[3]The feast of weeks.

[4]The question is whether the week long festivals ending with a
Sabbath preceded the weekly Sabbath (Kraus, Worship in Israel, pp. 83-
85; William A. Heidel, The Day of Yahweh: A Study of Sacred Days and
Ritual Forms in the Ancient Near East [New York: Century Co., 1929],
p. 438; Kiker, "The Sabbath in the Old Testament Cult," pp. 126ff.), or
vice versa (Ernst Kutsch, "Erwägungen zur Geschichte der Passafeier und
des Massotfestes," ZThK, LV [1958], 1-35). We will return to this question below, pp. 113-21. According to a similar theory the original
Sabbath (week) was one or two yearly seven-day periods which served to
complete a solar year measured by a pentecontad calendar. See above,
p. 7.

[5]Such intervals have been discovered in many parts of the world,
and some were found to be seven days long, although other durations seem
to be more common. These periods were delimited by market days. Though
no such market days have been found in the ancient Near East, some
scholars still have maintained that the Sabbath originated as such a
market day. Cf. Jenni, Die theologische Bergründung, p. 13; Martin P.

The year, month, and day are regulated by the movements of the sun, moon, and earth; but the recurrent seventh day cannot be derived directly from the movements of any celestial body. It is, therefore, natural that attempts should be made to establish an indirect association between it and the lunar phases, or a direct relationship between it and an original agricultural calendar based on the number seven. It is not our primary concern here, however, to evaluate these attempts,[1] but to examine the relationship between Sabbath and seventh day in the Old Testament literature. We will now turn our attention to it.

The Sabbath and the seventh day are identified in several Sabbath laws consisting of a three-part structure. First there is a command to work for six days, then a characterization of the seventh day as Yahweh's Sabbath, and as a holy day, and thirdly, a prohibition

---

Nilsson, Primitive Time-Reckoning (Lund: C. W. K. Gleerup, 1920), p. 334; Webster, Rest Days: A Study in Early Law and Morality, pp. 101-23. See below, pp. 123-24. Some parts of the Near East seem, however, to have had a five-day week, ḫamuštum. It was first described by A. H. Sayce, "Assyriological Notes--No. 3," PSBA, XIX (1877), 288ff. Since this initial discovery there has, however, been much disagreement about the exact meaning of the ḫamuštum. It has been proposed that it was a fifty-day period, perhaps reflected in the interval between the two spring harvest festivals in ancient Israel (Lev. 23:15-16). Thus Lewy and Lewy, "The Origin of the Week and the Oldest West Asiatic Calendar," pp. 1-152. Recently a ten-day period has been proposed and retracted by J. A. Brinkman, "New Evidence on the Assyrian ḫamuštum," Or, XXXII (1963), 387-94; "Note on Old Assyrian Ḫamuštum," JNES, XXIV (1965), 118-20. Finally, Tur-Sinai ("Sabbat und Woche," pp. 14-24) has argued for a six-day period, or one-fifth of a month. Recently the identification of the word with a five-day period has been defended by Balkan, "The Old Assyrian Week," pp. 159-74. According to Landsberger (Der kultische Kalender, pp. 96ff.) and Hehn (Siebenzahl und Sabbat, pp. 113ff.) neither the fifth, the sixth, nor the tenth day, if such a one existed (cf. Wilhelm Nowack, Lehrbuch der hebräischen Archäologie, I (Freiburg und Leipzig: J. C. B. Mohr, 1894), p. 215) had much cultic significance, a conclusion which agrees with the general nature of the texts (commercial).

[1]See above, p. 8.

against performing any work on that day.[1] Except for Dt. 5:13 (D), these laws all come from P, or are thought to have passed through the hands of the priestly writer. Moreover, the middle part of the structure, the one which identifies the seventh day as the Sabbath, gives indications of being a late construction,[2] though not necessarily from exilic or postexilic times, cf. Dt. 5:13. A direct identification of the Sabbath and the seventh day is also presupposed in other passages, but all of them are late.[3] In the distinctly early appearances of the Sabbath, on the other hand, it is not characterized as the seventh day,[4] and we simply are not told how frequently it occurred.

The question of the relationship between Sabbath and the seventh day is not exhausted by these passages. There are a number of other passages which refer to the seventh day without mentioning the Sabbath, notably the two laws (Ex. 23:12; 34:21) which have a two-part structure somewhat similar to the three-part structure discussed above, and consequently, we assume, related to it. First, there is the command to work for six days; and, secondly, a command to stop work on the seventh day, followed by some expansion and amplification. This two-part structure

---

[1] Cf. Ex. 16:26; 20:9-10; 31:15; 35:2; Lev. 23:3; Dt. 5:13. See below, pp. 161-65.

[2] Notably the expressions: "Solemn rest," "holy Sabbath," "Sabbath to Yahweh." As we shall see, these are characteristic of late Sabbath literature.

[3] Cf. Ex. 20:11; 31:16-17; Ezek. 46:1; Neh. 13:15-22.

[4] Is. 1:13; Am. 8:5; Hos. 2:11; II Kg. 4:23; 11:4-12. Ex. 16:29 may possibly belong here (see below, pp. 129-30), so also Ex. 20:8; Dt. 5:12, if these verses indeed belong to the earliest part of the Decalogue. See below, pp. 157-61; 165-73.

is also presupposed by the accounts of the creation Sabbath (Gen. 2:1-3; Ex. 20:11a; 31:17) where "the seventh day" but not "Sabbath" occurs. Now we will propose below that the three-part and the two-part regulations are related. Both of them contain regulations for the six days and for the seventh day, but the longer regulations have inserted an identification of the seventh day with the Sabbath within the simple form of the law. However, Sabbath is not a neologumenon with these relatively late three-part regulations, for this word appears within literature from the middle part of the monarchy, and perhaps from the beginning of the monarchy, or even earlier, though always without mentioning the seventh day. In the light of this situation we will examine first the "Sabbath," then the "seventh day," and finally we will discuss their relationship.

Etymological difficulties

A number of attempts have been made to find the origin of the word Sabbath (šabbāt) in languages other than classical Hebrew. We shall take brief note of some of these, and then examine the word in the Old Testament literature.

Arabic origins.--It has been proposed that Arabic culture provided the Near East with both the seven-day week as well as with the name šabbāt for the seventh day. The seven-day week should, according to this view, be derived from the interval between the moon phases, at which time the moon was at rest in its stations (šubtu). This rest of such an important heavenly body was to be imitated by man on earth on the seventh day which is called šabbāt (Arabic thabat from the root wathaba, meaning "sit"). The development of the root, it is proposed,

went through Accadian where the Arabic th is an š.[1] This attempt at an
explanation for šabbāt has won little support, partly because a strong
cultic influence on Ancient Israel from Arabia has not been demonstrated,[2] and partly because it now appears very doubtful that the
Sabbath can be directly related to the phases of the moon.

Accadian origins.--A more attractive proposal has it that šabbāt
and the Accadian šabattu are related, and that the Accadian form is primary.[3] To bring the two forms of the word into agreement, it is pointed
out that the double t (from an old feminine ending) is preserved in the
dageš forte in the third radical of šabbāt when a suffix is added,[4] and
that the double middle radical of šabbāt may have been caused by the
lost double t, or it may serve to retain the short vowel a.[5] Whatever
we may think of this etymological possibility, its value is limited for
several reasons: (1) Since the discovery of Pinches it is generally
agreed that šabattu can mean only one thing, namely, the day of the full

---

[1]Cf. Nielsen, Die altarabische Mondreligion, pp. 52-88; Georg
Hoffmann, "Versuche zu Amos," ZAW, III (1883), 121; Gesenius and Buhl,
Handwörterbuch, p. 805; Meesters, Op Zook naar de oorsprong van de
Sabbat, pp. 6-8.

[2]See, however, Ditlef Nielsen, ed., Handbuch der altarabischen
Altertumskunde, Vol. I: Die altarabische Kultur (Copenhagen: Nyt
Nordisk Forlag, Arnold Busck, 1927), pp. 242ff. Cf. Th. C. Vriezen, The
Religion of Israel, trans. by H. Hosking (London: Lutterworth Press,
1967), pp. 65-71.

[3]See above, n. 2, pp. 94-95; n. 1, pp. 96-97.

[4]E.g., šabbattô. See Jakob Barth, Die Nominalbildung in den
semitischen Sprachen (Leipzig: J. C. Hinrichs'sche Buchhandlung, 1894),
p. 24.

[5]Cf. Bauer and Leander, Historische Grammatik, p. 476; Barth,
Die Nominalbildung, pp. 323-24.

moon, or the fifteenth day of the month.[1] (2) Despite the efforts of
Meinhold and his followers, it is now generally agreed that the weekly
Sabbath existed in pre-exilic times; and, as we shall see, there is
little reason to believe that šabbāt ever referred to the day of the
full moon.[2] (3) The characterization of šabattu as a day for pacification of the gods (ûm nûḫ libbi) also does not find a parallel in the Old
Testament Sabbath which appears, as we shall see, originally to be a
secular seventh day, characterized primarily by abstention from work.
Consequently, the Accadian šabattu will contribute little or nothing to
our understanding of the Old Testament word, whether or not the two are
related etymologically.

Šabbāt and šebaᶜ.--Since the Sabbath is known above all else to
be the seventh day, it has been proposed that šabbāt is derived from
šebaᶜ (seven). This proposal was first made by the fathers Theophilus
Antiochenus and Lactantius,[3] but has been repeated in recent times by

---

[1]See above, n. 1, p. 3. Other suggested meanings of the word
have been given, but none has achieved much support. (1) Sabattu means
a day of judgment (šabattu-šapâtu-šapāṭu-šāpaṭ); (2) it means a day of
penance (šabattu-šabâtu, a word which may mean "beat ones breast"). Cf.
Zimmern, "Sabbath," p. 202; (3) it means a day of propitiation, and
only incidently is also the day of the full moon. Cf. Jastrow, "The
Original Character," pp. 313ff.; (4) it is related to an obscure word
šabattu which appears in the syllabaries with the equivalents "prepare a
festival," "pray," "petition." Cf. Landsberger, Der kultische Kalender,
pp. 132-33; Kraeling, "The Present Status of the Sabbath Question,"
pp. 220-21. It is not at all clear if this word is the same as that
signifying the full moon day (Landsberger) or a different word
(Kraeling), but in any case it does not bring us closer to the Hebrew
šabbāt, or to the Old Testament Sabbath.

[2]See above, n. 3, pp. 4-5. Also Meesters, Op zoek naar de
oorsprong van de Sabbat, pp. 28-34.

[3]Theophilus Antiochenus (ca. A.D. 180), Ad. Antolycum, II, 2, in
MG, VI, 1069. Lactantius (ca. A.D. 300), Institutionum Divinarum, VII,

Hirschfeld and Torrey, and in a somewhat modified form by Hehn.[1] There is, however, still no satisfactory explanation for the disappearance of the radical ᶜ which, incidentally, is a pronounced and forceful consonant in Hebrew.[2] On the other hand, the final t̲ could be explained as a feminine ending, and there is indeed evidence that šabbāt existed as a two-letter word šb̲, or šb̲ɔ, in Syriac and Aramaic.[3] Nevertheless, a definite link between šebaᶜ and šabbāt has not been established. It is also frustrating that both Hirschfeld, Hehn, and Landsberger,[4] all of whom derive šabbāt from šebaᶜ, do so via the Accadian equivalent where the final gutteral might easier disappear, in spite of the fact that šabattu, for all we know, never had anything to do with the number seven, or the seventh day.

14, in ML, VI, 782: "Dies sabbati, qui lingua Hebraeorum a numero nomes accepit, unde septenarius numerus legitimus ac plenus est."

[1]H. Hirschfeld, "Remarks on the Etymology of Šabbāth," JRAS, LIII (1896), 353-59; Charles C. Torrey, "Recent Hebrew Lexicography," AJSL, XXXIII (1916-17), 53; Johannes Hehn, "Zur Sabbatfrage," BZ, XIV (1917), 210-13; Siebenzahl und Sabbat, pp. 91ff.

[2]See, however, Hirschfeld, "Remarks on the Etymology of Sabbath," p. 356: "Now it is a very common phenomenon in Hebrew that a guttural in words of frequent use is so worn away as to disappear entirely." This judgment applies better to Accadian than to Hebrew, for here the gutteral ɔ4 (ᶜ) has a tendency to disappear and be replaced by a doubling of the preceding radical. See Arthur Ungnad and Lubor Matous, Grammatik des Akkadischen (4th ed.; Munich: Verlag C. H. Beck, 1964), pp. 22, 28 (pars. 14c, 22b). Hirschfeld concludes that the verb šābat was derived from šebaᶜ and that the noun šabbāt was derived from the verb by means of a popular etymology.

[3]Cf. Hirschfeld, "Remarks of the Etymology of Šabbāth," pp. 357-58; A. Dupont-Sommer, "L'ostracon araméen du Sabbat (Collection Clermont-Ganneau No. 152), Semitica, II (1949), 29-39, and especially, Sabbat et parascève a Éléphantine d'après des ostraca araméens inédits (Paris: Imprimerie Nationale, 1950), pp. 9-11.

[4]Landsberger, Der Kultische Kalender, p. 134.

A variation of the šabbāt-šebaᶜ hypothesis has been proposed by Landsberger, namely, that two times seven or šabᶜān (dual ending) received a feminine ending to indicate a period of time, i.e., it referred to a period of fifteen days as well as to the fifteenth day. This feminine form, šabᶜāntu, could easily become šabattu. However, the whole process is difficult,[1] and its results are not easily related to what we know of the Old Testament Sabbath.

The frustrations involved in tracing the etymology of the word šabbāt have led some scholars to despair of the whole undertaking,[2] while others have proposed that an original West-Semitic or Amorite word made its appearance in Hebrew, Aramaic, and Accadian, and that it developed different forms and meanings in each instance.[3] In any case, the etymological quest has been largely fruitless.

When we turn to the root šbt in the Old Testament literature, we immediately notice that it appears frequently both in the verb šābat and in the noun šabbāt. We will first examine the verb.

Šābat

The common verb šābat occurs in qal, niphᶜal, and hiphᶜil, but not in piᶜel, a fact which frustrates the attempts to derive the noun

---

[1]Landsberger himself finds objections to it, e.g., sibūtu (seventh) has s, šabattu has š, and finally he despairs of the whole undertaking.

[2]Botterweck, "Der Sabbat im Alten Testamente," pp. 135-36; Bostrup, Den israelitiske Sabbats Oprindelse og Karakter, pp. 37-43; Meesters, Op zoek naar de oorsprong van de Sabbat, pp. 6-16.

[3]Cf. Lotz, "Sabbath," p. 290; Albert T. Clay, The Origin of Biblical Traditions: Hebrew Legends in Babylonia and Israel, Yale Oriental Series, Researches, Vol. XII (New Haven: Yale University

šabbāt, with a double middle radical, from the verb in the intensive
stem.[1] Its basic meaning is "cease," "stop," "come to an end." It is
also frequently translated "rest" (Gen. 2:2; Ex. 5:5; 16:30; 23:12;
31:17; 34:21, Lev. 23:34-35) and "keep Sabbath" (Lev. 23:32; 25:2;
II Chr. 36:21).

The instances in which it is translated "rest" or "keep Sabbath"
all, except one (Ex. 5:5), deal with either the seventh day, the Sabbath,
or the sabbatical year; and it is tempting to think that the idea of
"Sabbath rest" has influenced this translation of the verb which
actually means "stop," "desist," or "cease," but not "rest," for which
another word is available, namely, nwḥ (rest).[2] Some of the above
instances may, therefore, be better translated by "stop," or "cease."
Ex. 23:12; 34:21 call for the farmer to stop his regular, even essential
activities, in order that rest (nwḥ) and refreshment (npš) may be available to the workers. Gen. 2:2-3 announces that God had completed his
work on the seventh day,[3] that he thus abstained from working on it,
and consequently blessed and hallowed it, i.e., the sanctification and

_____

Press, 1923), pp. 122-23; Dupont-Sommer, Sabbat et parascève, pp. 14-15;
W. G. Lambert, "A New Look at the Babylonian Background of Genesis,"
JThS, N.S. XVI (1965), 297.

[1]Cf. North, "The Derivation of Sabbath," p. 187; Kiker, "The
Sabbath in the Old Testament Cult," p. 43.

[2]Cf. Meesters, Op zoek naar de oorsprong van de Sabbat, p. 14;
Hehn, Siebenzahl und Sabbat, p. 101. See also Mahler, Handbuch der
jüdischen Chronologie, pp. 43ff.; de Vaux, Ancient Israel, II, 475.
"This [to stop] is the etymology which the Bible itself puts forward in
Gn 2:2-3."

[3]The meaning of wayekal (and he finished) is that the work of
creation had been finished on the seventh day, not that God finished it
up during that day. See above, n. 2, pp. 63-64. Cf. the translation of
Gen. 2:2 in N.E.B.: ". . . He ceased from all his work."

blessing is the result of a completed task, not of a rest. Ex. 31:17
likewise emphasizes that God stopped his creative activities on the
seventh day, and was rested or refreshed as a consequence.[1] Similarly,
man is to stop his work on the seventh day (vs. 14-15). Ex. 16:30
explains that the people finally abstained from gathering manna on the
seventh day, whereas they had formerly been occupied by this activity,
for remaining at home (vs. 29) in this context is simply the opposite of
going around gathering food.

"Rest" must, however, be the preferred translation in some
instances; but in such cases the translation is unquestionably influenced by the Sabbath institution as an institution of rest. In Lev. 26:
34-35 the land is given rest during the people's absence, in the sense
that the cessation of normal agricultural activities, which should have
been suspended every seventh year, is now guaranteed to the land for an
extended period of time. The same must be said about the translation
"keep Sabbath." Lev. 23:32 is a cognate accusative (tišbᵉtû šabbattᵉkem)
and it must be translated "you shall keep your Sabbath." Similarly,
Lev. 25:2 (wᵉšābtāh hāʾāreṣ šabbāt), "the land shall keep a Sabbath."
II Chr. 36:21 is partly parallel to Lev. 26:35, and the verb cannot be
translated "stop," or "cease" in either place. The translations "rest,"
or "keep Sabbath," under the influence of the Sabbath institution, are
both satisfactory. However, since these instances are late, it is likely
that the influence of the Sabbath rest on the verb šābat, giving it the
additional meanings "rest," and "keep Sabbath," are also late. There

----

[1]See, however, Ex. 20:11. "And rested (wayyānaḥ) the seventh
day." See below, pp. 197-99.

are no instances of these meanings of the verb in early literature,[1] and
in late texts not related to the Sabbath. When translating the verb
šābat with "rest," cessation from work, not relaxation, is meant.
In the light of this situation, what can be said about the
relationship of šābat and šabbāt? We have seen that there is good
reason to believe that the noun has influenced the verb, at least at a
late stage; but we cannot assume that the verb is a denominative, for
then we should have discovered its primary meaning to be "keep Sabbath."[2] Other scholars have attempted to derive the noun from the
verb.[3] This is a far more plausible hypothesis, but no satisfactory
explanation of the process has been given.[4]

---

[1]A possible exception is Ex. 5:5 which reads wᵉhišbatem ᵓōtām
missiblōtām (you make them rest from their burdens). The context, however, shows that the Pharaoh is requested by Moses to let the people off
for a three-day journey into the desert where a celebration was to be
made. The Pharaoh decided, for whatever reason, that they could not
stop their work, but that additional tasks should be placed on them. We
could, therefore, translate the phrase: you make them quit their burdens. Cf. N.E.B.: "You would have them stop working."

[2]Thus Hehn, Siebenzahl und Sabbat, pp. 98ff. Hehn, however,
assumes that šabbāt originally signified "completion" (as a derivative
from šebaᶜ), and subsequently gave rise to the verb meaning "keep Sabbath" and secondarily "complete," "stop," and the like. This, as we
noted, contradicts the Old Testament evidence. See also Budde, "Antwort
auf Johannes Meinholds 'zur Frage,'" p. 143; W. W. Cannon, "The Weekly
Sabbath," ZAW, XLIX (1931), 325-27; Langdon, Babylonian Menologies,
p. 96.

[3]Cf. de Vaux, Ancient Israel, II, 475-76; North, "The Derivation
of Sabbath," pp. 185-87; E. Kutsch, "Sabbat," Die Religion in Geschichte
und Gegenwart, ed. by Kurt Galling, et al. (3rd ed.; Tübingen: J. C. B.
Mohr [Paul Siebeck], 1958), V, 1259; Bostrup, Den israelitiske Sabbats
Oprindelse og Karakter, p. 43; Bentzen, Den israelitiske Sabbats
Oprindelse og Historie, pp. 10-11; Bohn, Der Sabbat im Alten Testament,
pp. 2-3; Barth, Die Nominalbildung, pp. 24, 145.

[4]It is compared to the process whereby the Accadian šabattu
should have developed, namely, from the verb šabâtu with the addition of

Šabbāt

Šabbāt is normally a feminine noun, although it also occurs as a masculine, notably under the influence of yôm,[1] in the expression šabbāt bešabbattô (Num. 28:10; Is. 66:23), and in some other instances (Is. 56: 2; 58:13).[2] Although the expression yôm-haššabbāt (the Sabbath day) is more frequent in later texts, it appears to be employed indiscriminately with šabbāt, and was perhaps used for emphasis, or was developed under the influence of "the seventh day."

There can be no doubt that the exilic and postexilic literature identified Sabbath and the seventh day. In a number of these instances we have noted that this identification is made explicitly. In this same literature šabbāt is also used for the sabbatical year (Lev. 25:2-7; 26: 34-35, 43, II Chr. 36:21). However, the early regulations regarding the sabbatical year (Ex. 21:2-6; 23:10-11; Dt. 15:1-8)[3] do not call it

a feminine ending (a)tu. Šabbāt is thus explained as a qaṭalat, which in Hebrew can appear with or without a double middle radical, attributed either to the preservation of the short vowel after the first radical, or to an original dageš forte which moved forward from the third radical. We would then have this development: šabbat+at>šabbatat>šabbatt> šabbāt, or šābat+t (feminine ending) > šabbāt. Cf. Bentzen, Den israelitiske Sabbats Oprindelse og Historie, p. 11. On the other hand, Bauer and Leander (Historische Grammatik, p. 476) completely reject any association between the verb and the noun, and de Vaux (Ancient Israel, II, 476) admits that the expected form should have been šebet, a stative word meaning "a day on which men cease to work."

[1]Ex. 20:8, 11; 31:15; Num. 15:23; 28:9; Dt. 5:12; Neh. 10:31; 13:5, 17, 19, 22; Jer. 17:21, 22, 24; Ezek. 46:1, 4.

[2]M. G. Slonim, "The Gender of Sbt (Sabbath) in the Hebrew Bible," JBL, LXX (1951), pp. iv-v.

[3]The cultic calendars in Ex. 23:10-19; 34:18-26, and Dt. 16:1-17 in connection with which the regulations for the seventh year are given, are probably all older than the one in H (Lev. 23). Cf. Kraus, Worship in Israel, pp. 26ff.; de Vaux, Ancient Israel, II, 470ff.; Helmer

šabbāt, and although there can be no doubt that the sabbatical year is
an old regulation, it is most likely that its characterization (Sabbatical) is adopted from the weekly institution.[1]

Šabbāt is also used for certain feast days, viz., the day of
atonement (Lev. 16:31; 23:32), the day of trumpets (Lev. 23:24), and the
first and last days of the feast of booths (Lev. 23:39). Here again it
is only P and H which call these yearly feast days šabbāt and šabbātôn,
and we may assume that the priestly circles responsible for this literature found certain qualities in the Sabbath institution, probably
abstention from work, which would justify the use of the name šabbāt for
these feast days. In this connection we have the difficult expression
"the morrow after the sabbath" (Lev. 23:11, 15, 16). The difficulty
lies in the identification of the word šabbāt, which may refer either to
one of the days in the spring harvest festival, presumably the first or
last day of the week of unleavened bread, or to a seventh-day Sabbath
falling within this festival period or somewhere near it; but since the
first and last days of this festival are nowhere called šabbāt, it seems
more natural to associate the expression "the morrow after the sabbath"
with a regular weekly Sabbath.[2]

Ringgren, Israelite Religion, trans. by D. E. Green (Philadelphia:
Fortress Press, 1966), pp. 185ff.

[1]In the cultic calendar in Ex. 23:10-19 the seventh year and the
seventh day are closely related, and although we cannot demonstrate
this, it is likely that the former is derived from the latter. Cf. de
Vaux, Ancient Israel, I, 174. "The cycle of seven years is obviously
inspired by the week of seven days, ending in the sabbath rest, whence
the use of the same word 'sabbath' to denote this year of rest and the
whole period. . . ."

[2]The Pharisees later considered it to be the first day of the
festival of unleavened bread, perhaps on the basis of Lev. 23:11 in LXX,

Finally, šabbāt occurs in pre-exilic literature, but less frequently. It appears in the initial statements of the fourth commandment,
and it is identified as the seventh day in the subsequent regulations of
this same commandment. Moreover, we find it in Is. 1:13; Hos. 2:11;
Am. 8:5; II Kg. 4:26, associated with new moon and other festivals, but
nothing can be concluded about the frequency of the Sabbath from this
association.[1] The same applies to the other clearly old usages of the

tî ʾepaúrion tîs prótis. Cf. Jacob Z. Lauterbach, Rabbinic Essays
(Cincinnati: Hebrew Union College Press, 1951), pp. 124-25. The
Boethusians (Sadducees), on the other hand, held that it was a weekly
Sabbath. See the discussion J. van Goudoever, Biblical Calendars (2nd
rev. ed.; Leiden: E. J. Brill, 1961), pp. 25ff. It is possible that at
one stage the feast of unleavened bread was not tied to any certain date,
as it is in Lev. 23:4-8; Dt. 16:1-8, and possibly in Ex. 23:15, where it
is combined with the passover and associated with the exodus from Egypt.
If that was the case, one would expect a close association between this
feast and the wave sheaf ceremony, for both were harvest celebrations.
In the text at hand, however, no temporal relationship exists between
the two occasions. That in fact would be difficult to achieve, for the
feast of unleavened bread is tied to a certain date in the month (the
date of passover), whereas the time of the wave sheaf is determined by
the harvest (Lev. 23:9-10; Dt. 16:9). Moreover, this occasion serves as
the starting point for counting the seven weeks to the feast of weeks
(Lev. 23:15; Dt. 16:9-10). Consequently, it would most likely coincide
with a weekly Sabbath, for seven weeks (lit. Sabbaths) between the two
harvests could best be counted were they regular weeks each ending with
a Sabbath. And so we assume that the whole period began with a regular
Sabbath. It is certainly puzzling why the wave sheaf should be brought
after a Sabbath. Noth has suggested that such a practice would allow a
full uninterrupted week for the harvest procedures (Leviticus, pp. 170-
71). Kiker ("The Sabbath in the Old Testament Cult," p. 117) accepts
the view that the Sabbath in question is not a weekly Sabbath, but the
last day of the festival of unleavened bread, making that festival a
preharvest celebration. He argues that it is not likely that new grain
would be introduced in the middle of the feast of unleavened bread, and
that the last day of the week-long festival was traditionally called a
Sabbath. To the first point we may observe that the feast of unleavened
bread is no longer a harvest festival in Lev. 23:4-8; Dt. 16:1-8; Ex.
23:15, but had it been the case, Kiker's observation would be valuable.
The second point is a presupposition which will be discussed below, pp.
113-21.

[1]See above, n. 1, p. 94.

word, e.g., II Kg. 11:5, 7, 9;[1] 16:18. Before returning to the relationship of these occurrences of the word in early texts to the seventh day
we shall examine the word šabbātôn.

Šabbātôn

This word occurs ten times in Exodus and Leviticus where it is
applied to the weekly Sabbath (Ex. 16:23; 31:15; 35:2; Lev. 23:3), to
the day of atonement (Lev. 16:31; 23:32), to the feast of trumpets (Lev.
23:24), to the first and last days of the feast of booths (Lev. 23:39),
and to the sabbatical year (Lev. 25:4, 5). It seems to be employed at
random,[2] and it can apparently be used both in apposition to šabbāt,[3]
and interchangeably with it.[4] However, the frequent association of
šabbāt and šabbātôn,[5] and two instances where it is equated with

---

[1] We cannot conclude from this passage that the Sabbath occurred
once a week (Budde, "The Sabbath and the Week," p. 8), for although we
learn that the guards were changed on the Sabbath, so that two-thirds of
the force were in the temple on that day, in distinction from the normal
one-third of the force on other days, we cannot make any assumptions as
to the frequency of the change of the guards. Presumably the companies
of guards assigned to special Sabbath duty in the temple would be
released the following evening, and would not stay there until the
following Sabbath before being released.

[2] Of the eight important days in Lev. 23 (the Sabbath, the first
and last days of the feast of unleavened bread, the feast of weeks, the
day of trumpets, the day of atonement, the first and last days of the
feast of booths) four are called šabbātôn (the Sabbath, the first and
last days of the feast of booths, the day of trumpets, the day of
atonement).

[3] Ex. 16:23, šabbātôn šabbat-qōdeš . . . māhār ("tomorrow is a
day of solemn rest, a holy sabbath . . ."). Cf. Ex. 35:2.

[4] Lev. 23:24, 39.

[5] Ex. 31:15; 35:2; Lev. 16:31; 23:3, 32; 25:4, 5.

112

šabbat-qōdes[1] suggest that it qualifies or intensifies šabbāt in some way.[2]

There is general agreement among Semitists that šabbātôn is a denominative of šabbāt.[3] The an-on ending is common in Hebrew nouns, and, according to Bauer and Leander, produces "Abstrakta, Nomina agentis, Adjektiva, Deminutiva."[4] Normally the first vowel is shortened in such nouns (qᵉtalon), but by doubling the middle radical it is preserved, normally as an i,[5] with the exception of šabbātôn which preserves the a.[6]

According to its usage the word does not carry any idea of propitiation, or other penitential implications; and it is not clearly a

---

[1]See above, n. 3, p. 111.

[2]Elliger, Leviticus, p. 201, "unbedingter Ruhetag"; Heinisch, Leviticus, p. 76, "ein Tag vollkommener Ruhe"; Koehler and Baumgartner, Lexicon, p. 948, "most solemn Sabbath"; Francis Brown, S. R. Driver, and Charles A. Briggs, Hebrew and English Lexicon of the Old Testament, 1907, p. 992, "Sabbath of Sabbatic obedience"; Gesenius and Buhl, Handwörterbuch, p. 806, "Vollständiger Ruhetag"; Hehn, "Zur Sabbatfrage," p. 204, "ein hochheiliger Sabbat"; Meesters, Op zoek naar de oorsprong van de Sabbat, p. 116, "Dit woort heeft een intensiever betekenis dan שבּת, waarvan het is afgeleid."

[3]Cf. Barth, Die Nominalbildung, p. 324; Koehler and Baumgartner, Lexicon, p. 948, "artificial development of שבּת"; Hehn, Siebenzahl und Sabbat, p. 93; Meesters, Op zoek naar de oorsprong van de Sabbat, p. 116; Bauer and Leander, Historische Grammatik, p. 498. For a contrary opinion see Jastrow, "The Original Character of the Hebrew Sabbath," pp. 332ff.; "Onשבּת השבּתם," p. 97. Jastrow associates šabbātôn with the Accadian šabáttum, meaning not a day of rest, or solemn rest, but a day of propitiation. Šabbāt in the sense of day of rest is a secondary development of the Old Testament word. It seems, however, that šabbātôn should be associated with an Accadian form šabbatānu, and not šabattu. Cf. Cazelles, Études sur le code de l'alliance, p. 92.

[4]Historische Grammatik, p. 498.   [5]Ibid.

[6]Ibid. See also Barth, Die Nominalbildung, p. 324.

superlative. Rather, it seems to describe that which really characterize the Sabbath, or any other day which has Sabbath qualities. In that
sense it has been termed a Verbal-abstractum, meaning "Sabbath keeping."[1]
We conclude, therefore, that šabbātôn describes the content of the Sabbath, i.e., it is an abstraction of "keeping Sabbath," used only in the
late literature of P and H.[2]

The seven-day period

We have noticed that in the earliest occurrences of šabbāt there
is no indication of the frequency with which this institution was
observed, while in the later literature it is identified directly with
the seventh day of the week. What then can we say about this seven-day
period?[3]

Both the Old Testament and other Near Eastern literature
(including the Ugaritic) offer many illustrations of occasional seven-
day periods,[4] but since none of them demonstrates the existence of a

---

[1]Cf. Bostrup, Den israelitiske Sabbats Oprindelse og Karakter,
p. 38.

[2]It is interesting that the verb šābat also received the meaning
"keep Sabbath" under the influence of the Sabbath institution in late
literature. There may well be a relationship between this development
and the derivation of the noun šabbātôn. Both words appear predomi-
nantly in P and H.

[3]The seven-day period is only one aspect of the larger question
concerning the number seven and its function, and it undoubtedly shares
in the qualities associated with the number seven, and thus it contributes to our understanding of the role of this number in the ancient Near
East. Cf. Hehn, Siebenzahl und Sabbat, pp. 1-90; "Zur Bedeutund der
Siebenzahl," in Vom Alten Testament: Festschrift Karl Marti, ed. by
K. Budde, BZAW, No. 41 (Giessen: Verlag von Alfred Töpelmann, 1925),
pp. 128-36.

[4]Cf. Gen. 7:4, 10; 27:29; 31:23; 50:10; Jos. 6:3-4; Jg. 14:12;

seven-day week (i.e., a continual seven-day period), they are of little
value for the Sabbath question. However, one occurrence of the seven-
day period has received special attention in connection with the Sabbath,
namely, the two annual seven-day festival seasons, the feast of
unleavened bread and the feast of booths.[1] In 1929 W. A. Heidel suggested that the Sabbath originated as the last day of the six-day spring
festival.[2] More recently Hans-Joachim Kraus has expanded this hypothesis by suggesting that the seven-day festival unit of the spring and
fall festivals was the forerunner of the week, in the sense that it
served to measure the proper time until the next gathering for such a
festival.[3] This practice is perhaps preserved in the regulation for
measuring the time between the two spring harvest festivals (Lev. 23:15;
Dt. 16:9-10). According to this procedure the seven-day periods would
run throughout the two half years independently of the lunar month.

 The theories of Kraus have been further expanded in a recent

---

Job 2:13. The fire of Baal's house burned out after having raged six
days (Baal cycle, II AB, VI, 21-32, Pritchard, ed., ANET, p. 143); the
army of king Krt reached Udum after six days of marching (Krt A, III,
105-9, Pritchard, ed., ANET, 144); king Aqht received his dream on the
seventh day of sacrifices (Aqht, A, I, 1-18, in Pritchard, ed., ANET,
p. 150); Utnapishtum sent out his dove from the ark after six days of
waiting (Gilgamesh, XI, 140-46, in Pritchard, ed., ANET, p. 94). See
also J. B. Bauer, "Die literarische Form des Heptaemeron," BZ, NF I
(1957), 273-77; Arvid S. Kapelrud, "The Number Seven in Ugaritic Texts,"
VT, XVIII (1968) 494-99; Samuel E. Loewenstamm, "The Seven Day-Unit in
Ugaritic Epic Literature," IEJ, XV (1965), 121-33.

[1]Ex. 23:25; 34:18; Lev. 23:6, 34-36, 40-43; Num. 28:17; 29:12;
Dt. 16:4, 13.

[2]The Day of Yahweh, pp. 438-39.

[3]Worship in Israel, pp. 81-87.

study by Charles W. Kiker.[1] In this study the Sabbath is examined in
the context of the festal calendars found in Ex. 34, 23; Lev. 23; Num.
28-29; Dt. 16. These calendars, Kiker agrues, contain "sabbatical
ideas,"[2] a fact attributed to the origin of the Sabbath as the last day
of the seven-day festival periods enumerated in these calendars. Ex.
34:21 thus refers to the last day of the feast of unleavened bread.[3]
Ex. 23:12, on the other hand, contains a "genuine Sabbath command,"
which was released from its cultic setting, presumably in verses 14-17,
because of a "stickwörtliche association" with the sabbatical year in
verses 10-11,[4] and because of its humanitarian motivation which fitted
the context of verses 6-11 better than that of verses 14-17.[5] But
originally it too referred to the last day of a festival period. Dt.
16:8 employs the Sabbath formula,[6] and yet, Kiker points out, it refers
especially to the feast of unleavened bread, not to the Sabbath.[7]

---

[1]"The Sabbath in the Old Testament Cult."

[2]Ibid., p. 67.

[3]Ibid., pp. 80-81. See also Meinhold, Sabbat und Woche, p. 32;
Henri Cazelles, "Ex 34,21 traite-t-il du Sabbat?" CBQ, XXIII (1961),
225: "Dans ces conditions, le tišbôt d'Ex 34.21, traduit par anapausis
dans le grec, semble correspondre non à un sabbat de toutes les saisons,
mais a une fête saisonnière chrôme, et le v. 21b se traduit tres
simplement sons ajouter un 'fur-ce' ou un 'mème': aux labours et à la
maisson, une fête chrôme."

[4]Kiker, "The Sabbath in the Old Testament Cult," p. 90.

[5]Ibid.

[6]The command to work during six days and to cease from working
on the seventh day. Dt. 16:8 uses this formula to regulate the use of
unleavened bread.

[7]Kiker, "The Sabbath in the Old Testament Cult," pp. 98-99.

Lev. 23:1-3 demonstrate, according to Kiker, that the Sabbath regulation belongs in a festal calendar,[1] for it shares with the other feast days certain expressions, notably "holy convocation," and you shall do no (laborious) work." In short, the Sabbath was originally simply one feast day among those mentioned in the cultic calendars.

These three studies thus conclude that the Sabbath originated as the concluding day of a seven-day festival period which occurred once or twice a year in very ancient times.[2] Why should this day have become the Sabbath? Kraus suggests that the two annual week-long festivals were associated with the day of the full moon which the Babylonian called šabattu. Ancient Israelites used this name to indicate the last day of the feast which began at the middle of the month and lasted a week. Subsequently, it was also used for the ensuing seven-day periods.[3] Kiker, on the other hand, proposes that the Sabbath, or the seventh day of any given period, was characterized as a time of transition, fulfillment, or turning, as a boundary time which led from one situation into another.[4] When the week was developed for unknown reasons, it was natural to identify its last day with the name and qualities of šabbāt.

---

[1] Ibid., p. 111. The festal calendar beginning in Lev. 23:1 is destinguished from the Festkalender which contains the descriptions of the yearly feasts.

[2] Possibly already among the Cannanites prior to Israel's entry in the country. Kraus, Worship in Israel, p. 87.

[3] Ibid., pp. 84-85.

[4] Kiker derives this understanding from the noun sabbat which is, he suggests, derived from two biliteral roots šb and bt with the combined meaning of "turn," or "cut off." In doing so he follows some hypothetical theories regarding biliteral Hebrew roots. "The Sabbath in the Old Testament Cult," pp. 44ff. See also Robert L. Cate, "An

Conclusion

How shall we evaluate these attempts to relate Sabbath and the
seventh day? First of all, it is really quite doubtful that the Sabbath
is as closely related to the festivals in the Old Testament literature
as Kiker maintains. Without considering Ex. 34:21 a gloss, we could
understand it as an isolated regulation independent of the festivals,
similar to verses 19-20.[1] Dt. 16:8 exhibits the Sabbath formula, but
makes no reference to the Sabbath. Lev. 23:1-3 are generally considered
a secondary addition to the festal calendar, and verses 11, 15, 16 are,
as we suggested above, best understood to refer to a weekly Sabbath.
Finally, Ex. 23:12, which is one of the oldest passages in question, has
by Kiker's own admission become a genuine Sabbath regulation. It is
thus very doubtful that we can demonstrate a relationship between the
Sabbath and the two annual festivals in the Old Testament literature;
but it is of course possible, as Kraus has suggested, that such a relationship is very ancient, perhaps of old Canaanite origin. We have

Investigation into the Origin of the Triliteral Root System of Hebrew
Verbs," (unpublished Th.D. dissertation, Southern Baptist Theological
Seminary, 1959). Kiker concludes by showing that the three main festivals (passover--unleavened bread, weeks, booths), with which the
original Sabbath was associated, were times of transition, or boundary
times (pp. 147ff.), and finally he suggests that this understanding of
Sabbath agrees with the Hebrew conception of time.

[1]It is correctly observed that this law is inserted between laws
regarding the feast of unleavened bread and the feast of weeks. This
does not mean, however, that vs. 21 applies only to these occasions, for
they do not include any seed time. However, the appearance of a Sabbath
law just before the regulations for the feast of weeks may be inten-
tional, serving to emphasize that the schedule of the harvest festivals
in the spring is dependent on the week (Lev. 23:15-16; Dt. 16:9-10).
Cf. Ernst Kutsch, "Erwägungen zur Geschichte der Passafeier und des
Massotfestes," ZThK, LV (1958), 17.

noted that seven-day periods were well known among the Canaanites, but
we have no clear instances of seven-day festival periods, or of such
periods with calendar functions, i.e., used to measure time. Moreover,
it is not at all certain that the spring and fall harvest festivals were
associated with the full moon to begin with,[1] and so we cannot assume
that the "Sabbath" of the festival week was in any way related to
šabattu. Finally, a seven-day festival period is not a particularly
suitable calendar unit for measuring time.[2] For these reasons, we

---

[1]There is general agreement that these festivals, which were
originally harvest festivals, were once scheduled by the ripening crop.
Ringgren, Israelite Religion, p. 185; Kraus, Worship in Israel, pp. 43-
45; de Vaux, Ancient Israel, II, pp. 490, 493, 496. They were perhaps
celebrated by the Canaanite community before Israel arrived in the land.
The passover, which was originally a feast for shepherds and which
Israel consequently would naturally have celebrated before the conquest
brought them in contact with the important agricultural cycle, was
probably always associated with the full moon. We may assume that when
the feast of unleavened bread was attached to passover (Dt. 16:1-8), it
too was associated with the moon, and the other festivals were tied into
the lunar calendar as well by analogy. Perhaps the distinction between
the preconquest shepherd society and the postconquest agricultural
society is drawn too sharply, but the general relationship between the
festivals may well be correctly portrayed by it. See however Judah B.
Segal, The Hebrew Passover: From the Earliest Times to A.D. 70, London
Oriental Series, No. 12 (London: Oxford University Press, 1963), p. 175.

[2]For a festival week to become a calendar unit for measuring
time, it must contain the quality of being able to delimit, i.e., as the
seven day period moves away from the festival week with its distinctive
festal activities, it must be able to conclude itself by having a last
day distinct from the preceding six days. One could speculate on this
hypothesis and suggest that the community stopped its activities every
seventh day and remembered the festival. But this is not very likely,
for the early regulations for the feasts (Ex. 23:14-17; 34:18-23) do not
call the celebrants to desist or rest, and the regulations for the seventh day make no mention of the festivals. Moreover, it is not
characteristic of Israel to "remember" her festivals. They are rather
the vehicle, but not the object of remembrance (Childs, Memory and
Tradition, p. 55). To measure the time between the feast of unleavened
bread and the feast of weeks, seven Sabbaths (seven-day periods) were
needed. It is quite possible, therefore, that Kraus has put matters on
their head, that the festival week and the weeks between the festivals

consider it quite doubtful that the seven-day week is derived directly from a seven-day festival period.[1] It is certainly possible that a common psychological orientation was responsible for the occasional seven-day period, the seven-day festival period, and the seven-day week, perhaps all related to the function of the number seven; but to demonstrate this would take us beyond the Old Testament literature, and beyond the purpose of this study. Any direct relationship between the seven-day periods and the seven-day week has not been shown and must remain sheer speculation. The pressing question still remains, how Israel learned to divide time into six working days followed by a seventh day without work. The Old Testament considers the phenomenon of the Sabbath a _fait accompli_. To attempt to pass beyond this point would

---

depend on the seven-day week and on the Sabbath, and not vice versa. Cf. Harrelson, _From Fertility Cult to Worship_, pp. 29-30.

[1]Even Kiker somehow admits this. No Old Testament evidence is available to demonstrate a development from a seven-day festival to a seven-day week, except that the last day, the Sabbath, is characterized as boundary time or transition time. However, the seven-day week is, of course, not explained by it, only the quality of the last day, which is also called Sabbath, i.e., once the seven-day week has been developed, the Sabbath or transition day, known from the seven-day festivals, could easily be used for the last day of the week also, for it is indeed a day of transition and of boundary. (See "The Sabbath in the Old Testament Cult," pp. 130-31). The problem with Kiker's hypothesis lies in the fact that (1) the origin of the seven-day week is not explained, and (2) the seven-day week is actually not conceivable without the particular qualities of transition or boundary associated with the Sabbath. In other words, the seven-day week cannot precede the seventh day with Sabbath qualities. If the Sabbath then preceded the seven-day week, and if it was originally the last day of a seven-day period, then we must derive the week from the festival week. This, however, brings us back to the views of Heidel and Kraus, beyond which Kiker has not really passed, despite his intentions to do so. That the Sabbath should have originated in a week-long festival period is a hypothesis which is only workable, as Kraus rightly understands, in traditions lying behind the Old Testament literature. We cannot trace the origin of the week in the Old Testament.

lead to a study of the origin of the week, but since the week is not
determined merely by the number seven, but equally much by the quality
of the seventh day, it is really impossible to separate the question of
the week from the Sabbath question. The origin of both is equally
obscure. We simply do not know precisely why Israel began to celebrate
the seventh day as Sabbath, and how she arrived at it.

It is possible, however, to attempt to sketch historically the
relationship between Sabbath and seventh day. First, there are the old
laws (Ex. 23:12; 34:21) which command work on six days and cessation
from work on the seventh. We are given no reason for this command,
although Ex. 23:12 does invoke a humanitarian concern, namely, a concern
with rest and relaxation for the laborer and the beast of burden. Rest
is thus a reason, or at least a result of the seventh-day regulation;
but it does not explain it. The creation Sabbath theme is perhaps
closer to the real explanation, which the Old Testament is capable of
giving for the seventh day. On this day God stopped creating, had completed his work, and rested and was refreshed (Ex. 20:11; 31:17). The
Old Testament understands the reason for the seventh-day Sabbath to rest
in a divine fiat. It does not remember when the Sabbath began and where
it originated. Perhaps we should take this to mean that the Sabbath is
older than the Old Testament literature and that its origin was as
obscure to it as it is to us.

In the late monarchial period and subsequent to the fall of
Jerusalem, the Sabbath was customarily identified with the seventh day;
but since this was done within the traditional Sabbath formula without
any apparent confusion arising from it, we may assume that šabbāt was

the technical term for the seventh day even in its earlier occurrences, viz., Is. 1:13; Hos. 2:11; Am. 8:5; II Kg. 4:23; 11:5, 7, 9; 16:18 and perhaps in J (Ex. 16:29).[1]

Was the seventh day always called Sabbath? Of this we cannot be certain, but since šabbāt was used commonly in the very early period of Israel's national existence with no reference of the seventh day, and was then identified freely with the seventh day in the history-conscious literature of D and P, we can reasonably assume that it always referred to the seventh day in the Old Testament literature and its traditions. It is puzzling, of course, that the very old Sabbath texts, Ex. 23:12; 34:21; Gen. 2:1-3; Ex. 31:17 and perhaps Ex. 16:29,[2] do not contain the noun šabbāt, but use the verb šābat to describe the day which delimits, completes the week and work, and consequently provides rest. It is just possible that the noun šabbāt was introduced or was developed from the verb, because it too conveyed the qualities of delimiting, completing, and thus providing rest.[3] This, however, must have happened in very early times.

---

[1]Šabbāt may not have been part of the original manna account. LXX reads "this day" (vs. 29a) and the Samaritan Pentateuch reads "the Sabbath day" (vs. 29b). Apparently there was some question about the appearance of šabbāt in this verse.

[2]See above, n. 1.

[3]De Vaux (Ancient Israel, II, 476) has proposed that if šabbāt is indeed derived from the verb šābat (stop, cease), its form šabbāt in the active would mean "the day which stops (transitive), which marks a limit or a division." This is indeed a plausible proposal, but since šabbāt in its earliest appearances in the Old Testament literature had already become a technical term for the seventh day, it must remain a hypothesis. Secondly, if we may draw a comparison with the corresponding Babylonian words, despite the etymological difficulties, we have the noun šabattu meaning the day of t̲ full moon, or the complete moon, and

B.   The Sabbath as Social Institution

The problem

To affirm that the Sabbath is a day of rest, i.e., a day without the performance of work, is carrying coals to Newcastle. Work is, therefore, always closely related to the Sabbath in one way or another; and it is the aim of this chapter to examine the way in which the Old Testament understands this relationship. We shall not ask about the kinds of work which are permitted on the Sabbath, and those which are not,[1] but we shall rather turn to the more fundamental question of the role of work and abstention from work in the Old Testament interpretation of the Sabbath.

Abstention from work, or at least certain kinds of work, may be

a corresponding verb šabâtu which seems among other things to mean "complete." We do not know, of course, if the noun was developed for the purpose of naming that which the verb described, but it does have some plausibility.

[1]The Old Testament does not address itself directly to this question. It is true, of course, that such questions must have been raised in Biblical times as they are today, for man cannot easily understand time without content, time in which there are no things or activities. Thus contemporary Sabbath keepers who explain that they cannot do thus and so on a certain day, because it is their Sabbath on which they do not work, are frequently asked, but what do you do on the Sabbath? with the correct implication that one has, of course, to do something on that day. However, since the Sabbath, as we saw, is characterized primarily as time, one day of it, it is reasonable to assume that time, not activities or things, is being emphasized by it. This means that to ask which activities one can or cannot perform and still take the Sabbath seriously would be to foreclose one's insight into the true relationship between Sabbath and work. In other words, if the Sabbath is attempting to overrule man's preoccupation with activities and things, one cannot seriously ask about it by posing such questions as are nurtured precisely by these preoccupations of ours. Cf. Abraham J. Heschel, "The Sabbath: Its Meaning for Modern Man," in The Earth is the Lord's and the Sabbath, Harper Torchbooks (New York: Harper & Row, Publishers, 1966), pp. 3-10.

done for a number of reasons, as can be determined by noting some theories regarding the original Sabbath rest.

The Sabbath may originally have been simply a "day off," when all work stopped, a position maintained by some interpreters who emphasize the humanitarian character of the day, a day of joy, recreation, and the return of full physical energies to man and beast.[1] Although we do know about complaints because of overwork in the ancient world,[2] there is no evidence that a Sabbath was devised to relieve such a situation. It is, therefore, generally assumed that regular abstention from work on the seventh day must also have some other reason than simply a desire for relaxation and leisure. Either it was necessitated by socio-economic considerations or caused by some magic, or taboo, or religio-cultic qualities of this day, so we are told.

The socio-economic considerations are founded in the so-called market days, the existence of which has been demonstrated in many parts of the world, though not in the Near East. According to the market day theory, the Sabbath originated as a day when agricultural work ceased in order that produce might be brought to market. This day also provided occasion for cultic and recreational activities which accompanied the

---

[1]Cf. Abram Menes, Die vorexilischen Gesetze Israels, BZAW, No. 50 (Giessen: Verlag von Alfred Töpelmann, 1928), p. 37; Pfeiffer, Religion in the Old Testament, p. 92; Rordorf, Sunday, pp. 12, 17. Says Rordorf: "In the oldest stratum of the Pentateuch the sabbath is, therefore, to be understood as a social institution. After six days of work a day of rest is inserted for the sake of the cattle and of the slaves and employers." This emphasis was lost, according to Rordorf, when the day was given theological interpretations subsequently.

[2]Cf. the complaint of the lesser gods who were once burdened by heavy work. Lambert and Millard, Atra-Ḫasis, pp. 43ff.

market in town.[1] The proponents of this view emphasize that market days are independent of the lunar phases, but do occur at regular intervals, and that Neh. 13:15-22; Jer. 17:19-26 and possibly Am. 8:5 associate, if not Sabbath keeping, then Sabbath breaking with marketing.

It is far more commonly assumed that the prohibitions against work on the Sabbath were brought about by religio-cultic qualities associated originally with this day. Either the Sabbath was a taboo day on which normal work was dangerous and would bring a disaster on the transgressor,[2] or it was a feast day when acts of propitiation should be

---

[1]Cf. Martin P. Nilsson, Primitive Time-Reckoning, pp. 324-46; Max Weber, Gesammelte Aufsätze zur Religionssoziologie, Vol. III: Das antike Judentum (Tübingen: Verlag von J. C. B. Mohr [Paul Siebeck], 1923), pp. 160-61; Eduard Meyer, Geschichte des Altertums, Vol. II, 2: Der Orient vom zwölften bis zur Mitte des achten Jahrhunderts (3rd ed.; Stuttgart: J. G. Cotta'sche Buchhandlung Nachfolger, 1953), p. 318; Webster, Rest Days: A Study in Early Law and Morality, pp. 101-23; Jenni, Die theologische Begründung, p. 13; de Vaux, Ancient Israel, I, 480; Kraeling, "The Present Status of the Sabbath Question," p. 228.

[2]Webster concluded that "the brief prohibitions of work found in the Pentateuch cannot easily be separated, by any subtleties of exegesis, from the numerous taboos with which the institution was invested." (Rest Days: A Sociological Study, The University Studies of the University of Nebraska, Vol. XI [Lincoln: Published by the University, 1911], p. 127). Two types of taboo have commonly been associated with the Sabbath. (1) The fire taboo which Israel's early cousins, the Kenites, introduced. It may be reflected in Ex. 35:3; Num. 15:32-36. See above, p. 5. (2) A taboo associated with the days when the moon changed phases. Cf. Nielsen, Die altarabische Mondreligion, pp. 52-88. In both instances one would refrain from working on the taboo day, because to do otherwise would bring certain disaster.

performed,[1] or celebrations should be engaged in.[2] These characteristics of the Sabbath will be discussed below. Here we are merely pointing to the fact that abstention from work on the Sabbath could be caused by one or more religious qualities of this day, or even by a combination of humanitarian and religious concern associated with it.[3]

We will now turn to a number of Old Testament passages dealing with Sabbath and work.

---

[1]The Babylonian šabattu is identified as a day when the god's heart is at rest. See above, n. 1, p. 96. Consequently the šabattu day might be given to acts of propitiation in order to achieve the appeasement of the god. This might involve abstention from certain functions, as well as participation in others of a cultic nature. Jastrow argued that Biblical man abstained from work on the Sabbath for just this reason. "The idea of 'propitiating' an enraged deity entered largely originally into the ordinance that became the central feature of Sabbath observance, namely, the command to abstain from labor. If the Sabbath was originally an 'unfavourable' day on which one must avoid showing one's self before Yahweh, it would naturally be regarded as dangerous to provoke his anger by endeavoring to secure on that day personal benefits through the usual forms of activity." ("The Original Character of the Sabbath," p. 323). Cf. Hehn, "Zur Sabbatfrage," p. 210; William R. Harper, Amos and Hosea, ICC, Vol. 23 (New York: Charles Scribner's Sons, 1905), pp. 232-33.

[2]It has been repeatedly emphasized that the Old Testament Sabbath was always a joyous occasion, in distinction from the gloomy and dangerous days in the Babylonian hemerologies. But also a festival might call for the suspension of ordinary activities without any taboo being invoked. According to this view, the Sabbath was always anchored in Yahwism and sanctified by Yahweh, i.e., it had no uncanny sanctity about it as a taboo day might have. Cf. Ernst L. Ehrlich, Die Kultsymbolik im Alten Testament und im nachbiblischen Judentum (Stuttgart: Anton Hiersemann, 1959), p. 78; Bostrup, Den israelitiske Sabbats Oprindelse og Karakter, p. 61; Enno Janssen, Juda in der Exilszeit: Ein Beitrag zur Frage der Entstehung des Judentums, FRLANT, No. 69 (Göttingen: Vandenhoeck & Ruprecht, 1956), p. 111; John Skinner and James Muilenburg, "Sabbath," Hasting's Dictionary of the Bible, ed. by F. C. Grant and H. H. Rowley (Rev. ed.; New York: Charles Scribner's Sons, 1963), p. 866; Kutsch, "Sabbat," col. 1259.

[3]Cf. Vriezen, "Kalender en Sabbat," pp. 188-89.

Neh. 13:15-22

This passage is important because it is extensive and can be accurately dated (second half of the fifth century B.C.). We learn that the men of Judah had been observed to harvest, gather in, and process their agricultural produce on the Sabbath. These activities must have been observed during an extensive period of time, for the crops of various seasons are mentioned. The men of Judah are not very well defined (lit., "In those days I saw in Judah the ones treading wine presses on the Sabbath"). Judah is undoubtedly the province over which Nehemiah was governor,[1] but the Sabbath breakers need not be members of the Jewish community, though they probably were,[2] since the other transgressors of the Sabbath (vs. 16) are clearly identified as foreigners. It is surprising, however, that Nehemiah does not correct this disrespect for the law by citizens of his province.[3] The only disapproval lies in the repetition and perhaps the tone of the words "on the Sabbath."

Worse than this, the Judean farmers market their produce in Jerusalem on the Sabbath. In this they are followed by Tyrian

---

[1] Vogt, Studie zur nachexilischen Gemeinde, pp. 70ff.

[2] The so-called Landjuden. Cf. Rudolph, Esra und Nehemia, pp. 205ff.; Galling, Die Bücher der Chronik, p. 253.

[3] We could suppose that those treading wine presses in Judah were faithless Jews who had not been in captivity and who disregarded the religious reforms sponsored by the returnees in Jerusalem, thus the vague reference to them and the embarrassing recognition of their disregard of the law. They might, of course, also be dwellers in the province who were displaced persons and who held no allegiance to the law, and on whom the reformers' activities had no effect.

tradesmen.[1] Both groups of traders sell their wares to the people of Judah (the sons of Judah),[2] and in the city of Jerusalem. The real culprits in the story, however, are the nobles of Judah, because they ought to know better than to let this situation exist (vss. 17-18). Their offense does not lie in the fact that they as feudal lords make their laborers work in their fields and operate their markets, but in the fact that they as nobles are held responsible for the behavior of the citizenry.[3] Nehemiah then takes up the responsibility neglected by the nobles, and puts an end to the Sabbath activities over which he had control, namely, the marketing in Jerusalem.

To the crucial question, why should the men of Judah and Jerusalem stop work on the Sabbath? we are told that to do otherwise would be to profane the Sabbath (vss. 17-18), i.e., not to keep it holy (vs. 22). Profaning the Sabbath (in this case by holding market on it) is a serious matter which was responsible for the captivity and the destruction of the city, and which could cause even greater disasters in the future (vs. 18). It is in this light that we must understand Nehemiah's concern with Sabbath breaking among the citizens of Jerusalem, whereas he is not equally bothered by the same offense among the Jewish and non-Jewish fringe groups.

---

[1] See above, n. 1, pp. 29-30.

[2] These Judeans are closer to the heart of Nehemiah. They appear to be city dwellers, returnees, and people who are closely attached to Judah, not just inhabitants of the Persian province of the same name. Cf. Vogt, Studie zur nachexilischen Gemeinde, pp. 68-69.

[3] Cf. Johannes Pedersen, Israel: Its Life and Culture (London: Oxford University Press, 1926-40), I-II, 34-40; de Vaux, Ancient Israel, I, 69-70.

Jer. 17:19-27

There are many similarities between this passage and the one in Nehemiah. Here kings and citizens of Judah and Jerusalem are admonished not to bear burdens on the Sabbath, not to carry them into the city, out of their houses, and not to work on this day. The object of these restrictions is to "keep the Sabbath day holy" (vss. 22, 24, 27). Failure to do so will involve the loss of life for the nation and for the individuals (vs. 21), as well as a destruction of the city (vs. 27). Compliance with the Sabbath regulations, on the other hand, will bring about continuation of the Davidic dynasty, and political and religious prosperity for the nation (vss. 24-26). In both of these passages the Sabbath occupies an important role in Israel's religious and political economy. Abstention from work on the Sabbath is required for the sake of the Sabbath, to keep it holy. To profane the Sabbath would bring about dissolution of the society by means of divine punishment.

This view of work and the Sabbath is shared by a number of Sabbath laws which have been composed by, or which passed through the hands of, priestly circles. They prohibit all work (kol-melā'kāh) on Sabbath.[1] Although it is not always stated, the context of these laws indicates that the object of abstention from work on the Sabbath is to keep the day holy. The Sabbath must be kept holy at all cost, and this is secured by abstaining from work on it. To refuse to do so would mean to reject one's religious duties in a most serious fashion, at the risk of death (Ex. 31:15; 35:2).

---

[1]Cf. Ex. 20:10; 31:14-15; 35:2; Lev. 23:3; Dt. 5:14.

Ex. 16:22-30

The account of the manna provision shows a more complicated
picture. It appears that an older story told of a double provision of
manna on the sixth day, and the absence of any manna on the seventh day,
with the instruction that a double portion should be gathered on the
sixth day (vss. 4-5). Verse 29, which purportedly is also from the old
story, reiterates that since Yahweh has given Israel the Sabbath, he
provides a double portion of manna on the sixth day, i.e., enough to
complete the food gathering for the week, and the people are admonished
not to go out and look for food on the seventh day. The result is that
the people rested, i.e., refrained from gathering, on the seventh day.
Nothing is said about tainting the holy Sabbath by attempting to gather
food on it. The call for the people to comply is a call for them to
recognize a work regulation forced upon them by the particular schedule
of the manna supply, and ultimately by the Sabbath institution. The
verses influenced by the priestly writer, on the other hand, expand this
story by centering the activities of the people around the "holy sabbath
to Yahweh" (vs. 23), rather than around the schedule of the manna provision. Thus the people gather twice the normal amount of manna on the
sixth day and come to Moses in surprise, only to be informed that nothing is amiss, but that since tomorrow is a Sabbath, they are to prepare
the double portion of manna on the sixth day (the leftovers would not
spoil this time), eat what they can (nobody gathers more than he can
eat), and keep the rest for the Sabbath. Thus while the J section,

which may well contain the oldest use of šabbāt in the Old Testament,[1]
warns against gathering manna on the seventh day, because Yahweh has so
arranged that man should not do that, the P section knows furthermore
that the seventh day is the holy Sabbath on which man just must not
work.

The question has been raised as to whether the Sabbath can
really belong properly in Ex. 16, prior to the Sinai narrative. It
seems that the old story takes its presence for granted. Yahweh has
given Israel the Sabbath, and consequently he schedules two portions of
manna on the sixth day. In the priestly stratum, on the other hand, the
double portion of manna comes as a surprise which has to be brought to
the attention of Moses who proceeds to give the reason for the phenomenon. Here the Sabbath is not commonly known to the people, and they now
have to learn to regulate their work according to its regulations. It
is, therefore, likely that the Sabbath did in fact belong in this pre-
Sinaitic story originally, and that P simply accommodated it by making
it a surprise appearance just before its proper introduction at Sinai.

Dt. 5:14-15

The Deuteronomic version of the fourth commandment has been a
particularly fruitful field for studying the relationship of Sabbath and
work. Thus it has been proposed that in this commandment the Sabbath is
in a special way released from theological interpretation and overlay,
and that it is given to anthropological, sociological, psychological, or

---

[1]Noth, Exodus, p. 136. However, see above, p. 121.

humanitarian concerns.[1] This judgment is based primarily on the so-
called reason for the Sabbath (vs. 15), but is it really dominated by
humanitarian concerns? "You shall remember that you were a servant in
the land of Egypt, and the LORD your God brought you out thence with a
mighty hand and an outstretched arm; therefore the LORD your God commanded you to keep the Sabbath."

We may compare the two recensions of the Sabbath commandment in
the Decalogue. In Ex. 20 the reason for Sabbath keeping (vs. 11) corresponds stylistically to verses 9-10, i.e., man is called upon to
schedule his work the way God schedules his, but it is also subordinated
to the previous verses by means of the preposition kî (for). Similarly
verse 11b, "therefore the LORD blessed the sabbath day and hallowed it,"
corresponds stylistically to verse 8, and it brings the command back to
the "holy Sabbath" where it began, while at the same time it follows
from verse 11a by means of ‹al-kēn (therefore).[2] The Deuteronomic
recension of the law is structured differently. We can see that by
setting it out in the following way:

> (a) Observe the sabbath day, to keep it holy, as the LORD your God
> commanded you (vs. 12).
>
> (b) Six days you shall labor, and do all your work; but the
> seventh day is a sabbath to the LORD your God; in it you
> shall not do any work, you, or your son, or your daughter,

---

[1]Cf. Morgenstern, "Sabbath," pp. 137-38; Skinner and Muilenburg,
"Sabbath," p. 866; Gerhard von Rad, Deuteronomy: A Commentary, trans.
by D. Barton (Philadelphia: Westminster Press, 1966), p. 58; Rordorf,
Sunday, p. 15; Gottlob Schrenk, "Sabbat oder Sonntag," Judaica II (1946),
178; Menes, Die vorexilischen Gesetze Israels, p. 37; Botterweck, "Der
Sabbat im Alten Testamente," pp. 138-41; et al.

[2]For an analysis of the structure of Ex. 20:8-11, see below,
pp. 170-71.

or your manservant, or your maidservant, or your ox, or
your ass, or any of your cattle, or the sojourner who is
within your gates, that your manservant and your maidservant may rest as well as you (vss. 13-14).

(c) (and) You shall remember that you were a servant in
the land of Egypt, and the LORD your God brought you
out thence with a mighty hand and an outstretched arm
(vs. 15a);

(d) therefore the LORD your God commanded you to keep the sabbath
day (vs. 15b).

In this structure (a) contains the opening command with the
characteristic Deuteronomic expansion: "as the LORD your God commanded
you."[1] (d) is the corresponding conclusion to the commandment. It is
strikingly similar to verse 12a; and, as in the Exodus recension, one of
its purposes is clearly to "wrap up" the whole commandment, a purpose
which has been necessitated in part by the lengthy expansions throughout.
(b) follows the Exodus recension except for the expansions, but (c) has
no parallel there. It is not subordinated to verse 14 (there is no kî,
only a conjunction we), but coordinated to what precedes it. This means
that the Sabbath is the occasion when man is commanded to refrain from
all work, and to remember his servitude in Egypt and Yahweh's deliverance, i.e., his historical origins. The ᵓal-kēn (therefore) sentence
(vs. 15b) is thus, in distinction from Ex. 20:11b, even less, if at all,
related to the preceding sentences, for they do not contain an indica-
tive statement, as in Ex. 20:11a, but an imperative statement.[2] This
means that verse 15b does not make verse 15a into the reason for Sabbath
observance. Rather, verse 15a simply represents Deuteronomy's interest

---

[1]Cf. Dt. 6:1; 13:5; 20:17.

[2]Cf. Childs, Memory and Tradition, pp. 52-53.

in the salvation history, the exodus deliverance in particular,[1] with
the implication that Israel is to remember her past experience on the
Sabbath. With this new dimension, Dt. 5:12-15 is seen to be very "theo-
logically" oriented with more than a simple humanitarian concern.[2] The
only real reason given for the Sabbath is that God commanded it.

There are, however, several overtones in this commandment, the
most important of which is, in our opinion, a humanitarian and social
concern. The expression "your ox and your ass" indicates that its
author was concerned with the extension of the Sabbath regulation to the
whole household. More telling is the expansion "that your manservant
and your maidservant may rest as well as you." Though we cannot conclude that the purpose of the Sabbath is to provide rest for the
laborers, we can say that whatever rest and freedom is provided by the
Sabbath is to be extended to the workers and to the whole household.
This emphasis we know from Ex. 20:9-10, but the expansion in Dt. 5:14,
which may have been added at a time when Israelite freemen were misusing
their servants or letting their servants do the tasks from which they
themselves abstained on the Sabbath, does have strong humanitarian
overtones.[3]

---

[1]See also Dt. 5:15; 6:12; 7:18-19; 15:15; 16:3, 12; 24:18, 22.

[2]Other studies have shown the fundamentally theological orientation of this version of the commandment. Jenni, Die theologische
Begründung, pp. 15-19. "Wir stellen somit im Deuteronomium eine
heilsgeschichtliche Begründung des Sabbats fest" (p. 18); Hulst,
"Bemerkungen zum Sabbatgebot," pp. 155-56; Reventlow, Gebot und Predigt,
pp. 57-58.

[3]Both recensions of the commandment define the sphere of the
Sabbath by including the whole household under its regulation. It is
possible that a humanitarian concern lies behind these specifications.

The same can be said about verse 15. Deuteronomy's preoccupation with the deliverance from Egypt and the rest which Israel must enter,[1] a theme which provides the theological horizon against which all its laws are given, is very likely responsible not only for verse 15, but also for the preceding expansion in verse 14b. In fact, it is likely that Deuteronomy's acute awareness of Israel's experience of servitude and deliverance is responsible for the humanitarian-oriented expansion (vs. 14b).

Ex. 23:12; 34:21

These two Sabbath laws are completely without overt religious implications. The latter commands that work[2] be stopped on the seventh day and emphasizes the importance of this regulation by the added reference to the busy sowing and harvest seasons. However, we are given no reason for this practice. Ex. 23:12, on the other hand, explains the requirement to cease with all work on the seventh day with the words: "that your ox and your ass may have rest, and the son of your bondmaid,

---

Cf. Bentzen, Den israelitiske Sabbats Oprindelse og Historie, pp. 55-56. It does seem, however, that Ex. 20:10b is concerned with protecting the Sabbath from transgression rather than with protecting the worker from overwork. Seen from this perspective Dt. 5:14b strikes the reader as an effort to point to the humanitarian or ethical value of the regulation to keep the Sabbath. The freemen of ancient Israel were not always as considerate towards their servants and slaves as the Sabbath laws and other regulations might suggest. Cf. Jer. 34:8-17.

[1]See below, pp. 221-25.

[2]The verb ᶜbd (work) is used primarily for agricultural work, and not for general activities in the sense of "undertaking," "business," "task," or "occupation." It is also used to describe worship, the service performed on behalf of God. Koehler and Baumgartner, Lexicon, pp. 670-71.

and the alien,[1] may be refreshed." That this regulation has a humanitarian concern is beyond question, but this is not a unique feature in
the Book of the Covenant (cf. Ex. 21:2-6; 22:21-27; 23:6, 9, 10-11).
Consequently, it has been suggested that the humanitarian concern is
imposed upon the Sabbath regulation by the general concern lying behind
a number of laws in the immediate context, whereas the real "reason" for
the seventh day and the sabbatical year (Ex. 23:10-11) is a mythical and
cultic understanding of land and people, namely, that these are not at
Israel's free disposal, but must after having been used be allowed to
return to their original state, by means of a rest, so that restoration
of spent powers can be accomplished.[2]

Such a conclusion cannot readily be drawn from our passages,
both of which contain completely secular regulations for the seventh
day. We can say, however, that as early as pre-monarchical times the
seventh day was characterized as a day without work, and that it was
concerned with the laborers. It is very likely that these early regulations, as well as Am. 8:5, rely on even older practices which the
complexities of society had made it difficult to observe any longer.
Thus business competition (Am. 8:5) made it problematic, expanding agricultural enterprises could barely afford the time off during the sowing
and harvest seasons, and the aquisition of servants made it tempting for

---

[1]The alien (gēr) is a displaced person who as a consequence may
have lost his civil rights and religious privileges. Koehler and Baumgartner, Lexicon, p. 192. This was certainly true in ancient Israel,
where the gērîm were reduced to common laborers, hiring out their services. Consequently, they were the object of Israelite charity (Ex. 22:
21; 23:9). Cf. de Vaux, Ancient Israel, I, 74-75.

[2]Noth, Exodus, pp. 189-90.

an Israelite not to apply the regulation to them (Dt. 5:14b). We cannot,
however, be certain that the seventh day originated with such humanitarian concerns for the worker, but only that when regulations were made
for this practice, socio-humanitarian considerations were invoked at a
very early time, as well as in the later Deuteronomic laws. Beyond this
point our texts do not take us.

Ex. 35:3; Num. 15:32-36

The two final passages we will examine regarding work and the
Sabbath prohibit the making of fires.[1] Why in particular should the
making of fires be prohibited on the Sabbath? Since all ancient peoples,
even the Kenites (smiths) were engaged in other work than making fires,
it is possible that we here have the remnants of a special fire taboo,
and not a prohibition of general work. The question is, did the Sabbath
originate in such a taboo?[2]

The Old Testament evidence for it is very poor. Ex. 16:23
refers to cooking and baking the manna on the sixth day, but it is even
possible that such food preparation with the accompanying fire making is
not altogether prohibited on the seventh day. Perhaps we are to understand that cooking and baking is to be done on the sixth day in order to
prepare food for that day. What is left over of the manna is then to be
set aside, for it will keep; and it will then be prepared and eaten on
the seventh day. The old stratum of the story only prohibits gathering

---

[1]Num. 15:32-26 presumably refers to a man who wanted to make a
fire. Cf. I Kg. 17:12.

[2]See above, p. 5.

food on the seventh day, but not preparing that which was gathered on the sixth day. Num. 15:32-36 relates that a man was caught picking up sticks on the Sabbath, presumably to make a fire for cooking or heat.[1] Now it is surprising that this tradition should have the whole community and Moses uncertain about the punishment of a man who had violated the Sabbath by working or by making a fire (Ex. 35:2-3). It is not surprising, however, that there should be doubt about whether a simple matter, such as gathering a few sticks, should be punished as Sabbath breaking. The real question is, can one collect a bit of firewood on the Sabbath, or is such an innocent act of work on the Sabbath a capital offense? Consequently, we cannot draw any conclusions about fire taboos from this passage. This leaves us with the categorical prohibition (Ex. 35:3) against kindling a fire on the Sabbath. It appears without any context; however, it is probably not included in this position by P for no reason at all. We have proposed that although the Sabbath regulation (Ex. 35:2) may be intended to emphasize that the new building activities should not take place on the Sabbath, nevertheless, this is not spelled out. Rather, the law (vs. 2) looks much more like a standard Sabbath prohibition; and it could well be that verse 3 is intended to make verse 2 applicable to the context, for verse 5 proceeds to call for donations of fine metal which would have to be smelted down.[2] It is not very sound, therefore, to conclude from the Old Testament literature

---

[1]Kenites who used fire commercially, as smiths would do, probably did not acquire their fuel by having a man pick up sticks in the field. The emphasis in this story is only slightly related to fire making, and not at all to the Kenites or smiths.

[2]Cf. Vriezen, "Kalender en Sabbat," p. 187.

that the Sabbath originated as a fire taboo day, for the prohibitions of fire making are in fact only prohibitions of work. It is perplexing, of course, that we should have these references specifically to fire making; and there just may be ancient regulations against fire making behind them, but such are not described in the Old Testament.[1]

Conclusion

One of the most fundamental Sabbath laws commands man to work six days and to refrain from working on the seventh day. In the later literature, notably in P, this law has been expanded in the following way: On six days work is commanded, but the seventh day is a Sabbath; on it work is prohibited.[2] In the early form of the law abstention from work is understood simply in terms of the seven day schedule, and probably as a means to achieve rest and restoration, both in a physical and in a mythical way. In the expanded laws, on the other hand, the term Sabbath provides adequate rationale for the work prohibition. This development illustrates a shift in the relationship between Sabbath and work. Now the prohibition of work on the seventh has become subordinated to the Sabbath institution, i.e., one does not work on the seventh day, because it is the Sabbath, and that is certainly something more than just a day without work. Neh. 13:15-22 and Jer. 17:19-27 understand the Sabbath as a guarantor of the continued existence of the

---

[1]In extra-Biblical literature such fire taboo days are not altogether unknown. Cf. Meesters, Op zoek naar de oorsprong van de Sabbat, pp. 49-53. See also Webster, Rest Days: A Study in Early Law and Morality, pp. 257-59.

[2]See below, pp. 161ff.

community, and remind the reader from two different viewpoints that
rejection of the Sabbath is directly responsible for the destruction of
the community by the hand of Yahweh. At the same time, abstinence from
work is a sign of genuine Sabbath keeping. In Dt. 5:12-15 the Sabbath
is clearly related to the history of the community as well. And finally,
Ex. 16:22-30, in its present form, also subordinates the schedule of the
manna provision to the Sabbath institution. In all of these instances
the Sabbath is the day when one abstains from work; but the object of
this is not to abstain from activities, i.e., to rest, but to keep the
Sabbath. That is to say, the Sabbath is no longer constituted by
abstention from work with the ensuing rest. The Sabbath is now in
existence even if man breaks it by working all seven days. Man cannot
abolish the Sabbath by refusing to stop his work, he can only disregard
it thereby and take the consequences of such an act.

This situation is not brought about merely by the fact that the
Sabbath had become the delimiting factor of a new calendar unit, the
week, which would persist for practical reasons, whether man worked for
six or seven days. Rather, the texts indicate that the Sabbath exists
independently of whether man works on it or not, because of its role as
a religious emblem. We shall examine this aspect of the Sabbath later.
In the early passages, however, abstention from work does constitute the
seventh day (Sabbath). This appears from the very structure of the laws
(Ex. 23:12; 34:21) which indicate that anyone who broke them by working
on the seventh day would in fact do away with it, since there is nothing
except abstention from work to identify it.[1] No definite reason for

---

[1]This also applies to the accounts of the creation Sabbath.

this characterization of the seventh day can be detected. We have noted
a humanitarian concern with the rest and relaxation of the workers;
there may be some mythical or taboo like elements hidden behind the
earliest Sabbath traditions, which would lead to abstention from work,
but they are no longer explicit; and thirdly, we noticed some overtones
associating Sabbath and freedom. However, this freedom is not a humanitarian or democratic principle, but a function of Israel's sacred
history. It is likely that also the rest and relaxation theme had
religious overtones.[1] Nevertheless, abstention from work stood very
close to the essence of the seventh day Sabbath in the earliest strata
of the Old Testament, whereas in later literature, already in D and certainly in P, that had become merely the way to recognize the self-
contained Sabbath institution.[2]

Am. 8:5 implies that the Sabbath was recognized, grudgingly by some, as
a day without work. The verb hišbattî (I will put to an end) may provide a word play with šabbattāh (her sabbaths), Hos. 2:11. If so, we
may conclude that also Hosea knew the Sabbath as a day of ceasing,
meaning resting from ordinary activities. Cf. Wolff, Dodekapropheton 1:
Hoshea, p. 46.

[1]This is, we noted, the case with Dt. 5:12-15. Ex. 23:12 is
found in a context with cultic, ethical, and judicial material; and we
may assume that its author was aware of the penetration of Israel's
religious life into her socio-economic activities. And yet Ex. 23:12;
34:21 are the most secular Sabbath regulations in the entire literature.
George R. Berry ("The Hebrew Word ⌐Η⅂," JBL, L (1931), 207-10) has
argued that this verb and its corresponding noun does not mean rest from
work, but from some kind of trouble. It is true that it refers to rest
from various kinds of distress, both physical and mental (Koehler and
Baumgartner, Lexicon, pp. 601-2), but trouble must include work, for it
is precisely work which is brought to an end that rest might prevail in
Ex. 23:12 and Dt. 5:14b, and, we will maintain, also in Ex. 20:11 dealing with the Yahweh's rest.

[2]It has been pointed out repeatedly (e.g., Rowley, "Moses and
the Decalogue," pp. 28f.) that the Sabbath, if it was originally a day
without work, could not have been observed among pastoral nomads, i.e.,

C. The Sabbath as Cultic Institution

<u>The Problem</u>

Although the Sabbath throughout the Old Testament literature is characterized as a day without work, we noted that this fact may depend on an even more fundamental attachment of the Sabbath to some religious or cultic element.[1] We shall now examine the relationship between the Sabbath and various spheres of the cult, beginning with the postexilic period, where our sources are most informative, and moving back into the earlier literature. It will be our objective here to seek the real or

---

prior to the settlement as far as Israel is concerned. This objection is quite irrelevant. This is not because the pre-settlement Israelites may have been semi-nomads or caravan nomads (cf. Albright, <u>Yahweh and the Gods of Canaan</u>, pp. 64-73) rather than pastoral nomads. These and other forms of nomadism would, of course, also require some Sabbath activities. It is irrelevant because it reveals an absolutist view of the Sabbath rest, a view which is not present everywhere in the Old Testament, nor in the New Testament for that matter. We must agree with Rowley (see above) that the Sabbath has had a history also in regard to the way in which it was observed. We have noticed that at one stage it provided the occasion for a journey with the assistance of a servant and a beast of burden, while at the same time it was considered a day without work, as the text (II Kg. 4:23) implies. This leads us to conclude that cessation from work on this day meant different things to different social and occupational groups, as it also does today. Pastoral nomads could, therefore, keep Sabbath, although not all their daily work could be put aside on this day; but semi-nomads, and even settled farmers in Canaan after the conquest, would also have some necessary tasks to perform every day of the week. It is, therefore, not impossible to accept the view that the earliest Old Testament Sabbath traditions, reaching back to the period of the pre-monarchical settlement and beyond into the nomadic communities, knew the Sabbath as a day without work. But this does, of course, not mean that there were not other motifs involved in this early Sabbath, e.g., a sacral view of rest and work (see below, pp. 149-50).

[1]This question has recently been explored with reference to the origin of the Sabbath by Kiker, "The Sabbath in the Old Testament Cult." See above, pp. 114-116.

ideal cultic role assigned to the Sabbath by the various strata of the
literature.

Sabbath sacrifices

A number of passages, all of them exilic or postexilic, make
mention of Sabbath sacrifices. Two of them (Num. 28:9-10; Ezek. 46:4-5)
specify the types of sacrifices required, but the specifications do not
agree. Num. 28 enumerates the sacrifices appropriate for the various
feast days listed in Lev. 23. The special Sabbath sacrifice is identical to that for ordinary days: two male lambs a year old, and two two-
tenths of an ephah of fine flour mixed with oil, and a drink offering.
Together they make up what is presumably a burnt offering (ʿōlāh)[1] and a
cereal offering (minḥāh). This was the usual type of offering made on a
feast day. We must assume that this special offering was made in
addition to the daily sacrifices, i.e., the daily sacrifices were simply
doubled on the Sabbath.[2] Ezek. 46 projects the Sabbath sacrifices of
the new temple to consist of six lambs and a ram for a burnt offering,
together with a cereal offering for the animals (an ephah for the ram
and as much as can be afforded for the lambs). Though the number of
animals is not identical in the two passages, both consist of the same
elements, namely, an ʿōlāh and a minḥāh. Unfortunately, we do not know
how old the regulation in Num. 28 is, and whether the one in Ezek. 46

---

[1]Vs. 9 does not indicate the type of offering, but vs. 10
explains: "This is the burnt offering of every Sabbath."

[2]Cf. Rolf Rendtorff, Studien zur Geschichte des Opfers im Alten
Testament, WMANT, No. 24 (Neukirchen-Vluyn: Neukirchener Verlag, 1967),
p. 15; Roland de Vaux, Studies in Old Testament Sacrifice (Cardiff:
University of Wales Press, 1964), p. 36.

reflects pre-exilic practices.[1]

According to Ezek. 44:17; 46:2, it is the prince who offers the sacrifice, or more likely provides the animals for it, and thus guarantees its performance. He is the envisioned king, perhaps with charismatic qualities, of the reunited land (Ezek. 37:15-28). At a later time, when re-establishment of the kingship is completely abandoned as a possibility, the Chronicler retrojects this same obligation of the king into the pre-exilic times (II Chr. 31:3).[2] The actual sacrificing was executed by the temple personnel, the priests (cf. Ezek. 46:2) and, according to the Chronicler, with the assistance of the Levites (I Chr. 23:30). The Chronicler's interest in the cause of the Levites is further apparent in the regulation that they should prepare the holy bread every Sabbath (I Chr. 9:32).[3] Here again we do not know how old these regulations and practices are.

The additional passages in Chronicles make mention of the burnt

---

[1] The six small animals corresponding to the six working days, and the one larger animal corresponding to the Sabbath could represent an idealistic view of the Sabbath offerings. However, there might be some actual basis for it, perhaps in the types of sacrifices to be brought, and even in the amount.

[2] This is surely not a pure invention of the Chronicler, for the king was in fact the protector of the cult in pre-exilic times, both that associated with the religion of Israel, as well as that borrowed from other nations (cf. I Kg. 3:3-4; II Kg. 16:10-14). In a sense the Jerusalem temple was both the royal chapel and the national cult center, and whereas many other cult places might have been maintained by the local population (an exception being perhaps Bethel and Dan in Israel), the Jerusalem temple seems to have been operated by the king. Moreover, we may presume that only the king could afford the great expense of providing continuous sacrifices. The Chronicler merely idealizes the royal support of the temple because that demonstrated to him the particular king's piety in a special way.

[3] See above, pp. 53-55.

offerings on the Sabbath. II Chr. 2:4-6 informs us that Solomon planned to build the temple for such offerings to be presented, but the parallel passage in I Kg. 5:2ff. lacks any reference to such sacrifices. Even more telling is the account of Solomon's burnt offerings on the Sabbaths, the new moon, and the three annual festivals, according to the commandment of Moses (II Chr. 8:12). Its parallel account in Kings (I Kg. 9:25) mentions only the burnt offerings and peace offerings presented three times a year.

From these passages it is clear that the regulations for special Sabbath sacrifices are an exilic or postexilic phenomenon, although we cannot exclude, of course, that some sacrifices, and perhaps the presentation of holy bread, were performed on the Sabbath in much earlier times.

Festal assemblies on the Sabbath

Was the Sabbath a day for festal assembly? This is an important question in the relationship between Sabbath and cult. We cannot answer in the affirmative on the mere assumption that anciently as presently Sabbath (Sunday) must have been the occasion for communal worship activities. In fact, our observation in the previous chapter, that the Sabbath was very early the occasion for field workers and household servants, as well as the members of the family, to be given time to rest (Dt. 5:14; Ex. 23:12), may lead to the assumption that the Sabbath was oriented towards the household, and not to the community at large. Ex. 16:29 (attributed to JE) exhorts everyone to stay in his place on the seventh day. In these regulations the Sabbath is, of course, treated as a religio-cultic occasion, but one having to do with abstention from normal activities. If, on the other hand, we were to interpret these regulations as an outcome of a religio-cultic orientation, we would easily be led to the idea that the Sabbath was a taboo day.[1] According to this view, each Israelite would sit indoors fearful to do anything that was prohibited and afraid even to go outside lest he should unwittingly perform such an act. This religio-cultic orientation is, however, not present in the passages which prohibit normal activities on the Sabbath; and it is, therefore, frequently claimed that the Old Testament Sabbath is, in fact, not a dangerous day of taboos, but a joyous day, or at least a day which provided occasion for joy.[2] On such a day we would expect some communal activity.

The word šabbāt appears in company with several other words for festal occasions: (1) Hos. 2:11, "her feasts (ḥag), her new moons, her sabbaths, and all her appointed feasts (môᶜēd)"; (2) Ezek. 45:17, "the feasts (ḥag), the new moons, the sabbaths, all the appointed feasts (môᶜēd)"; (3) I Chr. 23:31; II Chr. 2:4; 31:3; Neh. 10:33, "the sabbaths, the new moons, and the appointed feasts (môᶜēd)"; (4) Lam. 2:6, "appointed feast (môᶜēd) and sabbath"; (5) Is. 1:13, "new moon and sabbath and the calling of assemblies--(qᵉrōʾ miqrāʾ)"; (6) Lev. 23:3, "a holy convocation (miqrāʾ-qōdeš)."

The general word for feast is môᶜēd, whereas the word ḥag is

---

[1]See above, pp. 124-125.

[2]See above, n. 2, p. 125. Cf. Is. 58:13.

usually reserved for the three annual feasts.[1] Mô‹ēd and ḥag were
associated with the festal assemblies and were no doubt accompanied by
ritual activity,[2] cultic functions, sacrifices, and gatherings.[3] In (2)
and (3) above it appears that the Sabbath and the new moon share these
characteristics of the other feasts, for these texts contain identical
regulations of a cultic nature for all the various feasts, both the
yearly, the monthly, and the weekly. Nothing can be concluded from (1),
for Sabbath and new moon could be days of a quite different nature from
those characterized as ḥag.[4] We are only told that Sabbath, new moon,
ḥag, and mô‹ēd will be terminated by Yahweh; but we do not know if that
would involve the termination of festal assemblies in all or any of the
cases. In (4), however, the context indicates that the end of Sabbath
and mô‹ēd followed as a consequence of the destruction of Zion, specifically the temple, a fact which may lead us to suggest that the Sabbath
was associated with temple services in pre-exilic times. We have suggested, following Kutsch,[5] that the expression miqrā› (Is. 1:13) should
not be translated "assembly," but festival. This may also be the meaning of the expression miqrā›-qōdeš (Lev. 23:3). It seems, however, that

---

[1]Cf. de Vaux, Ancient Israel, II, 470-71; Ringgren, Israelite
Religion, p. 185.

[2]The root ḥg also means "dance," and "make procession." See
Koehler and Baumgartner, Lexicon, p. 275.

[3]This is implied in the oldest regulations for these feasts,
Ex. 23:14-17; 34:18-24.

[4]Am. 8:5 from the same time and locale as Hos. 2:11 couples
Sabbath and new moon as days on which no work is done, but no assemblies
are mentioned.

[5]See above, n. 2, p. 59.

a number of occurrences of this term, viz., Num. 28:18, 25; Is. 1:13;
4:5, presuppose the idea of an assembly in any case. Thus Is. 1:12
pictures people trampling across the temple court to appear before
Yahweh. And the legislation on the festivals (Lev. 23; Num. 28-29)
assumes that the temple or at least Jerusalem will be the scene of the
celebrations called miqrā²-qōdeš. And so whenever the Sabbath is celebrated at the religious center (temple or other cult center), we may
assume that some form of assembly took place.

  In addition to Is. 1:13, other pre-exilic material is available.
II Kg. 4:23 informs us that it was not customary to visit a prophet
except on a Sabbath and a new moon. We cannot assume with certainty
that an assembly took place at the prophet's residence, or that people
went there every Sabbath and new moon; but at least some people left
their homes on these days on a religious journey, perhaps as the
occasion arose. The obscure passage in II Kg. 16:18 suggests that the
king was in the temple on the Sabbath, and II Kg. 11:4-12 (II Chr. 23:
1-11) probably imply that a large group of worshippers were in the
temple also. They were thus at hand to acclaim the child king Joash,
and the extra military force deployed in the temple on this day was
responsible for controlling the crowds.

Sabbath and synagogue

  In the contemporary Jewish and Christian communities Sabbath and
Sunday are traditionally associated with synagogue and church. This
association of Sabbath and public acts of worship is very important to
our understanding of the Sabbath. Rowley has rightly observed that "in

post-exilic days, if there had been no synagogues, it is difficult to
see how it [the Sabbath] could have survived, and it is significant that
in our day impatience with the sabbath as a day of rest is the accompa-
niment of the widespread abandonment of the sabbath as a day of
worship."[1] This association of Sabbath worship and the synagogue is
very old and may go back into Biblical times; but, unfortunately, there
is no evidence of it in the Old Testament literature. We can only
assume that if the synagogue did indeed originate during the exile,[2]
then it would be natural to expect that the religious feast which could
be celebrated away from the land of Israel and its temple, namely, the
Sabbath, would be celebrated in the synagogue. Perhaps a very cautious
and reasonable position is adopted by Rowley and Kraus who suggest that
the exilic synagogue was a home synagogue, i.e., a gathering place in
private homes on the Sabbath.[3]

Conclusion

The attempt to abstract from the Old Testament traditions what
the Sabbath was really like in Israel has not been very successful. We
have seen that it is understood as a day without work throughout the Old

---

[1]Rowley, Worship in Ancient Israel, p. 241.

[2]Some scholars favor an exilic origin of the synagogue, or at
least an early form of it. Cf. Vriezen, The Religion of Ancient Israel,
pp. 244-45; Rowley, Worship in Ancient Israel, pp. 240-41; Janssen, Juda
in der Exilzeit, p. 111; Abram Menes, "Temple und Synagoge," ZAW, L
(1932), 268-76. Other scholars, noting that there is practically no
evidence of it, are very sceptical about the matter. Cf. Kraus, Worship
in Israel, p. 230; Kurt Galling, "Erwägungen zur antiken Synagoge," ZDPV,
LXXII (1956), 163-78. For an excellent survey of the whole problem, see
Rowley, Worship in Ancient Israel, pp. 213-45.

[3]Rowley, Worship in Ancient Israel, p. 224; Kraus, Worship in
Israel, p. 230. Cf. de Vaux, Ancient Israel, II, pp. 343-44.

Testament, but only a few passages understand the day solely in terms of abstention from work and the ensuing rest (for the laborer) and freedom (for everybody). The great majority of texts are clearly not concerned merely with abstention from work. When we consider the religio-cultic observations on the Sabbath, we find in the exilic and postexilic literature regulations for sacrifices to be offered on the Sabbath, performed in the temple, and sponsored by the king. As for the pre-exilic literature, on the other hand, we are led to believe that the Sabbath provided an occasion for gathering at the temple and perhaps at other sacred sites, such as the Carmel cult site (II Kg. 4:23). Moreover, the Sabbath is mentioned alongside other feasts, about which we know that assemblies and ritual and cultic acts were common procedures. This means that the Old Testament Sabbath traditions from the earliest to the latest can freely associate the Sabbath both with abstention from work and with festal activities.

This conclusion is based on very meager evidence, and any reflection on it must be cautious. The Sabbath, we may observe, was never simply a "free day," however much the Sabbath literature emphasizes abstention from work. It was very early a day on which man was drawn to a cultic site or institution. Perhaps it originally provided an occasion for man to dissociate himself from the battle to wrest a living from the earth, and also from other gainful activities. At the same time, the earth itself, the laborer, and the beast of burden were freed from man's aggressive activities. Thus the whole creation was provided with an occasion for regeneration. Yahweh himself had stopped his activities on this day, and thus the efforts of the earth and its life to come into existence had ceased. Such a period of reconstitution of life must have been considered very important. Even the busy harvest and plowing times were not allowed to interfere with it (Ex. 34:21). This function of the Sabbath as an occasion for reconstitution of spent powers and energies makes the day not just a catalyst, but an agent of redemption. The earth is freed from man's exploitation, the servants and the beasts are liberated from servitude, and the worker is himself liberated from his work by which he exercises both his mastery over the earth and his exploitation of it. Although the texts which relate the Sabbath to both work and the cultus do not take us quite so far, this dual association of the Sabbath in the early Old Testament literature suggests, even if tentatively, that some such sacral view of work and abstention from it may be part of the earliest Sabbath traditions. As the sacral sphere was associated with cultic sites, it was only natural that the Sabbath should also be associated with these.

D. The Sabbath as Law

Sabbath legislation

The majority of the Old Testament Sabbath material appears in the form of laws, or references to laws. This is not a unique situation, for the Old Testament generally contains many more regulations regarding Israel's cultic, religious, and social practices than descriptions of the same. We are not totally without non-legal references to the Sabbath institution; but, as we noted above, they do not give us a very complete picture of the role of the Sabbath in the Israelite community. Rather, it is the Sabbath laws which provide the most imaginative expositions of the role of the Sabbath in Israel's religious experience. These expositions will be discussed below, but first we will examine the formal aspects of the Sabbath laws.

At the outset we can eliminate a number of regulations dealing with cultic practices to be carried out on the Sabbath. Most of these regulations are late; and they deal with sacrifices and various temple ordinances on the holy days, including the Sabbath. Most of them tell us more about Israel's cultic practices than about the Sabbath itself.

The remaining Sabbath laws fall into several categories with reference to type and content, but nearly all of them belong to the so-called apodeictic type of law. Alt proposed in his study on Israelite law in 1934 that apodeictic law is uniquely Israelite in origin and was in existence prior to the conquest.[1] This limited view of Israelite law has now been abandoned by several scholars who argue that the origin of apodeitic law and especially apodeictic style cannot be limited to the Israelite community, or to specific religious components of the constitution of this community, viz., the covenant.[2] The general distinction between the functions of apodeictic and casuistic law, however, is probably still useful.[3] Casuistic law is case law, the outcome of actual

---

[1]"The Origins of Israelite Law," pp. 133ff.

[2]Cf. the recent studies by Gerstenberger, Wesen und Herkunft des "apodiktischen Rechts"; Hans Jochen Boecker, Redeformen des Rechtslebens im Alten Testament, WMANT, No. 14 (Neukirchen-Vluyn: Neukirchener Verlag, 1964); Fohrer, "Das sogenannte apodiktisch formulierte Recht," pp. 49-74; Rudolf Kilian, "Apodiktisches und kasuistisches Recht im Licht ägyptischer Analogien," BZ, N.F. VII (1963), 185-202; Henning Graf Reventlow, "Kultisches Recht im Alten Testament," ZThK, LX (1963), 267-304; Stamm and Andrew, The Ten Commandments, pp. 44-75.

[3]Casuistic law contains a statement of a hypothetical crime

152

cases heard by the elders holding court in the city gate. Apodeictic

law, on the other hand, is a statement of policy, providing the basic

guidelines according to which the community ordered its existence. It

was the purpose of casuistic law to insure that the general policy of

the community was upheld, as well as to take account of numerous special

situations which changing socio-economic and religio-cultic influences

brought on the community, not least in connection with the conquest.[1]

With one or two exceptions, the Sabbath laws are of the nature of

policy. No specific punishment is stipulated for breaking the laws

which are stated as unconditional commands.

---

together with the appropriate punishment. Laws of this type were used
in the courts. Apodeictic law contains categorical imperatives, generally in the form of prohibitions, often without a designated punishment
for the crime involved in breaking the law. It has been assumed that
this type of law belonged in the cultic sphere of Israel's life. Cf.
Alt, "The Origins of Israelite Law," pp. 116ff., 157ff.; George E.
Mendenhall, Law and Covenant in Israel and the Ancient Near East
(Pittsburg: The Presbyterian Board of Colportage of Western Pennsylvania, 1955), pp. 6ff. Also found in BA, XVII (1954), 26-46, 49-76;
Mowinckel, Le Décalogue, pp. 114ff. The cultic origin of apodeictic law
has recently been challenged (see above, n. 2, p. 151), but even if
apodeictic law originated in the patriarchal institutions (Gerstenberger), it probably functioned in most cases as community policy anyway.
It is unlikely, however, that we should distinguish so sharply between
the patriarchal institution and the priestly institution in nomadic
communities. Clan wisdom and clan religion were perhaps protected by
the same individuals. Cf. Reventlow, "Kultisches Recht im Alten Testament," pp. 278-79.

[1]According to Alt ("The Origin of Israelite Law," pp. 124ff.),
the contact with the Canaanite legal practices subsequent to the conquest
was responsible for introducing casuistic laws to Israel. This is
probably too simple a solution both from a form-critical and a chronological point of view. Recent studies of Israelite law have revealed a
variety of different forms of apodeictic as well as casuistic laws, and
there is good reason to believe that some forms from each category are
found on both sides of the conquest, and both inside and outside the
Israelite community. Cf. Gerstenberger, Wesen und Herkunft des
"apodiktischen Rechts," pp. 19ff., 23ff.

A specific Sabbath law: Ex. 35:3

This regulation deals with a specific type of Sabbath disruption:
"You shall kindle no fire in all your habitations on the sabbath day."
It is the only law of its kind; and although it may reflect an ancient
tradition associated with a fire taboo, its present position and function is probably determined by its context.[1] The unconditional demand
without a punishment stipulated characterizes it as an apodeictic type
law. It is often examined in connection with Num. 15:32-36. Assuming,
as we have done, that the issue in this passage is not with the making
of fires, although the sticks gathered were undoubtedly intended for a
fire, but with the trivial task of gathering a few sticks, then this
passage is actually not related to Ex. 35:3.[2] It demonstrates, however,
the passage from apodeictic to casuistic law. The community knew that
making fires, or more probably, just working was prohibited on the Sabbath; but the question of what to do with a specific man who possibly
prepared himself to make a fire, or who did an innocent sort of work in
order to prepare for necessary household duties, was not answered by the
general policy. From here on, however, it would be possible for the
community to formulate a case law regarding gathering sticks on the Sabbath for whatever purpose. If nothing else, this passage demonstrates
that the Israelite community could at one stage conceive of casuistic
Sabbath laws, although the passage is probably mostly hortatory in its
present position.[3]

---

[1]See above, p. 72.   [2]See above, pp. 136-38.

[3]If the context is at all determinative for the interpretation
of this passage, this must be our conclusion. Num. 15:27-31

154

Sabbath laws: type one

We now turn to a type of Sabbath law which occurs four times.

(a) Everyone who profanes it shall be put to death (Ex. 31:14a).

(b) Whoever does any work on it, that soul shall be cut off from among his people (Ex. 31:14b).

(c) Whoever does any work on the sabbath day shall be put to death (Ex. 31:15).

(d) Whoever does any work on it shall be put to death (Ex. 35:2b).

In his important essay, Alt identified a type of law ending with the words, "He shall be put to death" (môt yûmāt).[1] The classical form of this type may be illustrated in Ex. 21:12: "Whoever strikes a man so that he dies shall be put to death" (makkēh ʾîšʾ wāmēt môt yûmāt). This type of law, says Alt, cannot be considered casuistic. Its weighted style and ponderous emphatic language militate against this; but also its content, though it specifies both the crime and the appropriate punishment, is unlike what we find in casuistic laws. It rests on an unconditional principle, i.e., life for life, without regard for the other parties involved in the crime or its circumstances.[2] The recent re-evaluation

distinguishes between sin committed unwittingly and sin committed with a high hand. For the latter no atonement is available, and the culprit shall be "cut off from among his people" (vs. 31). Vss. 32-36 provide an illustration of the preceding regulation. What shall be done with a man who has committed a minimal offense against the Sabbath? The tradition (Moses) provides the answer. That man shall be put to death. We are to assume, therefore, that the man knew about the Sabbath regulations, and that capital punishment is the appropriate punishment for breaking the Sabbath wittingly by gathering sticks on this day. Vss. 37-41 conclude with an earnest appeal never to forget the commandments of Yahweh.

[1]"The Origins of Israelite Law," pp. 140-46.

[2]Alt identifies this type of law by both form and content. Its five short words should be spoken deliberately and emphatically with a

of the nature of casuistic and apodeictic law has questioned that the above type is in fact apodeictic,[1] and perhaps it would be most appropriate to call it "participial law" after the participle with which it begins; but Alt's basic view that this kind of law was in use in the earliest parts of Israel's history has not been effectively changed.[2]

Now with respect to the Sabbath laws, we must first of all distinguish between ancient apodeictic laws and the perennial apodeictic form.[3] Nevertheless, it is always significant when a law is cast in an old form as in this case. Secondly, the four laws do not follow an identical form, and a precise reconstruction of an archetype on the

---

caesura between subject and predicate, i.e., just before the fatal words môt yûmāt. Also the content is unique, for here, in distinction from ordinary laws, no consideration is given to the circumstances or motives involved in the crime. To whom can such a requirement be attributed? Alt's answer is that "it is Yahweh who demands a stern retribution for every drop of blood that is spilt" ("The Origins of Israelite Law," p. 141).

[1]Cf. Gerstenberger, Wesen und Herkunft des "apodiktischen Rechts," pp. 89ff.; Killian, "Apodiktisches und kasuistisches Recht," pp. 189, 197ff; H. Schulz, Das Todesrecht im Alten Testament. Studien zur Rechtsform der Mot-Jumat-Sätze, BZAW, No. 114 (Berlin: Verlag Alfred Töpelmann, 1969), pp. 71-84.

[2]Cf. Alt, "The Origins of Israelite Law," pp. 159-71; Gerstenberger, Wesen und Herkunft des "apodiktischen Recht," p. 25. Schulz has proposed that the môt-jûmāt clause represents a transformation of the original prohibitive form which arises in connection with the moment when a community assumes the responsibility of pronouncing a death sentence on someone. This argument is dependent on Gerstenberger's view that the Old Testament prohibitions have their source in clan or tribal ethic, but that view is not beyond question. See Das Todesrecht im Alten Testament, pp. 85ff.

[3]Apodeictic style is probably as old as mankind, and certainly does not assure us that the laws which use it belong to an early Israelite series of apodeictic laws. See Fohrer, "Das sogenannte apodiktisch formulierte Recht," pp. 49-52.

basis of one pattern may not be possible.[1] All four of them begin with a participial construction,[2] and two of them (Ex. 31:14a, 15) end with the standard emphatic formula môt yûmāt. Ex. 35:2b concludes with the non-emphatic yûmāt (he shall be put to death), whereas Ex. 31:14b has substituted it for the more euphonic "that soul shall be cut off from his people."[3] Ex. 31:14b, 15; 35:2b are particularly similar in content, and all understand the Sabbath as the day on which work (melāʔkāh) must not be done. Ex. 31:14b is the shortest prohibition; but it must be read in conjunction with verse 14a, "You shall keep the Sabbath, because it is holy for you." It is, therefore, not a pure form, a fact which may explain its brevity.

Thus although all these laws demonstrate marked differences and are of different length, they nevertheless are also similar to the standard type of apodeictic law identified by Alt in Ex. 21:12, 15-17

---

[1]See, however, Alt, "The Origins of Israelite Law," p. 144, n. 74. He reconstructs the original Sabbath law of this type as follows: ʕōsēh melāʔkāh bašabbāt môt yûmāt (everyone who works on the Sabbath shall be put to death). This reconstruction has the metre of the five beat verse. The first three words should be spoken slowly and deliberately, then follows the caesura, and finally the emphatic môt yûmāt. This reconstruction is hypothetical as far as the Sabbath laws are concerned, and it is patterned on Ex. 21:12; 31:15. Cf. Schulz, Das Todesrecht im Alten Testament, pp. 55-58.

[2]Ex. 31:14b, 15; 35:2b begin with kol-hāʕōsēh which really is a relative construction employing a participle as subject. Alt considers this a secondary development from the pure participial form (Ex. 31: 14a).

[3]This is a common phrase in P. Cf. Gen. 17:14; Lev. 7:20-21, 25, 27; 18:29; 19:8; 20:18; 23:29; Num. 9:13; 15:30. It is possibly an ancient expression applicable to the early community of the twelve tribes. Noth, Exodus, pp. 238, 241. For an analysis of it, see Walther Zimmerli, "Die Eigenart der prophetischen Rede des Ezechiel: (Ein Beitrag zum Problem an Hand von Ez. 14:1-11)," ZAW, LXVI (1954), 1-26.

and elsewhere. According to his examination of this type, the original form, which may have been used in one or more series of such laws, began with a participle and concluded with the clause môt yûmāt. In subsequent times, however, this pure form disintegrated, viz., by the added prefix kōl to the participle.[1] If this observation is correct, then these Sabbath laws cannot have been part of an original series as reconstructed by Alt, but it is remarkable that they have been preserved in a form which is recognized to be old.

Also Num 15:32-36 recognizes the antiquity of the regulation specifying capital punishment for Sabbath offenses, and together with Ex. 31:14-15; 35:2 suggests the existence of a tradition which specified that working on the Sabbath was an offense to which the community responded with môt yûmāt. Such a tradition would go back to very early times, perhaps nomadic times,[2] but no precise dating is of course possible.

Sabbath laws: type two

Another type of Sabbath laws simply commands to keep, observe, or remember the Sabbath. We have the following occurrences of it:

(a) How long do you refuse to keep (lišmōr) my commandments and my laws (Ex. 16:28).

(b) Remember (zākôr) the sabbath day, to keep it holy (Ex. 20:8).

(c) You shall keep (tišmōrû) my sabbaths (Ex. 31:13).

(d) You shall keep (šemartem) the sabbath (Ex. 31:14).

---

[1]Alt, "The Origins of Israelite Law," p. 144, n. 72; Gerstenberger, Wesen und Herkunft des "apodiktischen Rechts," p. 25.

[2]Koch, Die Priesterschrift von Exodus 25 bis Leviticus 16, p. 38.

(e) Therefore the people of Israel shall keep (šāmᵉrû) the sabbath (Ex. 31:16).

(f) Everyone of you shall revere his mother and father, and you shall keep (tišmōrû) my sabbaths (Lev. 19:3).

(g) You shall keep (tišmōrû) my sabbaths and reverence my sanctuary (Lev. 19:30).

(h) Observe (šāmôr) the sabbath day, to keep it holy (Dt. 5:12).

(i) Therefore the LORD your God commanded you to keep (laᶜᵃsôt) the sabbath day (Dt. 5:15).

The basic law, you shall keep the Sabbath day holy, is short and belongs in the apodeictic category of laws. It has also been suggested that it is a very old law, perhaps because the fourth commandment of the Decalogue opens with a law of this type. We have discussed the difference between the verbs in the two recensions of the commandment,[1] but have found no explanation really persuasive. All the other examples of this law, except Dt. 5:15, use the verb šmr (keep, observe), and it is just possible that Ex. 20:8 is the exception (an insignificant one) to the rule. Childs' suggestion[2] is very interesting, but it does not help us to relate the two recensions of the commandment chronologically, for zkr (remember) is used in its purely psychological sense (keep in mind, recall) both in pre- and post-Deuteronomic literature, although Deuteronomy, as Childs points out, uses it particularly to describe the relationship between Israel and Yahweh's acts of salvation.

Of the remaining laws, three (Lev. 19:3, 30; Dt. 5:15) are the simplest, commanding only to keep the Sabbath. The verb ᶜsh (Dt. 5:15) is chosen in accordance with a common pattern in Deuteronomic legal

---

[1]See above, pp. 83-84.   [2]See above, n. 2, p. 83.

material: observe . . . to keep. Dt. 5:12 and Dt. 5:15b thus provide
the outer framework of the fourth commandment.[1] Lev. 19:3, 30 come from
H but appear to be part of a tradition accumulated by H. Thus the association of the commandments regarding reverence for parents and
observance of the Sabbath is also present in the Decalogue, and it is
odd enough to lead us to believe that it belongs in the preliterary
tradition lying behind H.[2]

A second group of the laws (Ex. 28:8; 31:14; Dt. 5:12) commands
the observance of the Sabbath to keep it holy. Though the sanctity of
the Sabbath is old, this particular way of expressing it is probably
late and may be a secondary addition to the simple command.[3] Ex. 31:14
reveals a preoccupation with the question of the sacred and the profane
which is characteristic of P (cf. Ez. 44:24), and which undoubtedly
originated in the dynamics of the religious circles which influenced
both P and Ezekiel.

Finally, we have two laws (Ex. 31:13, 16) which require observance of the Sabbath because it is a sign or a covenant. Both laws occur
in P; but although they appear in the same context, they are not related
from a literary point of view, since the verbs of one are in the second
person and of the other in the third person. It is likely, however,

---

[1]Cf. Norbert Lohfink, Das Hauptgebot: Eine Untersuchung
literarischer Einleitungsfragen zu Dtn 5-11, Analecta Biblica, Investigationes Scientificae in Res Biblicas, No. 20 (Rome: Pontificio
Instituto Biblico, 1963), pp. 60-70; "Zur Dekalogfassung von Dt 5," pp.
21-22.

[2]On the close association of the fourth and fifth commandment in
the Decalogue, see Fohrer, "Das sogenannte apodiktisch formulierte
Recht," pp. 63-64.

[3]See above, n. 2, p. 85.

that both represent common ways of pronouncing the Sabbath regulation among priestly circles and that these and other traditional ways of referring to the Sabbath are here placed side by side in a mammoth effort of the priestly writer to say everything he remembered to say about the Sabbath.

Is it possible that any of these laws, or any part of them, should be considered old regulations, despite the fact that they appear almost exclusively in later literature (D, H, P)? We could ask, what does it mean to keep Sabbath? It means, according to these laws, to follow the Sabbath regulations regarding work and rest. The present laws are, therefore, secondary to the laws which regulated man's activities on the six days and on the Sabbath, and which protected him from profaning the sacred day. This point is clearly illustrated in the very structure of the Decalogue which opens with a command to keep the Sabbath and then specifies what this implies. This fact itself does not, however, make the command to "keep the Sabbath" late, for the Sabbath regulations to which it refers are very old. However, there are other reasons for considering it a secondary and probably late piece of Sabbath legislation. (1) It is strangely weak compared to the heavy and authoritative apodeictic Sabbath laws discussed above, as well as to the direct regulations to be discussed below. (2) It assumes that to keep the Sabbath is to abstain from working on it (Ex. 20:8-12; Dt. 5:12-15) but does not say so. Rather, it founds itself on the theological implications of this day on which no work is done, viz., the fact that the day is holy, unique, and represents the covenant. But these specific theological implications of the day are a later development in Old

Testament Sabbath theology. (3) The occurrence of it in the fourth commandment most likely does not belong to the so-called original Decalogue, for an analysis of the present commandment will show that the addition to the introductory command, "to keep it holy," corresponds stylistically to the concluding phrase of the commandment.[1] These two parts belong to the consciously constructed framework of the commandment as a whole and are probably not original. Nevertheless, the introductory command may well belong to a fund of Sabbath traditions. Its presence in Lev. 19:3, 30 supports this view; and its occurrence in Dt. 5:12, 15 gives support to the view that it is not a literary invention of P. It should more likely be ascribed to Levitical or priestly circles teaching the Sabbath regulations to Israel and encouraging her to "keep the Sabbath" during the centuries prior to the activities of P, i.e., in the eighth to seventh century B.C. or even earlier.[2]

Sabbath laws: type three

We now turn to another group of laws all of which are

---

[1]For an analysis of the style of the commandment, see below, pp. 170-71.

[2]Cf. Eduard Nielsen, "The Levites in Ancient Israel," ASTI, III (1964), 16-27; Reventlow, Gebot und Predigt, pp. 45-60. We are here dealing with priestly instruction which is essentially non-cultic. Cf. Gerhard von Rad, Old Testament Theology, Vol. I: The Theology of Israel's Historical Traditions, trans. by D. M. G. Stalker (New York: Harper & Row, Publishers, 1962), p. 193: "In addition, this festival also explains the non-cultic character of the Decalogue, on the basis of which so far-reaching conclusions used to be drawn. If the festival of the renewal of the covenant was a pilgrimage festival, then the exclusive concentration on the ethical is understandable. The people addressed by the Decalogue were, of course, the laity; and they were addressed with reference to their everyday affairs, their secular intercourse with one another in their communal life far and wide in the country, i.e., with reference to the life they had to live once the covenant was made and they had gone back to their homes."

characterized by a reference to the six-seven day scheme. First, we
have a number of laws with a three-part structure:

(a) Six days you shall labor, and do all your work; but the seventh
day is a sabbath to the LORD your God; in it you shall not do
any work . . . (Ex. 20:9-10a; Dt. 5:13-14a).

(b) Six days shall work be done, but the seventh day is a sabbath
of solemn rest, holy to the LORD; whoever does any work on the
sabbath day shall be put to death (Ex. 31:15).

(c) Six days shall work be done, but on the seventh day you shall
have a holy sabbath of solemn rest to the LORD; whoever does
any work on it shall be put to death (Ex. 35:2).

(d) Six days shall work be done; but on the seventh day is a sabbath of solemn rest, a holy convocation; you shall do no work;
it is a sabbath to the LORD in all your dwellings (Lev. 23:3).

(e) Six days you shall gather it; but on the seventh day, which is
a sabbath, there shall be none (Ex. 16:26).

The structure according to which these laws are built consists
of three parts. (1) Regulations for the six days: Six days shall work
be done, or, following the versions and the fourth commandment, six days
you shall work.[1] (2) Identification of the seventh day: The seventh
day, or on the seventh day, is a Sabbath (of solemn rest), holy to
Yahweh (your God). (3) Regulations for the seventh day: All who work
on the seventh day shall be put to death, or you shall do no work on the
seventh day.

Ex. 16:22-30 which, in distinction from the other four passages,
consists of narrative material, does not make direct use of this three-
part structure; but it clearly presupposes it. Thus the

---

[1] The Greek, Syriac, and Latin versions put the verb in the
active, perhaps following the Decalogue, or the verb in the subsequent
sentences of the law. The meaning of the law is not changed much, if at
all, by this variant reading.

characterization of the seventh day as "a day of solemn rest, a holy sabbath to the LORD" (vs. 23), or "a sabbath to the LORD" (vs. 25) corresponds to (2) above. The whole three-part structure is neatly preserved in verse 26, although its content is modified so as to correspond to the particular manna situation of this narrative. The three parts are as follows: (1) Six days you shall gather it; (3) but on the seventh day, (2) which is a sabbath, (3) there shall be none. Lev. 23:3 also shows a slight variation of the basic pattern, as it repeats the middle part (2) in the final addition "it is a sabbath to the LORD in all your dwellings." It was undoubtedly added for emphasis.

The three-part structured law is also found in Dt. 16:8. "For six days you shall eat unleavened bread; and on the seventh day there shall be a solemn assembly to the LORD your God; you shall do no work on it." This is, of course, not a Sabbath law; but it has adopted the so-called Sabbath formula with regulations for the six days and for the seventh-day Sabbath. There is no indication that this was the original setting of this formula.[1] It does not regulate the pattern of work and rest, as it does when used about the weekly Sabbath, but the manner whereby the feast of unleavened bread is to be conducted. The final prohibition of work is applied to Sabbath and festival alike, although we suspect that its application to the Sabbath is primary.

Two additional laws are somewhat similar to those cited above:

(f) Six days you shall do your work, but on the seventh day you shall rest; that your ox and your ass may have rest, and the son of your bondmaid, and the alien, may be refreshed (Ex. 23:12).

---

[1] Kiker, "The Sabbath in the Old Testament Cult," pp. 98-99.

164

(g) Six days you shall work, but on the seventh day you shall rest;
     in plowing time and in harvest you shall rest (Ex. 34:21).

Here we have a two-part structure consisting of: (1) Regulations for
the six days: Six days you shall work, or do your work; (2) Regulations
for the seventh day: The seventh day you shall rest, to which are added
elaborations answering the questions, when does it apply, to whom, and
why?

The similarity between this structure and the three-part structure discussed above is striking. Yet there are some differences also.
The identification of the seventh day as Sabbath is missing, and the
regulations for the seventh day are stated positively as commands, and
not by means of prohibitions or threats.[1]

In addition to these formal laws, the regulations for the six-
seven day scheme are also implied in several passages discussed
elsewhere, e.g., Gen. 2:1-3; Ex. 20:11; 31:17; Ezek. 46:1.

The frequent occurrences of this type of law in literature which
either belongs to P or which presumably has passed through the hands of
P should not lead us to suggest that it is a literary fabrication of P.
The repeated, very similar, but not identical appearances of it, on the
one hand, and the clearly related form found in the older laws (Ex.
23:12; 34:21) suggest that we are here dealing with a traditional formulation of a Sabbath law which dates back into Israel's early history.
It also appears to have gone through a development. Let us now look at

---

[1]A more limited survey of this type of law, referred to elsewhere in this paper as the Sabbath formula, is given by Kiker, "The
Sabbath in the Old Testament Cult," pp. 121ff. Here, however, it is
associated originally with the seven-day festival week of the feast of
unleavened bread, and only subsequently with the seventh-day Sabbath.

the history of the legal traditions which we have described in this chapter.

Development of the legal traditions

Reventlow has broken new ground in this area in his study of the laws in the Decalogue.[1] He rejects the procedure which by literary analysis attempts to extract the "original" law and to identify the subsequent additions to it. In its place he proposes that the present form of the laws should be attributed to repeated preaching upon the original law, in such a way that the final product of it represents an organic growth from the original command which is, therefore, now indistinguishable from the preaching that surrounds it.[2] This thesis has immediate implications for the Sabbath laws under discussion.

According to Reventlow, the Sabbath system, i.e., the system of six days ending with a special seventh-day Sabbath, originated in the general seven-day system of the priestly Torah, according to which the special feasts are structured. These feasts as well as the Sabbath originated in pre-Yahwistic cultures.[3] This leads Reventlow to the conclusion that the Sabbath is only a "special case" of a festival named

---

[1] Gebot und Predigt (1962).

[2] The growth of the Decalogue is sketched in the following way (Gebot und Predigt, pp. 93-95). (1) Apodeictic laws in two different series and some Thorastoff made up the basis. (2) The original Decalogue was thus a mixture of several strands. Its demands were announced at worship situations. (3) Illuminations and detailed applications (Näherbestimmungen) were added from a fund of priestly knowledge. (4) The apodeictic kernel was enshrouded in parenese and personal advice by means of continued proclamation of the laws.

[3] Gebot und Predigt, p. 55.

166

"Sabbath," because that is the word used in the priestly Torah to characterize a feast day on which abstention from work is required.[1] That the Sabbath must be understood in relationship to the festivals is then supported by a form and style analysis of the Sabbath laws and the regulations for the festivals, notably in Lev. 23 and Num. 28-29. It is noted that the festival regulations and the Sabbath laws share a number of expressions, e.g., "to the LORD,"[2] "you shall do no laborious work" (kol-mᵉleꜣket ꜥabōdāh lōꜣ taꜥasû),[3] "a holy convocation" (miqrāꜣ-qōdeš).[4] These expressions indicate, according to Reventlow, that the so-called additions to the fourth commandment and other Sabbath laws are in fact part of the priestly Torah, or instructional material, by which the laity was instructed regarding the feasts including the Sabbath.[5] Other

_____

[1]Ibid., pp. 51, 54.

[2]Lev. 23:3 passim; Ex. 20:10; Dt. 5:13.

[3]Cf. Lev. 23:7-8; 25, 28, 35-36. In these regulations the verb is consistently in 2nd pers. pl. qal. In the Decalogue the verb is in 2nd pers. sing. qal, a choice which is dictated simply by the common form of the verbs in the commandment. But also the form of the whole expression is different in the fourth commandment (lōꜣ-taꜥaseh kol-mᵉlāꜣkāh). Reventlow minimizes this difference (p. 50), but it is unmistakably present and important, when we think, as Reventlow would have us do, of these expressions as pithy laws shaped by much use. Even the formulation of it in the Sabbath law, Lev. 23:3 differs from its form in the festival regulations (kol-mᵉlāꜣkāh lōꜣ taꜥasû). Originally, claims Reventlow (p. 50), these formulations were impersonal, in niphꜥal (cf. Lev. 23:3; Ex. 12:16; 31:15; 35:2). Of this we cannot be certain, for we have the prohibition in the active form both in the fourth commandment and in Ex. 23:12; 34:21.

[4]See above, pp. 58-59.

[5]Thus the introductory statement "remember/observe the Sabbath day" is considered to be simply an opening statement by the priestly preacher or instructor, and not an old apodeictic law (Gebot und Predigt, pp. 55-56).

expressions belonging to the priestly instruction are also to be noted, viz., "a sabbath of solemn rest" (Ex. 31:15; 35:2; Lev. 13:3), "holy to the LORD" (Ex. 31:15; 35:2), "in all your habitations" (Lev. 23:3), and finally the threat, "whoever does any work on it shall be put to death" (Ex. 31:15; 35:2). We have suggested, following Alt, that it is an early type of Sabbath law, although it is here attached to the Sabbath formula by the hand of the priestly or Levitical teacher.

Having thus identified this instructional material in the festival regulations and the Sabbath laws alike, Reventlow proposes that the most fundamental part of the Sabbath laws is the prohibition: "You shall not do any work" (lō᾽ taʿaseh kol-melā᾽kāh), a prohibition which is shared, he argues, by both the Sabbath laws and the festival regulations. To this we must object, for the prohibition is an integral part of the larger Sabbath formula: "Six days you shall labor, and do all your work; but the seventh day is a Sabbath to the LORD your God; in it you shall not do any work . . ." (Ex. 20:9-10a). The symmetrical construction of it strongly suggests that we are here dealing with a carefully composed unit.

(1) Six days you shall labor, and do all your work (weʿasîtā kol-melaʾketekā);

(2) but the seventh day is a sabbath to the LORD your God;

(3) in it you shall not do any work . . . (lō᾽-taʿaseh kol-melāʾkah).

For this reason, it is more likely that the expression "you shall not do any work" belongs to the Sabbath laws in particular and originally, and to the festival regulations in general and by inference.

We have contended elsewhere that the Sabbath formula is not

derived from the festival regulations, but that it is a unique feature
of the seventh-day Sabbath. The most fundamental part of the Sabbath
legislation is the Sabbath formula which requires that work be done on
six days, and that no work must be done on the seventh day, or the Sabbath. We have further proposed that among the several occurrences of
this formula the laws in Ex. 23:12; 34:21 are the oldest. These two
laws do not contain the characteristic priestly expressions to which
Reventlow draws attention, but they do contain the six-seven day scheme.
For this reason, I think that Reventlow places the matter on its head,
when he argues that these shorter regulations represent a further
development of the typical priestly formulations.[1] It is much more
probable that the simple formulations of the regulation are the early
ones, and that the priestly circles subsequently expanded them by identifying the seventh day as Sabbath, by terminology borrowed from the
priestly Torah, and by various emphatic traditional prohibitions of work
on this day.[2]

---

[1]The fact that the later occurrences of this regulation demonstrate more uniformity than the earlier ones should not lead us to
reverse their chronological relationship, for it is the long and con-
stant use of such laws which creates uniformity.

[2]The exact process whereby the early formulations of the law
were transformed into the more complex ones is not easy to detect. The
basic form of the early law may, we have suggested, look like this: Six
days you shall work (taʿabōd), but the seventh day you shall rest
(tišbōt). The verb ʿbd, which refers primarily to toil with the soil
(Koehler and Baumgartner, Lexicon, pp. 670-72), may have been changed to
the more comprehensive term melāʾkāh or kol-melāʾkāh preceded by the
verb ʿsh (make or do). This would include all activities in work,
labor, business, service, etc. (Koehler and Baumgartner, Lexicon, pp.
526-27.) The fourth commandment, which uses both ʿbd and melāʾkāh, may
stand in the middle of this development. Under the influence of the
Sabbath institution which could now hold a stand on its own, the original prohibition, "on the seventh day you shall rest (tišbōt)," was

Now it must be admitted that there cannot be any doubt that the Sabbath laws were used in priestly proclamation and instruction, as Reventlow maintains. Expressions like "holy convocation," "to Yahweh," "solemn rest," et cetera should probably be attributed to such a usage of the laws. However, we are unable to see that they are only homilies on the original prohibition of work. In our view, the various Sabbath laws we have examined stand too close to the well defined Sabbath traditions to allow for this position. We have suggested three such traditional Sabbath laws. (1) Whoever works on the Sabbath shall be put to death; (2) you shall keep the Sabbath day; (3) six days you shall work, but on the seventh day you shall rest, or on the seventh day is Sabbath, in it you shall not do any work. The variations in the several occurrences of these laws are not due to preaching on the Sabbath, but to repeated enumeration of the basic Sabbath requirements, and perhaps also to the particular theological preoccupation of the literary recorder.

Reventlow's views about the development of the Sabbath laws are called further into question when we examine the structure of the passages on which he relies most heavily, namely, Ex. 20:8-11; Dt. 5:12-15;

---

changed into "the seventh day is a Sabbath." The identical radicals in the verb šbt (rest) and in the noun šabbāt (Sabbath) may have provided the catalyst in this development. Hereby the final prohibition was lost, and a new one needed to be added to complete the regulation. For this purpose one could use the initial command to work on the six days and simply prefix a negative (Ex. 20:9; Dt. 5:13; Lev. 23:3), or one could use the prohibition of work ending with the stern môt yûmāt (Ex. 31:15; 35:2). Finally, a variety of ornamentations were added, especially to the second and third parts of the law. The most noticeable continuity between the various Sabbath laws following this general pattern is the six-seven day scheme and the common concern with work.

Ex. 31:12-17. In the case of Ex. 20:8-11, we have the following
structure:

(a) Remember the sabbath day, to keep it holy (vs. 8).

   (b) Six days you shall labor, and do all your work; but the
        seventh day is a sabbath to the LORD your God; in it you
        shall not do any work, you, or your son, or your daughter,
        your manservant, or your maidservant, or your cattle, or
        the sojourner who is within your gates (vss. 9-10);

   (c) for in six days the LORD made heaven and earth, the sea,
        and all that is in them, and rested on the seventh day
        (vs. 11a);

(d) therefore the LORD blessed the sabbath day and hallowed it (vs.
     11b).

(a) is the general introduction to the commandment, stating the main
concern of the law, and it is one of the standard ways of referring to
the Sabbath. In its present position, however, it provides one of the
parts of the outer brackets of the commandment, the other of which is
provided by (d). Both speak of the "Sabbath day" rather than the
"seventh day" (b,c) and call it "holy." Similarly, (b) and (c) correspond to each other. (b) represents a traditional Sabbath law with
the six-seven day scheme, in which work is done during six days, but
abstained from on the seventh day with the ensuing rest, i.e., when the
reason for the regulation is given (c), it is specified that the worker
(here Yahweh) rests on the seventh day. The second part of (b), "you,
or your son . . ." is an expansion added to the basic regulation in
order to qualify it. It may indeed be attributed to a priestly instructor, following Reventlow, who answered the question, to whom does the
Sabbath law apply? or who admonished his listeners to do what they knew
had to be done, but had neglected to do, namely, to extend the Sabbath

privileges to the entire household. (c) provides a reason for (b)
through the subordinating particle kî (for), and (d) is made a consequence of (c) by means of the explanatory ᶜal-kēn (therefore). The four
parts of this commandment are thus terse traditional statements on the
Sabbath[1] (not preaching on it) which are structured in a sequence, as
well as arranged symmetrically around an axis between (b) and (c). The
fourth commandment is thus a purposeful and orderly construction made
from several Sabbath traditions.

We have examined the Deuteronomic recension of the fourth commandment already,[2] and discovered some differences in its structure,
e.g., (b) and (c) are here coordinated. There are also some further
expansions, notably verse 14b which gives a reason for extending the
regulation to the entire household. However, the parts of the commandment, introductory statement (vs. 12), the Sabbath formula (vss. 13-14)
with a double expansion, the command to remember the exodus deliverance
(vs. 15a), and the conclusion (vs. 15b), are structured just as tightly
as in the Exodus recension,[3] a fact which leads us to conclude that this

---

[1]For a discussion of the creation Sabbath (vs. 11), see below,
pp. 174-203.

[2]See above, pp. 130-134.

[3]Cf. Lohfink, "Zur Dekalogfassung von Dt 5," pp. 21-22. Here it
is suggested that the commandment is built up by a series of literary
symmetries in addition to the structural symmetry to which we have
pointed. It can be set out in the following way:

vs. 12 Observe the Sabbath day (šāmôr ᵓet-yôm haššabbāt).
vs. 12   as the LORD your God commanded you (ka²ašer ṣiwwekā YHWH
          ᵓelōhêkā).
vs. 14   the LORD your God (YHWH ᵓelōhêkā).
vs. 14   your manservant, or your maidservant (weᶜabdekā
                wa²ᵃmātekā).

172

too is a planned composition from beginning to end, and not the result
of a growth due to homiletic expansion.

In Ex. 31:12-17 we have a different situation. Here we get the
impression that the priestly writer has thrown in everything he remembered about the Sabbath. Thus we have the simple command to keep the
Sabbath in 2nd pers. pl. (vss. 14, 15) and in 3rd pers. sg. (vs. 16).
There are recollections of old laws ending in môt yûmāt (vss. 14-15), a
late form of the Sabbath formula (vs. 15), the theme of the creation
Sabbath (vs. 17), and several indications of the role of the Sabbath in
Israel's understanding of the covenant (vss. 13, 16, 17). Whether one
literary composition is responsible for this passage, we cannot say. It
is barely structured, if at all, and no attempt has been made to create
uniformity among its various parts. Ex. 35:2-3 reveals a similar situation, although on a smaller scale. Here is an impersonal command to
work six days which is followed by the austere prohibition ending with a
death penalty. In the next verse follows a prohibition of fire making
with its verb in the 2nd pers. pl. In addition to appearing in these
more extensive Sabbath passages, we find individual Sabbath laws following the same traditional pattern in various other places, viz., Ex.

vs. 14   that you (lᵉmā'ān).

vs. 14   your manservant, and your maidservant ('abdᵉkā
            waʾamātᵉkā).
vs. 15   the LORD your God (YHWH ʾelōhêkā).
vs. 15   therefore the LORD your God commanded you ('al-kēn
            ṣiwwᵉkā YHWH ʾelōhêkā).
vs. 15   to keep the Sabbath day (laʿaṣôt ʾet-yôm haššabbāt).

Lohfink concludes: "Die einheitliche Neugestaltung des Sabbatgebots
geschah also auf der Stilebene der Stichwortentsprechungen" (p. 23).

16:23, 25, 26; Lev. 19:3, 30; 23:3; 26:2. We can only assume that the writers had these laws in mind in a rather fixed form, especially Lev. 19:3, 30; 26:2, and recorded them at appropriate places.

These observations lead us to conclude that the Sabbath laws, rather than being the outgrowth of a general prohibition against working and a seven-day system, are traditional formulations falling into several categories which reappear with relatively little modification. Whatever variations we find must be attributed to a wide range of usage in the priestly circles who instructed the laity (Reventlow), and to the particular orientation of the literary artists. At the other end of the spectrum, we then have early traditional Sabbath laws. The type which concludes with the threat môt yûmāt probably dates back to the earliest period of Israel's history. The same may be said about the Sabbath formula which commands man to work on six days, and to rest from his work, i.e., cease, on the seventh day. The laws calling man to observe the Sabbath are probably secondary to the former two. We finally observed the way several of the legal and other Sabbath traditions have been united in the fourth commandment in the Decalogue, or have been assembled loosely in Ex. 31:12-17, while individual laws, also following the traditional patterns, appear at various appropriate places, sometimes seemingly out of context (Lev. 19:3, 30; Ezek. 22:8; 23:38), in other instances well adjusted to the context (Lev. 23:3). This only strengthens our assumption that the Sabbath laws in the Old Testament literature are really drawn from a fund of standard, and more or less fixed, Sabbath traditions.

E. The Creation Sabbath

Three passages associate the Sabbath with the divine rest
accomplished at the completion of creation. They are Gen. 2:1-3; Ex.
20:11; 31:17. In the examination of this unique function of the Sabbath
motif, two stages of it must be distinguished and explored: (1) The
traditions which existed prior to the present composition recorded in P;
(2) the interpretation of these traditions which was undertaken by the
priestly writer or his predecessors.

The divine otiositas

The motif most commonly attributed to the tradition behind the
passages under discussion is the divine _otiositas_ motif which is, we are
told, found in creation myths from many places on the earth.[1] It is
also found in Near Eastern creation myths; and we shall turn, therefore,
to some illustrations of it.

The Babylonian creation epic _Enūma eliš_, which is generally
assigned to the old Babylonian period (first part of the second millennium B.C.),[2] contains several references to the divine _otiositas_ motif.
Throughout the entire epic the various gods are attempting to achieve
rest, a privilege which is frustrated by the noisy activities of the
lower gods, or by duties involving hard labor, or by the mere fact that

---

[1] R. Pettazzoni, "Myths of Beginning and Creation-Myths," in
Essays on the History of Religion, trans. by H. T. Rose, Numen Supplement, No. 1 (Leiden: E. J. Brill, 1954), pp. 24-36. _Otiositas_ is used
here to describe the inactivity and rest of the creator god following
the struggle or excessive effort involved in creating the world or
ordering the chaos into a created cosmos, or following some other dis-
ruptive event.

[2] Pritchard, ed., _ANET_, p. 60; Heidel, _The Babylonian Genesis_,
pp. 13-14.

there is no place (temple) for the gods to rest. At the very opening of
the epic, before the creation is accomplished, the primeval waters Apsu
and Tiamat are disturbed by the tumult produced by the lower gods. Apsu
then exclaims:

> By day I find no relief, nor repose by night.
> I will destroy, I will wreck their ways,
> That quiet may be restored. Let us have rest.[1]

This initial threat to the lower gods is met by Ea who succeeds in dis-
arming and destroying Apsu and his counselor Mummu. Having thus
defeated his enemies we are told that he rests in "profound peace."[2]

However, rest is still denied the primeval sea Tiamat and her
associates; and so a new confrontation is staged with Tiamat and Marduk
as the chief contestants. The battle completed and the victory won,
Marduk sets out to create the world and to organize it. In the new cosmos (in distinction from the previously existent chaos) the gods who are
placed in charge of its various regions need not disturb the high gods
by their tumult, for they will all be at rest. The necessary and noisy
work will be performed by Marduk's special creation, man:[3]

---

[1]Pritchard, ed., ANET, p. 61 (I, 38-40). "Relief" may also be
translated "rest" (cf. Heidel, The Babylonian Genesis, p. 19). According to Speiser (Pritchard, ed., ANET, p. 61, n. 16) the prefixed š gives
the word an "elative force," hence the translation "relief." The result
which Apsu hopes to accomplish is expressed by Mummu his counselor:
"Then shalt thou have relief by day and rest by night" (I, 50).

[2]Pritchard, ed., ANET, p. 61 (I, 75).

[3]In Enūma eliš man is very much the brainchild of Marduk:
"Opening his mouth, he addressed Ea / To impart the plan he had conceived in his heart" (VI, 3-4).

> Verily, savage-man I will create.
> He shall be charged with the service of the gods
> That they might be at ease![1]

The lower gods (Anunnaki) are so delighted over their deliverance that

they decide to honor Marduk by building him a house:

> Let us build a shrine whose name shall be called
> "Lo, a chamber for our mighty rest"; let us repose in it!
> Let us build a throne, a recess for his abode!
> On the day that we arrive we shall repose in it.[2]

That man was created especially for the purpose of serving the

gods (carrying their yoke) thus giving them rest is a common motif which

is particularly prominent in the creation account of the Atra-Ḥasīs

flood story. Here the high gods (Anunnaki) make the low gods (Igigi)

suffer through excessive work day and night for forty years.[3] The lat-

ter decide to rebel against their superiors, they burn their tools, and

surround the temple of the high god Enlil in order to carry out a gen-

eral revolt. Their complaint is met by the high gods' proposal to

create man with this result:

> I have removed your heavy work,
> I have imposed your toil on man.
> You raised a cry for mankind,
> I have loosed the yoke, I have established freedom.[4]

The freedom thus provided is interferred with in due course by mankind

itself, because of the disturbing noises, equal to those which disturbed

Apsu and Tiamat, caused by man's toil:

---

[1]Pritchard, ed., ANET, p. 68 (VI, 7-8).

[2]Ibid., (VI, 51-54). B. Landsberger and J. V. Kinnier Wilson, "The Fifth Tablet of Enūma Eliš," JNES, 20 (1961), 154-79.

[3]Lambert and Millard, Atra-Ḥasīs, p. 45 (I, i, 37-38).

[4]Ibid., pp. 59-60 (I, v, 240-43).

> Twelve hundred years had not passed
> When the land extended and the peoples multiplied.
> The land was bellowing like a bull,
> The god got disturbed with their uproar.
> Enlil heard their noise
> And addressed the great gods,
> "The noise of mankind has become too intense for me,
> With their uproar I am deprived of sleep."[1]

Thus even the creation of man does not secure divine rest, although it does provide freedom for the lower gods. The epic then proceeds to describe the gods' final effort to attain rest by destroying mankind through various means, including a flood. Here, however, it seems that the theme of the epic shifts away from a concern with the gods to a concern with the survival of mankind; and it would be appropriate, therefore, to ask if the two concerns, i.e., divine *otiositas* and human survival, are related to each other. We will return to this question below.

In the Baal cycle we read that the high god El is glad when Baal is found to be alive, when vegetation and fertility return to the land. Then he exclaims:

> Now I will sit and rest
> And my soul be at ease in my breast.
> For alive is Puissant Baal,
> Existent the Prince, Lord of Earth![2]

The Irra or Era epic concludes with the counselor Išum advising Irra to cease with his rampage of destruction:

---

[1]*Ibid.*, pp. 73 (II, i, 1-8).

[2]Pritchard, ed., *ANET*, p. 140 ("Poems about Baal and Anath," I AB, iii-iv, 18-20). The first two lines are found in duplicate in Aqht A, ii, 12-15 (Pritchard, ed., *ANET*, p. 150). They are spoken by King Daniel as he is promised a son to succeed him on the throne. See also, Rene Dussaud, "Yahwe, fils de El," *Syria*, XXXIV (1957), 241-42.

Held, schweige, höre mein Wort!
[Fürwahr], jetz beruhige dich! Wir sind vor dich hingetreten,
Am Tage deines Zürnens wo ist der, der dir begegnet?[1]

Irra appears to agree that none has surpassed him in destruction and

that his wrath has been consummated; and he then agrees to rest in his

residence and be appeased, while Babylon, the object of his destruction,

enters a new age of prosperity.[2]

Finally, we may look at the old Egyptian creation account called

"The Theology of Memphis."[3] It is important for the study of the Old

Testament creation account in Gen. 1, because in it Ptah, the creator

god, performs his creative acts by the divine word. When it is all

accomplished we read: "And so Ptah was satisfied [or rested], after he

had made everything, as well as all the divine order (lit., every word

of the god)."[4]

Pettazzoni has suggested two ways in which the divine otiositas

motif could be explained.[5] (1) It could derive from a secondary devel-

opment in the myths of origins, in which the creator or original deity

is replaced by other more active gods who put the old inactive gods into

---

[1]Hugo Gressmann, ed., Altorientalische Texte zum Alten Testament
(2nd ed.; Berlin: Verlag Walter de Gruyter & Co., 1926), p. 229 (E,
17-19).

[2]Ibid.

[3]Pritchard, ed., ANET, pp. 4-6. The importance of this text is
enhanced by the fact that the god Ptah may have been well known in Syro-
Palestine as early as the middle of the second millennium B.C. Cf. Otto
Eissfeldt, "Die Wohnsitze der Götter von Ras Shamra," in Kleine
Schriften, II, ed. by R. Sellheim and F. Maass (Tübingen: J. C. B. Mohr
[Paul Siebeck], 1963), p. 505.

[4]Pritchard, ed., ANET, p. 5.

[5]Pettazzoni, "Myths of Beginnings and Creation-Myths," p. 32.

the background--a kind of divine retirement. (2) It could derive from
the essential nature of creative deities, being the "complement of their
creative activity":

> The world once made and the cosmos established, the creator's work
> is as good as done. Any further intervention on his part would be
> not only superfluous but possibly dangerous, since any change in the
> cosmos might allow it to fall back into chaos. Once the world is
> made, the existential function of the creator could be nothing but
> prolonging its duration and ensuring its unaltered and unalterable
> stability. The otiositas of the creative Being, . . . is the most
> favourable condition and the one naturally best suited to maintain
> the status quo.[1]

Although Pettazzoni adopts the second explanation, the illustrations of the motif which we have surveyed show support for both
explanations. In the Babylonian creation story Apsu and Tiamat are
clearly primeval gods "on the way out." They are brooding monsters
whose inactivity stands in marked contrast to the ebullient life carried
out by their offspring, the younger gods. Only the persistent disrespect of the younger gods for their repose brings them into action
again, and then only hesitantly. There is no doubt that the young gods
are there to stay, and that their vigorous activity should not be
stopped by the inactive old gods. This view seems to be shared by Apsu
and Tiamat themselves, for they really have grave doubts about interfering in the life of the young gods, and must repeatedly be prodded to do
so.[2]

---

[1]Ibid., pp. 32-33.

[2]Apsu first conceives of the idea of interfering in the life of
the noisy gods, but he needs to receive the moral support of his counselor Mummu before bringing it before Tiamat who would hear nothing of the
kind of intervention which Apsu proposed (destruction of the lower
gods). It is only at Mummu's continued encouragement that Apsu proceeds
with his plan (Pritchard, ed., ANET, p. 61). After Apsu's death Tiamat

The Baal cycle is not a creation myth, but it does portray El as a semiretired god.[1] His reaction to the death of Baal is one of sorrow and mourning, but he does nothing about it. He leaves his throne, to be sure, but only to sit on the footstool, and finally on the ground, as a sign of sorrow; yet he does nothing to rescue Baal. This is left to Anath.[2] The moment Baal is found alive, however, El resumes his otiositas, or semiretirement, without interruptions, sitting on his throne in peace. On the other hand, El's rest does correspond with favorable conditions in the world, although these are caused more directly by Baal.

At the same time we can see a relationship between the divine otiositas and the conditions in the world. In the Babylonian creation story Marduk crowns his creation of an ordered world by making mankind for the service of the gods. The liberated lower gods are then stationed in their respective positions in the world and the ordering of the cosmos is established. This even is sealed with the construction of Marduk's temple, a place of rest and repose, and with the victory banquet, at which occasion we are further assured that the world is now in order.[3] It seems, however, that a shift occurs in the rest motif of this epic, from the rest which Apsu and Tiamat sought to the rest which Marduk and his associates achieved. In seeking their rest Apsu and

---

fails to revenge her consort, and again has to be encouraged to do so.

[1]Albright, Yahweh and the Gods of Canaan, p. 120. "But by the time of the composition of the epics he had become otiose."

[2]Pritchard, ed., ANET, p. 139 (I AB, iv, 11ff.).

[3]Ibid., p. 69 (VI, 76-79).

Tiamat became the destructive force which threatens the existence of
the gods and promises to perpetuate chaos. Our sympathies are, therefore, shifted from the patient Tiamat who would rather sacrifice her own
rest than kill her offspring, to Marduk who secures the destruction of
chaos as well as the rest and security which Tiamat and especially Kingu
are threatening to destroy. That the rest following creation implies
the establishment and security of the world order is also implied in The
Theology of Memphis and in the Baal cycle.

There is no guarantee, however, that the stability of the world
order established by the divine _otiositas_ will persist. The Atra-Ḫasīs
epic follows the Enūma eliš epic to some extent. The lower gods revolt
against the high gods by quitting their work in the fields and on the
irrigation systems,[1] thus threatening the proper function of the world.
They are set free by the creation of man, that is, they are given rest
from their toil. Now it is the labor of man which secures the proper
function of the world. Man's work, however, proves to be no guarantee
for the status quo in the world. The noise of the multitude of the
people disturbs the gods, possibly because of a rebellion staged by man
against the gods, like that of the lower gods.[2] As a consequence, the
gods decide to destroy man, rather than to give him rest and freedom.
In a similar fashion the Irra epic shows that the god's rest is vulner-
able. In the face of the wrath and destruction of Irra, Marduk is

---

[1]This appears to be the nature of their work. Lambert and
Millard, Atra-Ḫasīs, p. 42 (I, i, 19-26).

[2]Thus when the gods' plans for destroying mankind fails because
of Enki's intervention on behalf of man, he is blamed for having "loosed
the yoke and established freedom" (Lambert and Millard, Atra-Ḫasīs, pp.
81-87, II, v, 19-31; vi, 28-29).

forced to leave his throne temporarily in search of some kind of solution to the impending destruction of his city. Such an act might be devastating to the stability of the world, as it is pointed out to him, and it is only when the angry god Irra quiets down that the prosperity of Babylon is secured.

We can say then that the gods seek rest, and that their rest implies stability for the world order. The gods rest because they want to see the world ordered. A chaotic world brings chaos into the pantheon itself and vice versa. But they also rest because they feel that to be a most comfortable situation which should not be disturbed. It appears to be a goal which, however, is never fulfilled permanently. Man too wants the gods to be at rest, except when the present world situation has become intolerable, when the yoke imposed upon man has become too heavy. Then he may call on his god to rouse himself and do something about the unfortunate situation (cf. Ps. 74:22; 94:2).

The divine rest and the seven-day creation

To what extent can this common motif of divine _otiositas_ be detected in the Old Testament literature? The closest Biblical parallels are found in some passages which portray Yahweh's rest in Zion:

> Arise, O LORD, and go to thy resting place,
> thou and the ark of thy might.[1]

> This is my resting place for ever;
> here I will dwell, for I have desired it.[2]

> Therefore I swore in my anger
> that they should not enter my rest.[3]

---

[1]Ps. 132:8; II Chr. 6:41. [2]Ps. 132:14. [3]Ps. 95:11.

> Heaven is my throne and the earth my footstool
> what is the house which you would build for me,
> and what is the place of my rest?[1]

Here we have the ark or throne of Yahweh identified as the place of his rest; and we learn that when Yahweh is at rest in Zion, national and political security is established, or, as in the case of Ps. 95:11, "my rest" refers to Israel's occupancy of the land.[2]

In the texts dealing with the creation Sabbath, on the other hand, we have a different situation, for here we are merely told in a disinterested way that God rested on the seventh day after having created during a six-day period. Why did he rest or desist on that day? The answer of the Old Testament is that he did so because that day is the Sabbath. Now there is, of course, no evidence of divine Sabbath keeping in extra-Biblical myths, and so the creation Sabbath could easily be considered a unique feature of the Old Testament. It is curious, however, that precisely the Old Testament should make Yahweh rest and even refresh himself after his creative work, for Yahweh is not a God who would tire or retire in the face of new and extraordinarily heavy activities, or before other aggressive powers, nor is the world's stability assured by his inactivity, but on the contrary by his activity within creation.[3] Nowhere in the Old Testament do we hear of seasons of

---

[1]Is. 66:1.

[2]For a discussion of these passages, see especially Gerhard von Rad, "There Remains Still a Rest for the People of God: An Investigation of a Biblical Conception," in The Problem of the Hexateuch and Other Essays, trans. by E. W. Trueman Dicken (New York: McGraw-Hill Book Company, 1966), pp. 94-102.

[3]The ongoing activity of Yahweh is realized in the course and events of history, as well as in the theophanies. The former may indeed

rest in the heavenly courts. When we do get a glimpse of the heavenly scene (Ps. 82; Job 1; I Kg. 22:19; Ezek. 1) we find Yahweh in council busily occupied with affairs of the world. Moreover, there is nothing in the Old Testament statements about the Sabbath which would warrant their application to the heavenly situation.[1] Why then should the priestly literature have Yahweh rest after creation? It has been suggested that the passages should be classified as a Sabbath etiology,[2] but this is not likely, for the passages do not contain the expected etiological elements, viz., expressions like, therefore the seventh day is called Sabbath, or therefore man is to celebrate the seventh day as a day of rest.[3] Moreover, there is not even an indirect suggestion to the effect that the story gives a reason for the Sabbath, or that Sabbath observance among men is commanded in the creation Sabbath. Ex. 20:8-11; 31:12-17 do, of course, assume a relationship between man's Sabbath and

---

not be unique in Israelite literature, but it is certainly important there. See Bertil Albrektson, History and the Gods: An Essay on the Idea of Historical Events as Divine Manifestations in the Ancient Near East and in Israel (Lund: Gleerup, 1967). For the latter, see Jörg Jeremias, Theophanie: Die Geschichte einer alttestamentilichen Gattung, WMANT, No. 10 (Neukirchen-Vluyn: Neukirchener Verlag, 1965).

[1]Gerhard von Rad pointed out some time ago that analogical thinking was common in the ancient Near East. This involves a "mythological conception of an all-embracing correspondence between the heavenly on the one hand, and the earthly on the other." "Typological Interpretation of the Old Testament," trans. by John Bright, in Essays on Old Testament Hermeneutics, ed. by Claus Westermann and James Luther Mays (Richmond, Va.: John Knox Press, 1963), p. 18. This sort of mythological speculation is practically absent in the Old Testament, and it is not present in the Old Testament Sabbath literature. An exception is Ex. 25:9, 40 where the heavenly model of the tabernacle is shown to Moses (cf. Enūma eliš, II, 113, Pritchard, ed., ANET, p. 69).

[2]See above, n. 1, p. 65.

[3]Cf. Jenni, Die theologische Begründung, p. 24.

God's, but both passages presuppose the creation Sabbath motif, rather than explain it.

Another and more realistic explanation of this quite strange motif in the creation account is that the divine rest motif in this account was part of its tradition. From the survey of the other Near Eastern creation accounts we may conclude that, for whatever reason, the creative deity rested at the conclusion of his creative work, immediately after the creation of man. This divine rest was also known, we may assume, to the priestly circles around the temple, in the sense that after the wars had been fought, and the nation had been established, Yahweh would no longer rage across the mountain tops mustering his hosts, but be at ease in Zion, the place of his choice. This rest pertained to the fulfillment of Yahweh's promise to Israel, but that promise was not fulfilled at creation.[1] Of a divine rest subsequent to the creation of the world we hear nothing, for the act of creation after which Yahweh will find rest is not the creation of a world or of mankind, but of the people Israel. That the creator should rest after making the world and mankind, but before making his people Israel, is to the Old Testament and to P a preposterous idea.[2] It must be said, therefore,

---

[1]Cf. von Rad, "There Remains Still a Rest for the People of God," p. 96. "This notion of 'rest' now comes to occupy an important place in the religious thought of Israel. It is thought of as a rest found by the weary nation through the grace of God in the land he has promised them."

[2]Cf. Is. 40:28. "He does not faint or grow weary." It is telling that this single expression appears in a chapter which has an even mixture of creation and salvation motifs. The prophet is asked, why does Yahweh disregard the affairs of men (vs. 27)? Has Yahweh retired from active Lordship? Not so is the reply, Yahweh is the creator and he does not tire (vs. 28).

that Gen. 2:1-3 is not portraying a divine _otiositas_, in the sense of a divine retirement from active engagement into the affairs of the world, but that the divine _otiositas_ motif is present in a unique way in Gen. 2:1-3, namely, as a creation Sabbath. There is, therefore, very likely a relationship between the creation Sabbath and the _otiositas_, but it is a broken relationship, for the author of Gen. 1:1-2, 4 understood the _otiositas_ simply as a Sabbath, the first Sabbath.[1] It is noteworthy that the Old Testament account of creation could withstand the temptation to develop a heavenly Sabbath as the antitype of the earthly Sabbath, but there is no speculation as to whether the divine Sabbath rest continued henceforth, or whether God returned to some other work on the following first day. The divine rest is discussed only in connection with the creation week. The association of Sabbath and creation thus explains to the reader of Gen. 2:1-3 what the divine _otiositas_ really means.[2]

One objection to this proposal has arisen from a suggestion that the seven-day scheme was attached to the creation account prior to the association between the seventh day and the creation Sabbath. We have indeed illustrations of the seven-day scheme in ancient Near Eastern literature, in which the seventh day brings about a turn in the foregoing activities, or a conclusion of the total activity.[3] Theoretically

---

[1]For the idea of a relationship between the _otiositas_ and the creation Sabbath, see now also W. G. Lambert, "A New Look at the Babylonian Background of Genesis," p. 297: "Therefore in seeking parallels to the seventh day, one must look not only for comparable institutions, but also for the idea of deities resting."

[2]Cf. Westermann, _Genesis_, p. 125.   [3]See above, n. 4, p. 113.

it would, therefore, be possible that the special role of the seventh
day is merely a by-product, under the influence of the Sabbath institution, of the seven-day scheme by which the creation account is framed.
For example, it has been suggested that the seven-day scheme reflects
the number of tablets (seven) of the Enūma eliš,[1] but the more important
proposal for associating the preliterary creation account with a seven-
day scheme is based on the assumption that the creation account belongs
to the cult liturgy of a New Year festival, i.e., an Israelite counterpart to the Babylonian New Year festival.[2] As in Babylonia, so it has
been thought that in Canaan the cosmic battle and creation motif was
celebrated cultically at this festal occasion.[3] In Israel this festival
would be associated with the old agricultural festival, presumably the
feast of booths, and would thus also extend over a seven-day period. It
has been proposed that this seven-day festival was the occasion for the
citation (and perhaps ritual enactment) of the creation account in

---

[1]Cf. John P. Peters, "The Wind of God," JBL, XXX (1911), 52.

[2]This festival has been discussed by Samuel H. Hooke, The
Origins of Early Semitic Ritual (London: Oxford University Press,
1938); Samuel H. Hooke, ed., Myth and Ritual: Essays on the Myth and
Ritual of the Hebrews in Relation to the Cultural Pattern of the Ancient
East (London: Oxford University Press, 1933); Ivan Engnell, Studies in
Divine Kingship in the Ancient Near East (2nd ed.; Oxford: Basil
Blackwell, 1967); Sigmund Mowinckel, Psalmenstudien II (Amsterdam:
Verlag P. Schippers, 1961); The Psalms in Israel's Worship, trans. by
D. R. Ap-Thomas (New York: Abingdon Press, 1962).

[3]Cf. John Gray, "The Hebrew Conception of the Kingship of God:
Its Origin and Development," VT, VI (1956) 270-71; The Legacy of Canaan:
The Ras Shamra Texts and their Relevance to the Old Testament, SVT,
Vol. V (2nd rev. ed.; Leiden: E. J. Brill, 1965), pp. 33-34; Sigmund
Mowinckel, "Psalm Criticism Between 1900 and 1935 (Ugarit and Psalm
Exegesis)," VT, V (1955), 24.

Gen. 1:1-2:3.[1] The creation account does thus not originate as a
literary composition, but as a cultic tradition performed once a year.

Two kinds of reservations should be made to this proposal: (1)
The particular nature of the Israelite New Year festival, which would
provide a setting for the creation liturgy, is now being reconstructed
more cautiously.[2] (2) As a consequence, the so-called cultic-
ritualistic elements in Gen. 1:1-2:3 are far less prominent than was
once thought, and as would be expected from a cultic tradition.[3] It is

---

[1]Cf. Samuel H. Hooke, In the Beginning, The Clarendon Bible:
Old Testament, Vol. VI (Oxford: Clarendon Press, 1947), pp. 35-36; Ivan
Engnell, "'Knowledge' and 'Life' in the Creation Story," in Wisdom in
Israel and in the Ancient Near East Presented to Professor Harold Henry
Rowley, ed. by M. Noth and D. Winton Thomas, SVT, Vol. III (Leiden:
E. J. Brill, 1955), pp. 104-5; Paul Humbert, "La relation de Genèse 1 et
du Psaume 104 avec la liturgie du Nouvel-An israélite," RHPhR, XV (1935),
1-27. Also in Opuscules d'un Hébraïsant (Neuchatel: Secrétariat de
L'Université, 1958), pp. 60-82; William G. Graham and Herbert G. May,
Culture and Conscience: An Archaeological Study of the New Religious
Past in Ancient Palestine (Chicago: University of Chicago Press, 1936),
p. 136. For a more sceptical position see Helmer Ringgren, "Är den
bibliska skapelseberättelsen en kulttext?" SEÅ, XIII (1948), 9-21;
Flemming Hvidberg, "The Canaanite Background of Gen. I-III," VT, X
(1960), 285-86.

[2]The envisioned New Year festival has two distinct foci portrayed in myth, liturgy, and ritual: (1) The enthronement of the king
or god, (2) the battle with the chaotic powers. The latter is a creation motif which is prominent in the Enūma eliš and is reflected in
several Old Testament passages, e.g., Ps. 74; 89; 93; 104. It is in
this part of the festival that Gen. 1:1-2:3 would have to be placed.
Unfortunately, the Old Testament evidence for such a festival in Israel
is very meager, limited mostly to certain Psalms. No liturgies or
descriptions of it are preserved, and it is reconstructed largely from
its Babylonian counterpart, a fact which should cause great caution in
the reconstruction of individual portions of a corresponding Israelite
festival.

[3]Humbert ("La relation de Genèse 1 et du Psaume 104 avec la
liturgie du Nouvel-An israélite") associates Gen. 1:1-2:3 with the New
Year festival for the following reasons: (1) the term behibbārē ʾām
(Gen. 2:4) has cultic overtones (pp. 66-67); (2) the acts of creation
are compressed into seven days corresponding to the number of days in

seriously questioned, therefore, whether Gen. 1:1-2:4 can be taken as a
liturgical cult text.[1] If this cannot be defended, we have no reason
for associating a seven-day scheme, distinct from the week concluding
with the Sabbath, with the creation account.[2] There is no visible stage

the festival week (p. 67); (3) the blessings pronounced on the living
creatures as well as on man reflect the agricultural and fertility concerns in the New Year festival (p. 69); (4) the dominion of man over
animal and plant life (Gen. 1:29) also reflects a concern with agriculture and fertility (p. 69); (5) the sanctification of the seventh day
is a cultic feature (p. 70); (6) Yahweh's triumph over chaos is
progressing from day to day (p. 73).

[1]Cf. Ringgren, "Är den bibliska skapelsesberättelsen en
kulttext?" It is agreed that the creation motif formed part of the New
Year festival liturgy, but Ringgren denies that Gen. 1:1-2:4 is such a
cult text. (1) Ps. 104 which as a hymn would lend itself better to
cultic use has no seven-day scheme; (2) Gen. 1:1-2:4 is so short an
account (compared to the Enūma eliš) that dividing it into seven parts,
one for each day of a festival, would seem strange; (3) it is clear that
the text reaches its conclusion and climax on the seventh day. This
might mean that it was used on the seventh day of such a festival, but
it is more likely caused by the seven-day motif itself; (4) it is
doubtful that a whole festival week should be associated with creation,
especially as it appears in the present demythologized account. Ringgren concludes, therefore, that Gen. 1:1-2:4 appears to protest against
cultic presentations of creation, and that it is not a cult text (p.
21). That the creation motif did occupy an important role in the cult
is suggested, however, on the basis of the creation psalms (Ps. 74; 89;
93; 104). Cf. Mowinckel, The Psalms in Israelite Worship, p. 169.

[2]The Sabbath and the seven-day scheme cannot be separated in
Gen. 1:1-2:4. The creation consists of eight acts (light, firmament,
dry land, vegetation, heavenly bodies, fish and birds, animals, and man)
or perhaps ten (Alfred Bertholet, "Zum Schoepfungsbericht in Genesis 1,"
JBL, LIII [1934], 237-40), and they are accommodated into six days,
whereas the seventh day is reserved for the creation Sabbath. The
divine otiositas, on the other hand, does not traditionally belong in
the creation event, but introduces a whole new situation, a post-
creation status quo. In Gen. 1:1-2:4 this situation is introduced
already within the seven-day creation schedule, namely, on the seventh
day which, therefore, determines the whole creation week, i.e., the goal
of creation is reached already within the seven-day scheme, namely, on
the last day. Thus Schmidt, Die Schöpfungsgeschichte, p. 69. "Die
Tageserzählung trägt nicht wie die Volksbestätigung oder die Billigungs-
formel ihrem Sinn in sich selbst, sondern bereitet Gen 2:1-3 vor."
Similarly, Westermann, Genesis, p. 125. "Was das Schema der sieben Tage

behind the present form of the account at which a seven-day scheme without a Sabbath can be detected. Moreover, Gen. 2:1-3 shows no traits of a tradition of this type, but is in fact in its present form a tightly knit literary unit. We shall now turn to an examination of it.

Gen. 2:1-3

We have examined the traditions behind the creation Sabbath in the Old Testament, namely, the divine *otiositas* and the Sabbath. We have further argued that a seven-day festival week most probably does not lie behind the seven-day creation sequence, ending in its completion on the seventh day. Now we shall turn to an analysis of the text itself. We can set it out in the following way:

(a) Thus the heavens and the earth were finished, and all the host of them (vs. 1).

(b) And on the seventh day God had finished his work which he had done (vs. 2a),

(c) and he rested on the seventh day from all his work which he had done (vs. 2b).

(d) So God blessed the seventh day and hallowed it (vs. 3a),

(e) because on it God rested from all his work which he had done in creation (vs. 3b).

These verses are a unit, almost poetic in character, with some liturgical qualities. The first line (a) is attached to (b) through the common verb. The next lines (b, c) belong together with identical conclusions and the same number of words (seven). The following lines (d, e) are also tied together by kî bô, and so are (c) and (e) with respect to

---

mit den Schöpfungswerken verbindet, ist nicht die Zahl sieben, sondern die Bedeutung des siebten Tag in der Woche."

content, whereas (b) and (d) have similarly structured beginnings.[1] In a word, the four lines form a tightly knit unit. Westermann has proposed that (b) and (d) contain the passage's essential understanding of the conclusion of creation, and that (c) and (e), the divine rest motif, is a secondary step beyond the conclusion reached in (b) and (d).[2] But it is not necessary that we should divide the verses up in this way. Rather, the lines rise to a cresendo climaxing in (d) with an anticlimax in (e), i.e., (a) is introductory or perhaps it concludes the preceding verses; (b) states what God did with reference to the six days; (c) states what he did with reference to the seventh day (rested, desisted); (d) reaches the climax with blessing and sanctification of the seventh day; (e) finally brings us back to (b). Thus it is (c) and (e) which signify that the acts of creation had stopped, a circumstance which leads God to bless and sanctify the seventh day. Gen. 2:1-3 is, therefore, a unified composition which does not let the reader bracket out any traditions within it with any degree of certainty.[3]

---

[1](b): wayᵉkal ᵓelōhîm bayyôm haśśᵉbîᶜî. (d): wayᵉbārek ᵓelōhîm ᵓetyôm haśśᵉbîᶜî.

[2]Westermann, Genesis, p. 232. "Damit hat P seine eigene Sinngebung des Abschlusses der Schöpfung eindeutig und ausreichend gegeben." "Jetz aber kommt noch ein zweiter Schritt hinzu. Der Satz 3a, der für P von grösster Wichtigkeit ist, wird in einen diesen Satz kommentierenden und dadurch zugleich hervorhebenden Rahmen gefügt, in die fast gleichlautenden Sätze 2b und 3b." See also von Rad, Die Priesterschrift, p. 16. Here the passage is divided up into Pᴬ (vss. 2, 3b) and Pᴮ (vss. 1, 3a). This is a doubtful procedure, and the author has not followed it up in his Genesis commentary. Other scholars have found glosses in the verses, viz., 2a is a gloss on 2b (Gunkel, Genesis, p. 114; Simpson, "Genesis," p. 498). None of these attempts have successfully disputed the unity of this passage. Cf. Schmidt, Die Schöpfungsgeschichte, p. 155, n. 2.

[3]This is a warning against attempting to distinguish too sharply

Verse 1 concludes the creation account and it may be considered
part of a hypothetically reconstructed creation tradition in existence
before the seven-day scheme became part of it. The fact that this conclusion is preserved here where it is essentially not needed may,
therefore, correspond to the tendency of the whole narrative to preserve
the traditions.[1]

Verses 2-3 combine the conclusion of creation and the seven-day
scheme. This happens in two steps. Firstly, we learn that the work of
creation had been completed by now; and secondly, that God rested from
his creative work. Only in the second statement (c) do we have the
divine rest motif appearing, but it is not really a divine rest any
more, for it stands in close parallel to (b) which simply informs us
that all the work of creation had been accomplished. Moreover, the verb
here is not nwḫ (rest) but šbt (cease). Finally, when we compare (d)
and (e) we notice that God blessed and sanctified the seventh day
because he rested on it. This rest, however, is not relaxation from
physical exhaustion, but resting from work, in the sense of turning away
from work; and it is on the basis of this that the day is blessed and

---

between that which is received (traditum) and the package in which it is
passed on (actus tradendi). Apparently the author of Gen. 1:1-2:4 did
not distinguish sharply between the two. See the study by Schmidt, Die
Schöpfungsgeschichte, and Westermann's critique of it, Genesis, pp.
115ff.

[1]See also the last pleonastic expression, "because on it God
rested from all his work which he had done in creation." It is possible
that the two verbs reflect an attempt to combine creation terminology
(bārāʾ) and Sabbath terminology (ʿāsāh). Cf. Schmidt, Die Schöpfungsgeschichte, p. 156, n. 5. It is also possible that two different
conceptions of the creative activity are reflected here, i.e., by spoken
word and by performed act. Westermann, Genesis, p. 111; Schmidt, Die
Schöpfungsgeschichte, p. 160.

hallowed. So much for the structure of the passage.

Two observations regarding the content may now be made. (1) The passage is saturated with expressions characteristic of the Sabbath literature.[1] (2) It does not really enforce or command recognition of the Sabbath institution. This strange situation lends some support to the proposition made above concerning the initial introduction of the Sabbath into the traditional creation account, namely, as a means to interpret the divine _otiositas_ motif. It shows that the main concern of Gen. 1:1-2:4 is with creation, and not with the Sabbath. If the creation account had been of cultic origin and framed by a seven-day schedule appropriate to a seven-day long festival period, we might assume that Gen. 2:2-3 came about in its present form because of a concern with the Sabbath institution.[2] But such a concern is indeed expressed very mutely, and the presence of the verses here can be much better explained by assuming, as we have done in this paper, that they serve to give interpretation to the creation tradition, and not vice versa. It is worth noting also that Gen. 2:1-3 does not use the noun šabbāt, but only the verb šbt (cease).

At the same time it is also puzzling that here we have the only reference to the Sabbath in P without any implication that the Sabbath

---

[1] To the Sabbath terminology belong mᵉlaʾketô, ʿsh (Ex. 20:9-10; 31:14-15; 35:2; Dt. 5:13-14); the verb šbt (Ex. 23:12; 34:21; 31:17); "in the seventh day" (Ex. 16:26, 29, 30; 20:10; 31:15; 35:2; Lev. 23:3; Dt. 5:13); "bless" and "hallow" (Ex. 20:11); cf. the expression "holy to Yahweh" (Ex. 16:23; 31:14) and the several occurrences of "keep the Sabbath day holy" (Ex. 20:8; Dt. 5:12).

[2] E.g., a concern to authenticate the Sabbath institution and authorize its regulations, or to provide an etiology for the Sabbath institution.

institution must be observed, or even given recognition. The immediate

solution to this puzzle is that the Sabbath could not appear prior to

the Sinai lawgiving in P's chronology,[1] and that Gen. 2:1-3 is, there-

fore, not concerned with the Sabbath institution at all, but only with

God's rest.[2] This means that the creation Sabbath is not conceived of

as a socio-religious, or a cultic phenomenon. Rather, it is here

released from its religious and cultic attachment and put to new use in

the structure of the priestly account of creation. It explains the

divine _otiositas_ as the seventh day of creation on which the creator has

completed, and therefore stops, his activity. However, it is impossible

to put the Sabbath to such a startling new use without its being

affected in the process. Perhaps this was intended in the first place,

but it certainly cannot be overlooked.

---

[1]Ex. 16:4-5, 22-30 provide an exception. However, we should
remember that Ex. 16 refers to the events just preceding the Sinai lawgiving, and the priestly interest in the Abrahamic covenant (Gen. 17:
1-14) would not find a reference to the Sabbath just prior to Sinai
problematic. The Sabbath was after all to become the sign of the
covenant (Ex. 31:12). Notice, however, that the Sabbath comes as a surprise in Ex. 16:22-23. Cf. Walther Zimmerli, "Sinaibund und Abrahambund
(Ein Beitrag zum Verständnis der Priesterschrift)," ThZ, XVI (1960),
287. Also in Gottes Offenbarung: Gesammelte Aufsätze zum Alten Testament (Munich: Chr. Kaiser Verlag, 1963), p. 215. Cf. von Rad, Die
Priesterschrift, p. 57.

[2]Cf. von Rad, Die Priesterschrift, pp. 168-69: "Gegen die
weitverbreitete Meinung, Gen. 1 münde in ein Sabbatgebot aus, muss aber
nachdrücklich Protest erhoben werden. Mit keinem Wort ist in diesem
Abschnitt der Sabbat verbindlich gemacht. . . . Also um eine
Verbindlichmachung und Ausgabe eines Gesetzes geht es hier gerade nicht,
sondern vielmehr um den Hinweis auf eine Ruhe, die vor dem Mensche da
war und auch ohne ihm da ist. . . ." Cf. Noth, Überlieferungsgeschichte
des Pentateuch, pp. 261-62; Schmidt, Die Schöpfungsgeschichte, p. 157:
"Die Ruhe bleibt wie die ganze Schöpfung allein eine Tat Gottes. Von
eine 'Schöpfungsordnung' der Ruhe oder gar des Wechsels von Arbeit und
Ruhe kann also keine Rede sein."

We have a clear illustration of how the creation Sabbath influenced Israel's thought about the weekly Sabbath in Ex. 20:11; 31:17.
Here it is argued that the creation Sabbath provides an example for man's Sabbath keeping, and that its purpose is to give the Sabbath keeper rest. These inferences are not drawn in Gen. 2:1-3, but it is probably accurate to say that the blessing and sanctifying of the seventh day implies that it, as well as the other creations, are now readied to function in the life of the community and of man generally.[1] That the Sabbath should thus itself benefit from its function in the creation account is in agreement with the role of the total creation account in P, namely, as _preparatio_. As it is a preparation for the sacred history of Israel, so the creation Sabbath is a preparation for Israel's sacred Sabbath institution.

Finally, we may ask if the probable association of the divine _otiositas_ and the creation Sabbath motifs should not lead us to the

---

[1]Cf. Karl Elliger, "Sinn und Ursprung der priesterlichen Geschichtserzählung," _ZThK_, XLIX (1952), 122. "Aber dieser Gipfel wird doch überhöht durch einer zweiten, die Erschaffung des Sabbats zunächst noch nicht im Menschlich-geschichtlichen Bezirk, sondern als Ruhe Gottes jenseits, aber bereits zur Entfaltung ihrer Segenswerkung im Diesseits." Thus also Gerhard von Rad, _Genesis: A Commentary_, trans. by John H. Marks (Philadelphia: Westminster Press, 1961), p. 60. "Even more, that God has 'blessed,' 'sanctified' . . . this rest, means that P does not consider it as something for God alone but as a concern of the world. . . . The way is being prepared, therefore, for an exalted good, actually the final, saving good. Nothing of this is apparent to man. . . . But once a community and a tabernacle are present, at such time they will then be bound to observe this rest of God." In short, it is suggested that Gen. 2:2-3 does not contain a reference to the Sabbath institution, but that more than just the creator's rest is implied. Cf. Westermann, _Genesis_, p. 236. "Dies ist sehr mehr als bloss ein Hinweiss auf den später in und für Israel eingesetzten Sabbat; in der Heiligung des siebten Tages ist eine Ordnung für die Menschheit gesetz, nach der die Zeit in altägliche und heilige, in Arbeits- und Ruhezeit gegliedert ist."

following suggestion: Just as the gods seek rest and in doing so assure
a stable world order, so also man seeks and needs rest because it too
contributes to a stable world order. This suggestion is intriguing for
it follows the pattern of analogy between heavenly and earthly things, a
pattern well known in the ancient Near East. In this instance, however,
that pattern is actually broken. The Sabbath is not a heavenly Sabbath,
nor a divine Sabbath, but the creation Sabbath; and even if it originally stood in a relationship to the divine *otiositas*, that relationship
is severly strained in the Old Testament, for here it is after all only
a Sabbath, namely, the seventh day, lasting twenty-four hours, and not a
perpetual rest. It does not, therefore, insure that henceforth the
world order is stable. Actually, it only signifies that now the creation is completed, and that the creator has ceased his work. However,
it is the completion of this good creation, and not the cessation of the
creative activity through a divine *otiositas*, which assures a stable
world order. Here we must remind ourselves that it is not the rest
(cessation from work) which concludes creation, but it is the concluded
creation which occasions both rest and the Sabbath. Moreover, the Sabbath is not here given to man directly, but only by inference; and when
we do find it among men, it does not serve to insure a stable world
order. Its sphere of influence is merely the human situation, including
perhaps the animal life and the fields, but not the world as a whole.

Now on the other hand, we have suggested tentatively (above, p.
148) that the earliest Sabbath traditions may have included a sacral
view of work and abstention from work, that the Sabbath provided an
occasion for regeneration of the earth and its inhabitants and a

reconstitution of the powers of life. It is also correctly observed that Ex. 20:11; 31:17 make the creation Sabbath into an example for man's Sabbath. But this example seems to limit itself to the time of the Sabbath (seventh day), the nature of Sabbath keeping (cessation of labor), and the result of Sabbath observance (rest and refreshing). Nothing is said directly about the effects of this rest and cessation on the once established world order. If we, therefore, compare the effects of the divine _otiositas_ on the world order with those of the Sabbath on the earthly situation, we should probably think of the Sabbath institution per se, and not of the creation Sabbath in particular. On the Sabbath, the earth, animals, and man received rest, refreshing, and reconstitution of lost powers (the Old Testament understands the latter in a completely secular way), so that we may say that the day secured the proper function and maintenance of the world. Such a function of the creation Sabbath is not made explicit, but perhaps it may be implied.

Ex. 20:11

The use of the creation Sabbath motif in Ex. 20:11 and Ex. 31:17 is far less imaginative than in Gen. 2:1-3. We have already discussed the general structure of the fourth commandment of which Ex. 20:11 is the last verse.[1] Verse 8 is the general introduction, stating the main concern of the law. Verses 9-10 contain the specific stipulations which fall into an established pattern. Verse 11a is also patterned after the standard Sabbath law and corresponds to verses 9-10. Finally, verse 11b

---

[1]See above, pp. 169-171.

corresponds to verse 8; and although it is attached to verse 11a by
means of ʿal-kēn (therefore), it also provides a conclusion to the commandment as a whole which is built up symmetrically according to the
pattern a, b, b1, a1.

Ex. 20:11 demonstrates both similarities and dissimilarities to
Gen. 2:1-3. Ex. 20:11b corresponds fairly closely to Gen. 2:3a, but Ex.
20:11a shows some divergence from the Genesis passage, notably in the
choice of verbs, nwḥ (rest)[1] for God's (Yahweh's) activities on the seventh day, and ʿsh (make) for his creative activities on the six days.
The addition "the sea, and all there is in them" is an expansion which
is foreign to Gen. 2:1-3 where the sea is not created. It serves to
include everything in the three-part universe within the sphere of
Yahweh's creative activity. Gen. 2:1-3, on the other hand, operate with
a two-part cosmos, heaven and earth.[2] The direction of a relationship,
assuming that such a one exists, between Gen. 2:1-3 and Ex. 20:11 has
been discussed with no convincing results appearing as yet,[3] and it is
very likely that we should think of both as having arisen from a common
fund of priestly instruction.[4]

---

[1]See above, n. 1, p. 140.

[2]Noted already by Karl Budde, Die biblische Urgeschichte: Gen.
1-12,5 untersucht (Giessen: J. Ricker, 1883), pp. 493ff. See also Ps.
115:15; 121:2; 124:8; 134:3; II Chr. 2:12. The three-part cosmos is
found in Ps. 146:2; Neh. 9:6.

[3]A dependence on Gen. 2:1-3 immediately suggests itself. Thus
Noth, Exodus, p. 164; Jenni, Die theologische Begründung, p. 20. See,
however, Nielsen, The Ten Commandments, p. 41; Reventlow, Gebot und
Predigt, pp. 59-60; A. van der Voort, "Genèse I, 1 a II, 4a et le psaume
CIV," RB, LVIII (1951), n. 1, pp. 325-26.

[4]Cf. Hulst, "Bemerkungen zum Sabbatgebot," pp. 159-62.

The purpose of the creation Sabbath theme here is to provide a reason for the Sabbath regulation in verses 9-10, and not as in Gen. 2: 1-3 to bring the creation account to a specific conclusion. Whereas Gen. 2:1-3 refers only to the seventh day on which all the creation was completed and all creative activity stopped, with no mention of the previous six-day period, Ex. 20:11 contrasts the six days of creative activity with the seventh day of rest. The main point of Ex. 20:11 is clearly to draw this distinction, for that is the whole argument of the commandment, namely, that verse 11 is parallel to and provides an analogy to the same distinction in verses 9-10. This circumstance is sufficient explanation for the choice of verbs (ʿsh, nwḥ), for they reflect the practical aspect of the regulation in verses 9-11. In other words, the pattern whereby man works for six days and stops his activities on the seventh day with the ensuing rest is observed by Yahweh. There is no theological speculation as to how Yahweh works and rests; in fact, it is doubtful that we should think of Ex. 20:8-11 as deriving one Sabbath (man's) from another (Yahweh's). Rather, it stresses that Yahweh once rested on the seventh day, that he consequently blessed and hallowed it, and that man should thus also refrain from working on it. What we have here is a practical inference drawn from the creation Sabbath with reference to man's Sabbath. There is thus no reason to postulate an old anthropomorphic tradition (Yahweh rested after creation or entered an _otiositas_ after his work) behind this verse. It is a good illustration of an argument from a proof text.

Ex. 31:17

Here the creation Sabbath motif plays an even more obscure role
than in Ex. 20:11. The whole passage (vss. 12-17) contains a collection
of Sabbath laws which center around three concerns: (1) The Sabbath
should be kept holy continually; (2) no work must be performed on it;
(3) it is a covenant and a sign between Yahweh and Israel. In the last
verse then, we have the reference to the creation Sabbath: "It is a
sign for ever between me and the people of Israel that in six days the
LORD made heaven and earth, and on the seventh day he rested, and was
refreshed." Formally this verse shows affinities to both the other
passages. It follows Gen. 2:1-3 in having a two-part cosmos (heaven and
earth), and in the use of the verb šbt; but it clearly intends, along
with Ex. 20:11, to emphasize that God rested and was refreshed (npš) on
the seventh day, in distinction from his six days of creative activity.
In the light of this, we would expect the creation Sabbath to appear in
the immediate context of verse 15 where the six-seven day schedule is
imposed upon man. But this is not the case. Rather, it follows after a
reference to the Sabbath as a covenant (vs. 16) and as a sign (vs. 17a),
and it is connected to these references by means of the particle kî
(for). This construction is identical to the one found in Ex. 20:11;
but whereas the particle there serves to combine the work-rest schedule
of the creation week with that of the regular week, it here connects the
work-rest schedule with the Sabbath as a covenant sign. Now it is
extremely difficult to find any causal relationship between Yahweh's
rest and the covenant sign; and it is quite plausible that the rationale
behind the position of verse 17 in this passage is to be . ·nd in its

similar position, though in a different context, in Ex. 20:8-11. We have argued elsewhere[1] that Ex. 31:1-17 contains a collection of Sabbath traditions strung together very loosely. The creation Sabbath is one such tradition. It is severed from its natural context and placed at the end of the passage, probably by analogy with Ex. 20:8-11, where it provides a fitting climax to the whole passage. Thus the creation Sabbath not only provides a reason for man's Sabbath observance, but here serves as a fundamental Sabbath tradition on the basis of which a comprehensive Sabbath theology may rest.

Conclusion

How are these three passages related, and what is their provenance? It is very difficult to determine a relationship between them, firstly because they function quite differently, and secondly because they contain both late and traditional traits. We have already noted the predicate, "who made heaven and earth," attached to God,[2] as well as some expanded forms of it.[3] Apparently this was a traditional though not demonstrably early way of referring to the work of the creator. We have further noted the expression: "In six days God made, . . . but on the seventh day he rested." That way of referring to the Sabbath is also very old. It has also been suggested that Ex. 20:11; 31:17 contain some old elements, notably the choice of verbs,[4] but very little can be

---

[1]See above, pp. 69-71, 172.

[2]Ps. 115:15; 121:2; 124:8; 134:3; II Chr. 2:12.

[3]Ps. 146:6; Neh. 9:6.

[4]ᶜsh (make) is used about the work of God in creation (Gen. 2:

concluded from this observation; and we definitely cannot maintain that these are old anthropomorphic images of God. The function of the verbs excludes this. The creation Sabbath provides a reason for, or an analogy to, man's Sabbath which involves both an end to work and rest, ideas which are expressed very well by the so-called anthropomorphic verbs. In other words, the verbs nwḥ (rest) and npš (refreshed) accentuate the analogy between man's Sabbath and the creation Sabbath by describing the latter in terms of the former.

The question as to when the account of creation and the Sabbath were first united is very hard to answer; but recent studies of the creation account in Gen. 1:1-2:4 indicate that it probably did not take place in late exilic or postexilic times, but a great deal earlier, in pre-exilic times.[1] It is this tradition which enabled the fourth

---

2-3) although the proper verb for this action is brɔ (create). It is, however, used in the Sabbath laws about the work done on the six days (Ex. 20:9; 23:12). nwḥ (rest), npš (refreshed) is never used about Yahweh in the sense of resting from strain, but it is part of the Sabbath vocabulary, however. Therefore, just as the Sabbath has conditioned the creation account, so the Sabbath has conditioned the creation Sabbath and placed it at its service.

[1]A growing number of voices now object to attributing as much theological activity to the exile as has traditionally been done. It is assumed that Gen. 1:1-2:4 is the product of repeated interpretation of a tradition which, though it cannot be reconstructed, probably consisted of a statement of the creative acts. See Schmidt, Die Schöpfungsgeschichte, pp. 160ff. The elaboration of it by means of creation through the divine word is very likely also pre-exilic. See Klaus Koch, "Wort und Einheit des Schöpfergottes in Memphis und Jerusalem," ZThK, LXII (1965), 273; Schmidt, Die Schöpfungsgeschichte, pp. 169-78. It is also possible that the seven-day scheme was associated with creation in the tradition available to the writer of the present account. See Bauer, "Die literarische Form des Heptaemeron," pp. 276-77; Ackroyd, Exile and Restoration, pp. 35-36. However, we cannot be certain of this. It is generally assumed that the increased concern with the Sabbath as "holy time" originated during the exile, when the "holy place" had lost its importance. Recently Ackroyd (Exile and Restoration, p. 35) has taken

commandment to use the creation Sabbath as an analogy for the regular Sabbath and which slipped into the conclusion of the Sabbath laws in Ex. 31:12-17. Gen. 2:1-3, on the other hand, shows no concern with Sabbath observance, and does not mention the six days of work (although it is, of course, implied), but is mainly concerned with what happened after creation had been completed. This could well have been an important concern in pre-exilic priestly circles who were acquainted with Egyptian and Mesopotamian creation accounts.

We have suggested that the combination of creation and Sabbath is Israel's answer to the divine *otiositas* motif. This must remain a hypothesis; but it is supported by the observation that the creation Sabbath, on which an enormous amount of support for the Sabbath institution could easily be established, not least during the exile when creation themes were important, appears only two times outside the creation account, and one of them (Ex. 31:17) quite accidentally, it seems.

F. The Sabbath and the Covenant

In exilic and postexilic times the Sabbath played an important role in Israel's understanding of her covenant relationship with Yahweh.

---

exception to this by claiming that the evidence favoring a close association of Sabbath and the exile is not really very convincing. For a discussion of these views, see below, pp. 235ff. Ex. 20:11; 31:17 do, of course, testify to the importance of the Sabbath in P by making the creation Sabbath into the reason for man's Sabbath observance, but it seems that we are here dealing with traditions which are not related directly to Gen. 2:1-3, but which depend on the seven-day structure of the creation account and perhaps were modified so as to provide an analogy to the weekly Sabbath. It is not likely that an exilic priestly writer should have spun all this out of whole cloth. Unfortunately, we have no way of knowing the nature of the earliest creation Sabbath

Both the weekly Sabbath institution and the sabbatical year will be
examined as we explore the way in which the Sabbath came to occupy one
of the most sacred chambers in Israel's religious understanding, namely,
the covenant relationship.

The Sabbath as holy

Historians of religions have attempted to explain the holy as
that aspect of human experience which is saturated with reality or
being,[1] or as the irrational mystery (_mysterium tremendum_) before which
man shudders in terror.[2] The holy, however, invades human experience
and attaches itself to places and times, whereby these become imbued
with a special power which in turn affects the rest of human experience.
In the words of Johannes Pedersen, holiness becomes a regulating principle in life and dominates the whole of life.[3] It is no wonder,
therefore, that a breach of holiness caused by the action of one member
of the community could be punished by death, for such an action would
bring the whole community into disarray.

The Sabbath, the seventh day of the week, was a time in which
holiness was concentrated. It is, therefore, called a "holy Sabbath"

---

traditions, but it must have associated God's resting after creation
with the seventh-day Sabbath.

[1]Mircea Eliade, _The Sacred and the Profane: The Nature of
Religion_, trans. by Willard R. Trask, Harper Torchbooks (New York:
Harper & Row, Publishers, 1961), pp. 12-13.

[2]Rudolf Otto, _The Idea of the Holy: An Inquiry into the Non-
Rational Factor in the Idea of the Divine and Its Relation to the
Rational_, trans. by John W. Harvey, A Galaxy Book (New York: Oxford
University Press, 1958).

[3]Pedersen, _Israel_, III-IV, p. 287.

(Ex. 16:22; 31:14-15; 35:2; Is. 58:13),[1] and Israel is required to keep it holy (Ex. 20:8; Dt. 5:12; Jer. 17:22, 24, 27; Ezek. 20:20; 44:24; Neh. 13:22). It is also called a holy convocation (Lev. 23:3). The holiness of the Sabbath is attributed to an act of divine sanctification in Gen. 2:3; Ex. 20:11; but it is perhaps emphasized most strongly in several passages which warn against profaning the Sabbath (Ex. 31:14; Ezek. 20:13, 16, 21, 24; 23:38; Is. 56:2, 6).[2] It is generally assumed that the Sabbath is kept holy when Israel refrains from working on it,[3] and conversely, Israel desists from work on that day in order to keep it holy. The above texts occur in late literature, and it may be asked if the holiness of the Sabbath is not a special exilic or postexilic element. Pedersen has argued that this is not so, but that the holiness of the Sabbath in early Israel was too overwhelming to be questioned, and that it, therefore, was generally respected.[4] Thus the Sabbath is the occasion for a visit to a holy man (II Kg. 4:23), or the temple (II Kg. 11:4-12), or a day on which the oppressor might contemplate his continuing fraud, but whose holiness he would not break by working. Even the

---

[1]The etymology of the common Semitic word qōdeš is not at all certain, but it has been proposed that it is related to the root qd, or qdqd (crown of head), or to the root ḥdš (new), or perhaps to the Accadian word qadašu (shine). However, the more elemental meaning of the word is "separation" according to James Muilenburg, "Holiness," The Interpreter's Dictionary of the Bible, ed. by G. A. Buttrick, et al. (New York: Abingdon Press, 1962), II, 617.

[2]Profane (ḥl, ḥll) is the antonym of holy (qdš). Cf. Muilenburg, "Holiness," p. 617.

[3]This is most obvious in Neh. 13:15-22; Jer. 17:19-27, but it is also implied in the structure of the fourth commandment, as well as in Gen. 2:3; Ex. 20:11; 31:17.

[4]Pedersen, Israel, III-IV, pp. 288-89.

humanitarian concern (Ex. 23:12; Dt. 5:14-15) is explained in terms of
the Sabbath's holiness, for it is due to this quality of the day that
man and beast may rest on it and gather strength from its power.[1]

The Sabbath may thus be considered an institution to which holiness was attached from time immemorial. That was expressed through
abstention from secular work, through the rest whereby special power
from the holy would be made available for the continued life in non-holy
time, and probably also through some form of cultic activity. In later
times, however, Israel's continued contact with strangers released her
from the impact of the holiness of this day, with the result that the
prophets (Jer. 17:19-27) and priests called upon Israel to preserve the
holiness of the Sabbath. Failure to do so, though it might not produce
instant disaster for the culprit, would eventually cut him off from the
life-giving source of holy time.

The Sabbath to Yahweh

In discussing the priestly theology of the cult, von Rad maintains that "no cultic celebration was solemnized for Israel, but they
were all 'for Yahweh.'"[2] By this he means that in the cult Israel was
called upon to recognize Yahweh's right to and claim upon her. This
right of Yahweh was demanded in realistic and actual areas of human
existence, viz., holy places, holy men, holy times, and holy objects.[3]

---

[1]Ibid., p. 290.   [2]Old Testament Theology, I, 242.

[3]The yearly festivals were "for Yahweh" (Lev. 23:6 passim), so
was the passover (Ex. 12:11, 27, 48; Lev. 23:5), and the Sabbath (Ex.
16:23, 25; 31:15; 35:2; Lev. 23:3; 25:44). The Nazirite separated
himself to the Lord (Num. 6:2, 5-6).

To say that the Sabbath is "for Yahweh" does not mean, however, that it gives something to Yahweh, viz., honor or praise. It does not provide benefit for Yahweh, or secure his rights or fair share in any way.[1] On the contrary, the Sabbath is in the oldest traditions the property of, and for the benefit of, the people Israel (Is. 1:13; Hos. 2:11; Ex. 23:12; 34:21; Dt. 5:14; II Kg. 4:23). The same is true about the later passages (Jer. 17:19-27; Neh. 13:15-22). In one sense the Sabbath is, therefore, lākem (for you), cf. Ex. 31:14; 35:2.[2] What then is meant by naming the Sabbath "for Yahweh" (Ex. 16:23, 25; 20:10; 31:15; 35:2; Lev. 23:3) or "my/thy Sabbath(s)" (Ex. 31:13; Lev. 19:3, 30; Is. 56:4; 58:13; Ezek. 20:12 passim; 22:26; 23:38; 44:24; Neh. 9:14)? It probably indicated that on this day Yahweh's presence was particularly manifest. In fact, the holiness of the day, which was recognized by the abstention from work on it, depended on the recognition of the real presence of Yahweh on that day. Thus when he removed himself from Israel ("set the daughter of Zion under a cloud," Lam. 2:6), one immediate consequence was the cessation of the Sabbath; and when Is. 1:13 pictures worshippers trampling the temple courts on the Sabbath, he adds that Yahweh will refuse to be present on such occasions.

---

[1]See especially Klaus Koch, "Die Eigenart der priesterschrift-lichen Sinaigesetzgebung," ZThK, LV (1958), 44. Koch rejects von Rad's statement quoted above. "'Keine kultische Begehung wurde für Israel, alle wurden 'für Jahwe' gefeirt'. . . gelt nicht für P." On the con-trary he claims: "Ist der Kult in weitem Masse zugunsten des Menschen da, alle Heiligkeit ist es ausschliesslich." This is correct, but Koch's further argument is not convincing, namely, that the expression "for Yahweh," which occurs so frequently in the cultic regulations, is not indigenous to P whereas the less frequent lākem (for you), Ex. 30:32, 37; 31:14; 35:2, reflects the true concern of P.

[2]Ibid., pp. 44-45.

"For Yahweh" is, therefore, another way of expressing the holiness of the Sabbath. It was used in pre-exilic times (cf. Dt. 5:13; Ex. 20:9-10) but became very prominent in exilic and postexilic texts, probably because "holiness" and "divine presence" on the Sabbath became a secondary experience, i.e., it was a thing which was sought, but scarcely felt. Now the consequences of breaking the Sabbath by working on it had to be taught to the people (Jer. 17:19-27; Neh. 13:15-22), for they were no longer experienced immediately, as was the case formerly (Num. 15:32-36). "My/thy Sabbath(s)" conveys the same idea, although we are here meeting the additional motif that Yahweh gave Israel the Sabbath (Ex. 16:29; Ezek. 20:12 passim) with the understanding and intention that she must not profane it. Moreover, the tradition attaches the Sabbath even more closely to Yahweh when we are told that not only he himself as creator shares in the holiness of the Sabbath, rests on it, and gathers strength (is refreshed) from it, but more importantly, he created it at the conclusion of his creative activity and made it holy, i.e., filled it with this special content (holiness) which would eventually be available to Israel and to mankind as a whole.

The Sabbath as a sign and a covenant

The much celebrated identification of the Sabbath as a sign that Israel remains in the covenant appears only five times:

(a) You shall keep my sabbaths, for this is a sign between me and you throughout your generations, that you may know that I, the LORD, sanctify you (Ex. 31:13).

(b) Therefore the people of Israel shall keep the Sabbath, observing the Sabbath throughout their generations, as a perpetual covenant (Ex. 31:16).

(c) It is a sign for ever between me and the people of Israel that in six days the LORD made heaven and earth, and on the seventh day he rested, and was refreshed (Ex. 31:17).

(d) Moreover I gave them my sabbaths, as a sign between me and them, that they might know that I the LORD sanctify them (Ezek. 20:12).

(e) And hallow my sabbaths that they may be a sign between me and you, that you may know that I the LORD am your God (Ezek. 20:20).

A sign provides recognition of a certain fact, or guarantees its reliability. Prophets used a sign (ʾôt) to guarantee the certainty of their words,[1] and Moses is told to confirm his claim to be Yahweh's messenger by performing signs before the Egyptians and the enslaved Hebrews.[2] Reliance on signs can, of course, be misleading, for it is in the actual fulfillment, or lack thereof, of the prophetic oracle that its truthfulness is discerned, and not in the sign itself.[3] In short, the sign must not usurp the place of that which it signifies. Rather, its function is to provide understanding, to give knowledge, to bring about recognition. Zimmerli has argued that the expression "and this shall be a sign to you" has the same function as the following: "by this you shall know."[4] A sign means to the individual who has received

---

[1] Cf. II Kg. 19:29; 20:8; Is. 7:11, 14; 38:7.

[2] Ex. 4:8-9, 17, 28, 30.

[3] Jer. 28:5-11; Dt. 13:1-5.

[4] I Sam. 14:8-10 concludes: "And this shall be the sign to us." Zimmerli comments: "Der Schlussatz liesse sich mit genau dem gleichen Recht formulieren: 'Darum werden wir erkennen, dass Jahwe sie in unseren Hand gegeben hat.'" He asks, "Dürfen wir umschreiben: Erkennen heisst: sich durch ein Zeichen die Gewissheit einer Sache geben lassen?" The answer is yes. Walther Zimmerli, "Erkenntnis Gottes nach dem Buch Ezechiel," in Gottes Offenbarung: Gesammelte Aufsätze zum Alten Testament (Munich: Chr. Kaiser Verlag, 1963), pp. 92-93. Cf. Carl A. Keller,

it that he now knows, or at least has been given opportunity to know, that which is implied in the particular sign.

We have proposed that the references in Ex. 31 and in Ezek. 20 to the Sabbath as a sign do not demonstrate literary dependence of P on Ezekiel, or vice versa; but that both writings are relying on a common tradition.[1] The two references are alike, but there are also some differences, e.g., Ex. 31:13 addresses Israel in the 2nd pers. pl., whereas Ezek. 20:12 uses 3rd pers. pl.; Ex. 31:13 adds the favorite priestly expression "throughout your generations";[2] Ex. 31:13 is a law requiring Sabbath observance, whereas Ezek. 20:12 narrates that Yahweh gave his Sabbaths to Israel. That this Sabbath theme could be put to such different use shows that we do not have a case of literary dependence. Rather, we are dealing with an idea, differently expressed, but whose basic claim is that the Sabbath is related to Israel's covenant relationship with Yahweh. The sign is always between Yahweh and Israel. Through it Israel recognizes or knows that Yahweh is her God and that he sanctifies her, that is, restores her as a holy people. But why should Israel gain this certainty through a sign which she herself produced? This, however, would be to miss the point, for the Sabbath is Yahweh's and he gives it to Israel for a sign. At the same time, Israel must

---

Das Wort OTH als "Offenbarungszeichen Gottes": Eine philologisch-theologische Begriffsuntersuchung zum Alten Testament (Basel: Buch-druckerei E. Hoenen, 1946); A. R. Johnson, The Cultic Prophet in Ancient Israel (Cardiff: University of Wales Press, 1962), pp. 52-53.

[1]See above, pp. 44-45.

[2]Gen. 17:12; Ex. 12:14, 17; 16:32, 33; 29:42; 30:8, 10, 31; 31: 13; Lev. 3:17; 6:18; 10:9; 22:2; 23:14, 21, 41; 24:3; Num. 9:10; 10:8; 15:14, 15, 21, 23; 18:23; 35:29.

keep the Sabbath in order that it may become such a sign (Ezek. 20:20). Though Yahweh is nowhere said to seek understanding regarding Israel's intentions through this sign, it is demonstrably a sign with a double function, for it stands between Yahweh and the people Israel assuring both of the other side's loyalty. It is no wonder then that it could also serve as a vehicle of the covenant (Ex. 31:16). The expression "between me and you," which describes the function of the sign, is also a covenant formula in P (Gen. 9:12; 17:2).[1]

In addition to these passages, we have other indirect evidence that the Sabbath functioned as a covenant between Yahweh and Israel during the Exile and in postexilic times. Jer. 17:24-27 assures the community which keeps the Sabbath that it will participate in two events, both of which are a part of Israel's covenant concept. (1) Kings will continue to occupy the throne of David in a perpetually inhabited Jerusalem.[2] (2) The neighboring nations will recognize Jerusalem and come to worship at the temple, a theme which is also present in Is. 66:23.[3] Neh. 13:18 charges that the catastrophe of the exile and the

---

[1]Cf. Zimmerli, "Sinaibund und Abrahambund," pp. 210-11.

[2]Yahweh's covenant with David and his house is explained in the succession story (II Sam. 9-I Kg. 3), and in the royal psalms. It was also adopted by some prophets (Isaiah, Haggai, and Zechariah) and the historians (the Deuteronomist and the Chronicler). Cf. von Rad, Old Testament Theology, I, 312-18; Leonard Rost, "Sinaibund und Davidsbund," ThLZ, LXXII (1947), 129-34; Martin Noth, "God, King, and Nation in the Old Testament," in The Laws in the Pentateuch and Other Studies, trans. by D. R. Ap-Thomas (Philadelphia: Fortress Press, 1966), pp. 145-78, especially pp. 174-74; Kraus, Worship in Israel, 189-200; Masao Sekine, "Davidsbund und Sinaibund bei Jeremia," VT, IX (1959), 47-57; A. H. J. Gunneweg, "Sinaibund und Davidsbund," VT, X (1960), 335-41.

[3]This theme is related to the former, but is rather more complex, including within it the motif of the mountain city, the

212

destruction of the city was caused by the forefathers profaning the
Sabbath, and the nobles of the city are warned that even greater disasters will fall upon the community, if it continues to profane the day.
Similar covenant overtones are present in Is. 56:2-6. We have proposed
that these verses apply best to the early part of the restoration
period,[1] when a number of eunuchs and foreigners were contemplating to
return to Jerusalem, but were sceptical about their status in the newly
organized covenant community in Jerusalem. Would such foreigners who
had "joined themselves to Yahweh" be separated from his people (vs. 3),
and would the eunuchs be useless outcasts (cf. Dt. 23)? The assurance
of the prophet is that any eunuch and foreigner who loves Yahweh, who
does his will, who keeps the Sabbath, and who holds fast to the covenant
will be ingrafted into the community so securely that his initial handi-
caps will be completely eliminated, i.e., the eunuch will receive a name

inviolability of Zion, and a variety of eschatological imagery. It was
associated with the Davidic covenant tradition, perhaps at first by
Isaiah. Cf. Gerhard von Rad, "The City on the Hill," in The Problem of
the Hexateuch and Other Essays, trans. by E. W. Trueman Dickens (New
York: McGraw-Hill Book Company, 1966), pp. 232-42. The gathering of
all the people is an occasion for worship, instruction, bringing riches
and glory to Zion, and for rejoicing (Jer. 17:26; Is. 2:2-4; 25:6-12;
66:1-22; Mic. 4:1-4, Zech. 14). Zech. 14 identifies this occasion
specifically with the fall festival of booths, the traditional covenant
festival. Cf. Walter Harrelson, "The Celebration of the Feast of
Booths According to Zech xiv 16-21," in Religions in Antiquity: Essays
in Memory of Erwin Ramsdell Goodenough, ed. by Jacob Neusner, Studies in
the History of Religions, Vol. XIV (Leiden: E. J. Brill, 1968), pp. 88-
96; Kraus, Worship in Israel, pp. 201-3. The association of Sabbath and
new moon in Is. 66:23 is unusual in the late literature, and may reflect
the author's preoccupation with traditional worship seasons in the old
temple (cf. Is. 1:13). The implication would be that Sabbath and new
moon are now acceptable worship seasons in the restored community.

[1]See above, pp. 37-38.

better than that secured by sons and daughters (vs. 5), and the foreigner will have access to the holy mountain (vs. 7). In both instances
the Sabbath is one of the things which identifies the outsider who
observes it as a covenant member.[1] Is. 58:13-14, a passage which we
have assigned to the same general period as Is. 56:2-6,[2] promises joy
and the heritage of Jacob to the Sabbath keeper. We may conclude,
therefore, that in exilic and post-exilic times the Sabbath was looked
upon as a gift from God which, when observed, guaranteed a continual
relationship between Yahweh and Israel in a very practical and realistic
way. Thus, Jer. 17:21 warns, "Take heed for the sake of your lives."

A Sabbath for the land

The sabbatical year and the jubilee year may both stand in some
relationship to the seventh-day Sabbath. The oldest regulation for the
former is found in Ex. 23:10-11. It is structured like the Sabbath
regulation (vs. 12), a fact which suggests some relationship between the
two. For six years the land shall be sowed and harvested, but the
seventh year it must lie fallow. Whatever grows on it without man's
attention shall feed the poor, and when these have satisfied their needs,
the fauna may eat what is left. This applies to the fields, vineyards,

---

[1]A close approximation between Zech. 14:16-21 and Is. 56:2-6;
66:23 has been proposed by Benedikt Otzen, Studien über Deuterosacharja,
Acta Theologica Danica, Vol. VI (Copenhagen: Prostant Apud Munksgaard,
1964), p. 211. However, there are also some differences between the
passages. The eschatological apocalyptic setting of Zech. 14 is missing
in Is. 56, and the Zechariah passage does not impose any conditions on
the foreigners, it only demands that they come to worship. Is. 56, on
the other hand, is concerned with the practical relationship of foreigners and eunuchs to the community in postexilic Jerusalem.

[2]See above, pp. 38-39.

and olive groves. Opinions vary as to the origin and purpose of this
practice; but there is general agreement that it is old,[1] and that it
was originally not a purely agricultural and economic institution.[2] No
doubt several motifs stand behind it. In its Israelite version there is
certainly a socio-humanitarian consideration involved, but it has been
suggested that originally the institution was motivated by religio-
cultic ideas involving a restitutio in integrum (a return to the
original state), that is, the land is to be given back its original
rest, while it lies undisturbed by man for one year during which it can,
so to speak, regenerate its lost energies. This is accomplished not
merely through a natural process, a lying fallow, but through the liberation of the productive powers of the earth (often symbolized by a
fertility god) from the hand of man.[3] At the same time the sabbatical
year liberates man from the toil of the soil, or from kinship with

---

[1]It is believed by most scholars that the sabbatical year is an
ancient institution, possibly originating in preconquest Canaanite
circles. It is also assumed that Israel adopted the practice very
early, perhaps when she came into contact with the agrarian communities
after the conquest, and that the practice was largely neglected in later
times, for there is scarcely any Biblical evidence for it apart from the
legislative texts. Cf. Kraus, Worship in Israel, pp. 70-76; de Vaux,
Ancient Israel, I, 173-75; Hans Wildberger, "Israel und sein Land,"
EvTh, XVI (1956), 412.

[2]Its purpose was not merely to increase productivity. Thus Beer
and Galling, Exodus, p. 119. It is generally assumed that the regulation was not applied to all the fields at once, at least this was not
the expectation in ancient times, but that individual pastures and
orchards were left fallow after six years of farming. Procksch,
Theologie des Alten Testaments, p. 112; Jepsen, Untersuchungen zum
Bundesbuch, p. 47; Kraus, Worship in Israel, p. 71.

[3]Noth, Exodus, pp. 189-90; Pedersen, Israel, I-II, p. 480; von
Rad, Deuteronomy, p. 105.

it,[1] and lets him eat from what it produces without his effort, while the dispossessed are also free to use the land to satisfy their needs.

Ex. 23:10-11 suggests that the sabbatical year was practiced in Israel in premonarchical times, adapted, no doubt, at the time of the conquest. At this time it became oriented towards the particular Israelite religious understanding.[2] Our passage in Ex. 23:10-11 emphasizes that the land must be given rest and released from human interference every seventh year, and that during this year the land must be given into the possession of the dispossessed. Lev. 25:1-7, 18-22 repeats the same regulations with some expansions.[3] It reiterates the demand to let the land rest on the seventh year, here clearly identified as a Sabbath,[4] and adds that the harvest of the sixth year will be blessed so as to provide amply for the fallow year's spontaneous, but smaller yield. Finally, Dt. 15:1-6, 12-18 requires the release of all debt which may have resulted in the loss of personal property or personal freedom, i.e., in the case of a man who has sold himself into slavery. This last regulation regarding personal freedom is also found

---

[1]David S. Shapiro, "The Sabbatical Year," Tradition, VII (1965), 45-56.

[2]Alt suggests the time when Israel was transferring from a semi-nomadic to an agricultural economy, as the only time when the various elements of this institution could flow together, e.g., abstention from work every seventh year and recognition of Yahweh's sole ownership of the land ("The Origins of Israelite Law," p. 165). Alt's suggestion that the institution was "introduced" in this economically mixed community has been questioned (cf. Kraus, Worship in Israel, pp. 71-72). Perhaps we should rather speak of a reorientation of an older practice.

[3]Cf. Reventlow, Das Heiligkeitsgesetz, pp. 123ff.

[4]A Sabbath of solemn rest (šabbātôn), vs. 4; a Sabbath to Yahweh, vs. 2b, 4; a Sabbath of the land, vs. 6.

in Ex. 21:1-6, whereas the agricultural emphasis is missing in this passage.[1]

Closely related to the sabbatical year is the jubilee year (Lev. 25:8-17; 23-55; 27:16-25; Num. 36:4). The exact relationship between these two institutions is not easily determined, but the way the jubilee year is calculated[2] has led some interpreters to believe that it is a secondary development of the sabbatical year.[3] The regulations for the jubilee year include those for the sabbatical year, e.g., the land is to lie fallow (vs. 11), financial indebtedness is to be forgiven (vs. 28),

---

[1]Cf. Gerhard von Rad, Das Gottesvolk im Deuteronomium, BWANT, No. 47 (Stuttgart: W. Kohlhammer Verlag, 1929), p. 30. Kraus has proposed (Worship in Israel, pp. 71-72) that by the time of Deuteronomy the ancient agricultural regulations had become totally impractical and utopian, wherefore the change to a socially oriented regulation. This observation on the part of Kraus and von Rad is important; however, we must remember that the agricultural regulations are preserved in Lev. 25, and that the social regulations appear already in the Book of the Covenant (Ex. 21:1-6). Moreover, the release of all debt and slave labor after six years is perhaps as impractical and utopian as to let the fields lie fallow. It is also possible that the older laws regarding the land and slaves were expanded to include indebtedness because of the proliferation of the economy in the areas of trade and commerse during the monarchy. Only in this way could the strictures of the regulations for the sabbatical year be applied with fairness to the whole of society. That the complex urban economy required different regulations than those operating in the rural family estates is evidenced by the special urban regulations for the jubilee year (Lev. 25:29-34). Cf. von Rad, Deuteronomy, pp. 105-6.

[2]It occurs after seven weeks (Sabbaths) of years, or seven times seven years (Lev. 25:8). Cf. the calculation of the feast of weeks (Lev. 23:15-16).

[3]It has been suggested that the jubilee year was instituted to restore the sabbatical year by transferring the neglected obligations of the seventh year to the fiftieth year. Alt, "The Origin of Israelite Law," p. 166; Kraus, Worship in Israel, p. 73; de Vaux, Ancient Israel, I, 177. It is also possible that the jubilee year is an early institution, although the regulations in Lev. 25 are not earlier than late pre-exilic. Noth, Leviticus, pp. 184-85; Reventlow, Das Heiligkeitsgestez, p. 139.

slaves who paid their debt by entering servitude are to be released
(vss. 39-40), but the main emphasis lies upon "restoration," restoration
of all property, particularly real estate, to its original owner.[1] The
reasoning behind this is again Yahweh's ownership of the land (vs. 23).
As for the practical implications of the jubilee year, we have little or
no information. There is no indication in Biblical literature that it
ever functioned.

We will now examine the relationship between these regulations
and the Sabbath, and the implications of this relationship for our
understanding of Israel's thoughts about the Sabbath. We have already
noted that the Sabbath formula appears in the regulations for the sabbatical year (Ex. 23:10-11; Lev. 25:3-4),[2] but we will suggest that the
relationship between these institutions goes deeper than the mere formal
similarities suggest. The regulations for the sabbatical year and the
jubilee year have two foci: (1) The relinquishing of man's use of the
land; (2) the liberation of man from poverty and bondage. In the following section we will treat the first of these.

On the occasion of the sabbatical year, ancient man recognizes
that he does not have unlimited right to the land, that he cannot
exploit it at will, that he can only use his agricultural skills to

---

[1]The exceptions to this practice are brought about by the complex city life (Lev. 25:29-34).

[2]To the compilor of these regulations, the Sabbath and the
sabbatical year must have been related. However, we cannot conclude
from this that one originated from the other. Notice that the regulation in Ex. 23:10-11 uses the two-part Sabbath formula adopted to the
sabbatical year, whereas Lev. 25:3-4 makes use of the three-part Sabbath
formula.

force productivity of the land for a time, and that after this he must
let it return to its rest, that is, its natural state. Whether or not
he really expects a regenerating process to occur during this year of
rest, brought about by a natural process, or by a recuperation of the
innate supernatural powers of the land,[1] he definitely recognizes that
the land is being given to him as a possession, but not for exploitation.
In the Old Testament literature the rightful owner of the land is Yahweh
who demands that Israel relate herself to the land in this particular
way, namely, as a "stranger and sojourner."[2] And yet at the same time
the land is given by Yahweh to Israel as an inheritance.[3] These two
affirmations correspond, according to von Rad, to two traditions which

---

[1]The laws for the sabbatical year do not explain this. It is
generally accepted that Old Testament man had no way of coercing
fertility upon the ground. His relationship with the earth is expressed
in secular terms, viz., to till the ground, to plant, sow, and reap.
Cf. Harrelson, From Fertility Cult to Worship, p. 14. "God was the
giver of fertility, but Israel could not coerce fertility or even
participate in the process through cultic acts. The task of man was
radically secularized. Man was to till the soil, remove the rocks, and
clear additional acreage." This disenchantment of earth, i.e., freeing
it from the sphere of the sacred is a much celebrated theme in the Old
Testament, which has now also been exploited by secular theologians.
Cf. Harvey Cox, The Secular City: Secularization and Urbanization in
Theological Perspective (New York: Macmillan Company, 1965), pp. 21-24.

[2]Lev. 25:23.

[3]Cf. Ex. 15:17; Lev. 25:23; I Sam. 26:19; II Sam. 14:16; Jos. 22:
19; Ps. 68:9; 79:1; Jer. 2:7; 16:18; 50:11. See especially Wildberger,
"Israel und sein Land," pp. 404-22; Gerhard von Rad, "The Promised Land
and Yahweh's Land in the Hexateuch," in The Problem of the Hexateuch and
Other Essays, trans. by E. W. Trueman Dickens (New York: McGraw-Hill
Book Company, 1966), pp. 79-93; Old Testament Theology, I, 296ff. This
same theme is emphasized in the cultic regulations for the first born
(Ex. 23:19; 34:26; Lev. 23:10), and tithe (Num. 18:21-24; Dt. 14:22;
26:12).

are fused in the late Old Testament literature.[1] Both of them seem to be related to the Sabbath, though at some distance.

Yahweh's land.--Two late passages (Lev. 26:34-35, 43; II Chr. 36:21) associate the Sabbath, the land (Yahweh's land), the sabbatical year, and the covenant themes. Although the land is never identified as Yahweh's land in Lev. 26,[2] Israel is clearly Yahweh's vassal in the land, and she can be removed to her enemies' land at Yahweh's discretion (vss. 32-33). Yahweh is in complete control of the land, and Israel may occupy it only as long as she fulfills whatever conditions are set for such occupancy (vss. 3-4, 14-17, 21-22, 27-28, 40-42). The conditions are that Israel obey the commandments, statutes, and ordinances, and that she honor the covenant. If she refuses to fulfill Yahweh's conditions, catastrophes will fall upon her in increasing severity, until a climax is reached with the deportation (vss. 31-33).

In verses 34-35, a new theme appears. The land becomes an active participant in the conflict, and its participation centers around the Sabbath. Verse 34 promises that as a consequence of the exile "the land shall enjoy its sabbaths." The Sabbath in question is the

---

[1]The theme of Yahweh's ownership to the land may have originated in the cultic realm. Von Rad, "The Promised Land and Yahweh's Land," p. 88; Old Testament Theology, I, 300; Wildberger, "Israel und sein Land," p. 418. This motif was then, through the common interchange of ideas, connected with the historical motif of "Yahweh who gives the land as Israel's possession," a motif which is central in the Pentateuch. The result of this fusion of themes is the view of Israel as "strangers and sojourners" (Lev. 25:23; Gen. 23:4).

[2]It is always "the land" (vss. 4, 6, 13, 20, 25, 32, 34, 43), except vss. 20, 33, which have "your land," but it is not identified as Israel's inheritance either.

sabbatical year which has been transformed to the land's Sabbath analogous to man's Sabbath. We have suggested that the verb rṣh should be translated by its second meaning, "be restituted," "be made good."[1] The land, as well as man and beast, it is argued, is entitled to its Sabbaths with the rest they imply. The land was deprived of this rest while Israel occupied it, but will have it restored during the captivity of the people. This implies, of course, that Israel was responsible for denying the land its Sabbaths and its rest. However, the emphasis is not upon Israel's neglect, but upon the rights of the land. This is further stated in verse 43 which explains that although Israel repents and gains Yahweh's favor, the land will remain desolate and be repaid for its lost Sabbaths, despite the fact that its inhabitants are no longer under Yahweh's curse (vs. 42). II Chr. 36:21 further explains that the land kept Sabbath during the seventy years of exile, and that this long Sabbath was a reimbursement of lost Sabbaths.[2]

The regulations for the sabbatical year are enforced by means of the destruction of the land, termination of its productivity, and Israel's expulsion from it. Moreover, the seventh or sabbatical year, whose recognition is Israel's responsibility towards the land, has here been transformed into a Sabbath for the land as an inherent right of the land. Thus the recognition of the land's Sabbath has entered into Israel's covenant relationship with Yahweh. When Israel honors the

---

[1]See above, n. 3, p. 80.

[2]For the seventy-year period, see above, n. 4, p. 57. The fact that it would take seventy years to fulfill the lost Sabbaths may contain the idea of complete or total restitution, corresponding to 490 years of neglect of the sabbatical year.

covenant, she will dwell in the land and harvest its yield (Lev. 25:4-7); when she repudiates the covenant, on the other hand, her efforts will be in vain (Lev. 26:16-20), the land will not yield, and she will be ejected from it. The measure of her rejection from the land will correspond to the number of Sabbaths due to the land (Lev. 26:35; II Chr. 36:21), and conversely, the opportunity for the land to keep its Sabbaths determines the solidity of the covenant relationship between Israel, Yahweh, and the land. It seems as if this interpretation of the old seventh or sabbatical year has taken place under the influence of the Sabbath institution. We suggest, therefore, that the influence of the Sabbath on the interpretation of the sabbatical year led to the incorporation of the latter into Israel's understanding of the covenant vis-a-vis the land.[1]

Israel's land.--In an essay written in 1933, von Rad discusses the conception of "rest" in the Bible.[2] He argues that it originated in Deuteronomy where "this 'rest' (מְנוּחָה) is not peace of mind, but the altogether tangible peace granted to a nation plagued by enemies and weary wandering. . . . The life of the chosen people in the 'pleasant land,' at rest from all enemies round about, the people owning their love for God and God blessing his people--this is the epitome of the state of the redeemed nation as Deuteronomy sees it."[3] This theme is

---

[1]Formally Lev. 26:34-35, 43; II Chr. 36:21 demonstrate reliance on Sabbath terminology. See above, n. 4, p. 215. Both passages also have the land "keep Sabbath" (šbt).

[2]"There Remains Still a Rest for the People of God," pp. 94-102.

[3]Ibid., p. 95.

present implicitly in the Pentateuch, in the form of a promise, and it
occupies an important role in the Deuteronomistic history.[1] Von Rad
finds that the theme was also adopted by the Chronicler, but with a
difference. The rest is here granted repeatedly to pious kings (Solomon,
I Chr. 22:9; Asa, II Chr. 15:15; Jehoshaphat, II Chr. 20:30).[2] Moreover,
a new feature appears, namely, that Yahweh is finding rest among his
people (II Chr. 6:41-42).[3] The Chronicler has aptly combined the
Deuteronomistic idea with his own in I Chr. 23:25. "For David said,
'The LORD, the God of Israel, has given peace to his people; and he
dwells in Jerusalem for ever.'" A final important passage is Ps. 95:11.
"Therefore I swore in my anger that they should not enter my rest." The
theme of Israel at rest is certainly present here, but that she should
enter God's rest is something new. According to von Rad, the verse has
no eschatological overtones, but refers to a "personal entering into its
God."[4] However, the moment the Deuteronomistic identification of Israel
at rest with the establishment in the land is made, the rest must be
characterized by a measure of contingency because of the vicissitudes of
the nation, and it is then natural to resolve it in the future through
hope. Deuteronomy itself, looking at the rest from beyond the establishment and dissolution of the monarchy, is in fact confessing that the
rest has not yet been entered.

---

[1] Cf. Jos. 21:43-45; I Kg. 8:56.

[2] "There Remains Still a Rest for the People of God," pp. 97-98.

[3] Ibid. See also, Ps. 95:11; 132:8, 14; Is. 66:1.

[4] Ibid., p. 99.

We must ask then if this rest is at all associated with the Sabbath. Such an association was indeed made subsequent to the time of the Old Testament literature, when ideas developed which associated the Sabbath with an eschatological situation at the end of the present world,[1] or with a present reality extending into the future and governed by the experience of the present.[2] Two themes combined to make up this eschatological or cosmic Sabbath: (1) the rest promised to Israel upon taking possession of her inheritance, and which she did not effectively receive; (2) the idea that the history of the world would reach a period (possibly 1,000 years) of Sabbath rest, corresponding to the rest following God's creation of the world. Is there any indication that these themes were combined in Old Testament literature?[3]

We have already seen how the rest was not accomplished during the monarchy. Deuteronomy confesses this silently, and the Chronicler

---

[1]Cf. Hermann L. Strack and Paul Billerbeck, Kommentar zum Neuen Testament aus Talmud und Midrasch (Munich: C. H. Beck'sche Verlagsbuchhandlung Oscar Beckm 1922-28), IV, Part II, 839-40. See also Rordorf, Sunday, pp. 48-51; Theodore Friedman, "The Sabbath: Anticipation of Redemption," Judaism, XVI (1967), 443-52.

[2]See Heb. 3-4. The argument is that in the beginning God rested at the conclusion of his creative work, and then made this same rest available to man, in particular to the people Israel. This is inferred in a negative way from Ps. 95:11. Israel forfeited her right to the rest in the wilderness, and did in fact not obtain it, when she entered the land under Joshua, for David said: "Today, when you hear his voice, do not harden your hearts" (Heb. 4:7). This "today" has now arrived, according to Hebrews, and so its author concludes: "So then, there remains a sabbath rest for the people of God. . . ."

[3]Cf. Jenni, Die theologische Bergründung, p. 19. "So bleibt doch noch ein anderen Gedanke als Bindegleid zwischen Sabbatfeier und Heilsgeschichte zu erwarten.
Dieser Gedanke scheint mir nun der Gedanke der מְנוּחָה, der 'Ruhe,' zu Sein."

admits that the rest appears and disappears. The contingency of the
rest is further emphasized in Ps. 95:8-11. As a result of her rebellion
in the wilderness, Yahweh had sworn that Israel should not enter his
rest; and we may understand the Psalmist to imply that this rest is,
therefore, still ahead of Israel. Ps. 132 is really a prayer to Yahweh
imploring him to find his rest in Zion "for David's sake." Thus we must
conclude that, although the rest for Israel is understood as having been
accomplished when Israel took the land in possession, nevertheless, it
was not really accomplished effectively at this occasion; and so it
became a part of Israel's hope, a thing of the future.

It is possible that the additional theme of Yahweh's rest in
Israel came about because of this situation. The two themes are
related, for Yahweh's resting place is Jerusalem, and his presence there
makes the city and the land secure (Ps. 132:11-18). Yet there is a
difference, for entering Yahweh's rest is a more personal experience
than merely living safely within the land.[1] There is no indication that
this rest was ever identified with the Sabbath in the Old Testament.
That identification comes about in subsequent times with help of the
creation Sabbath motif.

Finally, we may ask, if the rest accomplished at creation is
related to Israel's rest. We have argued that Gen. 2:1-3 is more
closely related to creation than to the Sabbath, although it certainly

---

[1] "'Sie sollen nicht kommen zu meiner Ruhe.'הׄוּחֻמ--das ist die
'Ruhe' des Landbesitzes, wie sie vor allem im deuteronomischen
Schrifttum hervortritt (Dt. 12:9). Aber es ist noch mehr: Jahwes Ruhe
--ein Heilsgut, das nicht material, sondern personal, nämlich in Gott
selbst seinen Grund und seine Mitte hat." Hans-Joachim Kraus, Psalmen,
BK, Vol. 15, 1-2 (Neukirchen-Vluyn: Neukirchener Verlag, 1960), p. 662.

has implications for the Sabbath institution as well as for the creation account, e.g., it is universal, was created at the beginning, and so it is fundamental to Israel. But its main function is to provide a particular conclusion of the creation account. The creator, having completed his work, is at rest. He no longer disturbs the elements, the sea has been put in its place, and he brings forth no new creatures. The whole creation is thus also at rest on the seventh day, a day characterized by completion, sanctity, and blessing. This rest is not, however, an eschatological Sabbath period in embryo; it is merely a seventh day. And yet it is not called "Sabbath," but it may have some typological overtones. Moreover, it has a cosmic outlook, related as it is to the creation of the world.

We have then several themes in the Old Testament which in Jewish and Christian times were united to form a universal and eschatological Sabbath period of rest. They are the rest which Israel enjoys, but mostly waits for, Yahweh's rest which is more personal and less materialistic than the rest in the land, and the creation Sabbath with its universal and cosmic overtones. It remained for Jewish and Christian writers to put these together and to interpret that universal and absolute rest for which the covenant community longed as a Sabbath.

The Sabbath and liberation

The second focus of the sabbatical year and the jubilee year has to do with man's liberation from poverty and bondage by restoring to him his formerly held possessions and freedom.[1]

---

[1] See above, p. 217.

The question before us is, whether the Sabbath entered Israel's understanding of liberation from debt and bondage. This would appear to be the case with the Sabbath law in Dt. 5:12-15 which reminds Israel that she had been liberated from servitude in Egypt. However, closer examination reveals that verse 15 does not, in fact, provide a reason for the Sabbath, but for the humanitarian attitudes towards servants which are involved in the Sabbath regulation in this commandment and in Ex. 23:12.[1] The command to remember the liberation from Egyptian slavery is repeatedly appended to humanitarian regulations in Deuteronomy.[2] Nevertheless, some relationship is implied between the humanitarian Sabbath law and the deliverance from slavery. Nielsen has concluded from this that the Sabbath commandment in Deuteronomy originated during the Babylonian captivity, when the people "even in impoverished Judaea, were lanquishing under the yoke of the Babylonian tyranny."[3] This judgment is, however, based primarily on the fact that Nielsen dates the commandment in Deuteronomy later than that in Exodus. But since we cannot be certain of this, the exilic dating of Dt. 5:12-15 is very doubtful.[4] To be sure, the captivity did give rise to thoughts about the deliverance through a new exodus from the house of bondage

---

[1]See above, pp. 130-134.

[2]Cf. Dt. 5:15; 15:15; 16:12; 24:18, 22.

[3]The Ten Commandments, p. 40.

[4]Nielsen argues (The Ten Commandments, pp. 40-41) that the simple structure of the commandment in Exodus has been lost in Deuteronomy, where particularly the "reason" for the Sabbath (vs. 15) is formulated in a far weaker fashion than in Ex. 20:11. This point is quite well taken, but even if the observation is correct, we still cannot conclude that Dt. 5:12-15 is exilic.

(II Isaiah), but Dt. 5:15 implies precisely that Israel is free, and
that as a consequence she ought to extend the privileges, which this
freedom entails, to her servants. The humanitarian concern in Dt. 5:
12-15 involves giving the laborers rest from their work, while the
deliverance from Egypt is to be remembered as Yahweh's act of giving
rest to Israel from her servitude (cf. Ex. 5:5). The Sabbath is
related to the redemptive acts of God in history, but it is the rest
rather than liberation accomplished thereby which Israel remembers and
shares on the Sabbath.

Liberation is an important theme in the sabbatical year (Ex. 21:
1-6; Dt. 15:12-18; Jer. 34:8-17), but the liberation of the servants on
this occasion is never thought of as a Sabbath for them the way the
land's release from human interference was understood as a Sabbath for
it (cf. Lev. 25:2-7).

There is one last theme which is possibly related to the above.
From early times the Sabbath appears to have been an occasion of joy
(Hos. 2:11; Lam. 2:6; Is. 58:13). This association of the Sabbath with
joy probably contributed, together with the responsibility placed upon
those whom Yahweh delivered from slavery, to the general concern with
the slaves and servants on the Sabbath. Deuteronomy maintains that for
such a festal occasion of joy to be accomplished all the members of the
community would have to participate.[1] The Sabbath as a frequently

----

[1]Cf. Jenni, Die theologische Begründung, p. 17. "Sicher sind es
nicht allgemeine Erwägungen über Menschenwürde und soziale Gerechtigkeit,
die den Deuteronomisten zu solcher Haltung bestimt haben. Es ist
vielmehr der Himweis auf die Heilsgeschichte, wie er sich gerade auch in
Dtn. 5, 15 findet, der hier weiterfürt. Darum soll der Israelit seinem
Sklaven die Ruhe gönnen, weil Gott sein Volk aus der Sklaveri in Ägypten

recurrent feast day is thus an important occasion on which servant and
landlord were equally free to rest and worship. Liberation, freedom,
and worship are intimately related in Israel. The Sabbath as an occasion for freedom is, therefore, one of the great social and economic
equalizers. The poor man does not get any poorer on it, the servant
does not serve any more, the rich does not get richer, the stranger and
the sojourner are no longer strangers and sojourners (Ex. 23:12; Is. 56:
3, 6), and the eunuch secures a memorial equal to that of the head of
the family (Is. 56:4-5). This equality of the Sabbath keepers cannot be
overruled by kings or nobles, for any special claims they may make for
themselves fall away on this day (Jer. 17:19-27; Neh. 13:15-22). Ezek.
46:2-5 says that the prince and the people shall alike worship at the
gate of the inner court which is opened on this special occasion.[1] It
is appropriate, therefore, that Deuteronomy should command the Sabbath
keepers to remember the exodus as the occasion when Yahweh delivered the
people from servitude and made it into one nation bound together in a
covenant.

---

in die Ruhe im gelobten Land gefügt hat. Durch diese gnädige Heilstat
hat Jahwe sich ein Heiliges Volk geschaffen. Dieses Gottesvolk, um
dessen Reinhaltung das Deuteronomiums kämpft, soll als Ganzes am Kultus
teilnehmen. Darum ist auch der Sklave nicht nur zur Teilnahme am Fest
berichtigt, sondern geradezu aufgefordert." Cf. von Rad, Das Gottesvolk im Deuteronomium.

[1]Cf. Vriezen, "Kalender en Sabbat," p. 189. Vriezen draws
attention to an old text from Gudea of Lagash published in Bruno
Meissner, Babylonien und Assyrien, II (Heidelberg: Carl Winters
Universitätsbuchhandlung, 1925), p. 94. "Während 7 Tage wurde kein
Getreide gemahlen, die Dienerin stellte sich gleich ihrer Herrin, der
Diener ging mit seinem Herr Seite an Seite."

The Sabbath and Torah

The involvement of the Sabbath in Israel's covenant relationship would naturally lead to an understanding of the Sabbath as law (Torah).[1] Law and covenant were closely associated in Israel from ancient times, as Alt and Mendenhall have pointed out,[2] in such a way that the law identified the stipulated code of conduct on which the covenant partners had agreed. Since the Sabbath came to be understood as a sign of the covenant, or a context within which the covenant relationship was realized, we would expect the Sabbath to enter the realm of Israelite law. Its presence in the Decalogue is, no doubt, an indication that the Sabbath law is covenant law.

Moreover, it has been pointed out frequently that the Sabbath as law entered a new development in connection with the deportation and cultic deprivation following the fall of Jerusalem in 586 B.C.[3] Stated simply, it is claimed that the Sabbath, which was formerly understood as a covenant law, now became interpreted in a legalistic way, i.e., the Sabbath laws now achieved a status in the community independent of the old covenant, or nearly so, because that covenant had been terminated with the destruction of the city and the temple. The veneration of the Sabbath by observing its regulations became an end in itself, an act of obedience which was considered pleasing to the deity. Observance of the

---

[1]See Gunnar Östblom, Tōrā in the Old Testament: A Semantic Study (Lund: Håkon Ohlssons Boktryckeri, 1945).

[2]See above, n. 3, pp. 151-52.

[3]For an evaluation of the historical development of the Sabbath traditions and interpretations relative to the exile, see below, pp. 235ff.

Sabbath laws, rather than genuine concern with the Sabbath, became a

sign of a religious man. To be sure, the Sabbath is not the only pre-

exilic institution which is thought to have developed in this way, but

it is one of the most important ones, it is claimed, because by its very

nature it was easily able to survive the termination of the Jerusalem

cult.[1]

Was the Sabbath really understood in this way in exilic and

postexilic literature? First of all, it is correct that Sabbath laws

---

[1]Since Wellhausen's reconstruction of Israel's history it has been customary to characterize the exilic and postexilic community as a community of the law. This has, no doubt, been furthered by the identification of the ideas of the emerging Judaism with the legalism of the Pauline law-grace polarity. It has been thought that the Sabbath lent itself to legalistic overtones, because the Sabbath institution was an important one in the exilic and postexilic communities. Cf. Noth, "The Laws in the Pentateuch," pp. 65ff. Skinner and Muilenburg, "Sabbath," p. 866, state: "None the less it is important to observe that, for whatever reason, a profound transformation of the character of the Sabbath emerges in the writings of the Exilic and post-exilic period. The obligation of rest, from being a necessary concomitant of acts of worship, or a means to a higher end, becomes an end in itself, a form of self-denial, pleasing to the Deity as an act of implicit obedience to His positive command." Similarly, Kornfeld, "Der Sabbat im Alten Testament," p. 25. "Während des babylonischen Exils 586-539 v. Chr., nachdem Jerusalem mit dem Tempel zerstört war, trat an Stelle der ehemaligen Kultfrömmigkeit die gewissenhafte Beobachtung der noch erfüllbaren Gesetze, welche zu ihrem Mittelpunkt jenes der Sabbatheiligung hatten." Recent studies, however, have questioned that law ever was severed from its moorings in the covenant in the Old Testament literature, and that law ever became simply an end in itself for the religious community. This is not to deny the important role of law in this period. The law was codified, interpreted, and canonized, but the fundamental role of law in the community's religious understanding had not changed much thereby. It was still a function of the covenant, although that became more difficult to define as a result of the catastrophe in 586 B.C. In the words of Zimmerli, "Die Auferweckung Israels aus dem Grab des babylonischen Exils in der Gestalt des Judentums enthält für die Gemeinde des alten Bundes die Zusage, dass Gott sein Bundesversprechen nicht zurückgenommen habe. Die Drohung des 'Gesetzes' wurde neu von der Zuwendung Gotten überleuchtet." In "Das Gesetz im Alten Testament," in Gottes Offenbarung: Gesammelte Aufsätze zum Alten Testament (Munich: Chr. Kaiser Verlag, 1963), p. 274. Cf. Hans-Joachim Kraus, "Zum

and concern with the Sabbath occur most frequently by far in the literature of this period. If we remember, however, that according to the
common view of the history of the Old Testament literature most of it
came into writing during this time, then the frequent mention of the
Sabbath becomes less unusual. Both the priestly writings and Ezekiel,
where the Sabbath appears so frequently, are interested in cultic and
religious matters, not just the Sabbath, but also in festivals, sacrifices, cultic functions, personnel, purity, et cetera. The reason for
the enormous preoccupation with the collection of laws of this type is
not that these laws suddenly were practiced scrupulously, but that the
religious leaders of this time came to understand the involvement of
Yahweh in every sphere of the community's life which, consequently, had
to be regulated accordingly.[1] The Sabbath was just one of these spheres.

Some of the Sabbath laws do seem, however, to indicate that the
Sabbath regulations occupied a unique role among the many other cultic
and religious laws. Ezek. 20:11-12 names the laws which Israel received
at Sinai as "my statutes, . . . my ordinances," and adds, "Moreover I
gave them my sabbaths" (cf. vss. 19-20). Here the Sabbath appears as an
addition to the law. By the observance of it man shall live (vs. 11),
but the Sabbath is also a sign between Yahweh and the people Israel that
he sanctifies them (vs. 12), that he is their God (vs. 20). The Sabbath
is of supreme importance, transcending that of the statutes and

---

Gesetzesverständnis der nachprophetischen Zeit," _Kairos_, XI (1969),
122-33.

[1]To attempt to demonstrate this view would take us too far
afield. For a recent discussion, see Ackroyd, _Exile and Restoration_,
p. 255.

ordinances, in the thought of Ezekiel, for it stands at the very core of
the covenant relationship. This view of the Sabbath is not spelled out,
but nevertheless implied in Neh. 9:13-14. Here again we are taken back
to Sinai: "And thou didst make known to them thy holy sabbath and command them commandments and statutes and a law by Moses thy servant."
The authors of both these passages must have believed the Sabbath to be
a unique part of the Sinai law. In both instances, the Sabbath is given
special attention; but what kind of attention, we might ask? Certainly
the Sabbath has not been made into a special law. There is no legalism
in the references to it, and it is not to be observed for its own sake;
rather, it is elevated above "mere law." Thus, by the law man lives,
but the Sabbath is a sign that Yahweh sanctifies Israel. The law was
given or commanded, but the Sabbath was made known to Israel. The
Sabbath is thus elevated for special attention, but it is not being put
deeper into the law; rather, it is being placed above it as a special
sign of the covenant people.

Now we have some references to the Sabbath which seem to imply
that the mere obedience of it would secure Yahweh's special favors for
Israel, notably Jer. 17:19-27 and Neh. 13:25-32. This is undeniable.
We must probably recognize, however, that both passages originated with
a specific breach of the Sabbath regulations, and that their aim was
primarily to correct this mistake of Sabbath desecration, not to secure
any special favor by doing so. This is implicit in Neh. 13, for Nehemiah is particularly angered by the people who make sport of the Sabbath.
The Jeremiah passage originated in a similar situation, but was subsequently reworked with a specific theological point in mind, namely, to

provide an explanation of the destruction of Jerusalem and Judah. We
may not conclude from these passages, however, that the Sabbath in
particular was responsible for the fortune of Jerusalem, or that it
attracted the attention of Nehemiah and the interpreters of Jeremiah in
a unique way. In Is. 58:13-14 we have no indication that a situation of
Sabbath breaking was directly responsible for the attention the Sabbath
receives here. It is simply stated that Sabbath observance will be
rewarded by Yahweh, and although it is not the only matter which is
rewarded, it is nevertheless tempting to think that the Sabbath occupied
an important role in the mind of the prophet; perhaps we are here close
to a legalistic view of the Sabbath. However, seen in its context, Is.
58:13 appears merely as one of the ways according to which a true fast
must be carried out. A real fast, says the prophet, involves a high
religious and social sensitivity. It has the double meaning of self-
denial and joy, two themes which are also present in verse 13. Is. 56:
2-6 also have a high view of the Sabbath. The man who keeps the Sabbath
is blessed. Its role is therefore central to the author of these verses,
although the eunuchs and aliens are, of course, also expected "to keep
the hand from doing evil." Sabbath keeping, though important, is not
the only and ultimate sign of true religion. Thus, in the subsequent
verses of Is. 56, Sabbath keeping is just one of the simple things which
will unite such unfortunates as eunuchs and foreigners to the covenant

---

[1]Nehemiah was as angered by the transgressions of other of
Israel's ancestral laws, as of the Sabbath laws. Cf. Neh. 13:23-27
(mixed marriages); Neh. 5:1-13 (taking mortgage). An illustration
similar to Jer. 17:19-22 is found in Jer. 34:8-22 where the observance,
or lack thereof, of the sabbatical year is related directly to the
Babylonian war and its consequences.

community.

Finally, the strict demands on Sabbath obedience have been pointed to as evidence of a legalistic view of the Sabbath. As we have already suggested, the most strictly formulated Sabbath laws are probably the earliest. In the late period, on the other hand, the community was quite unable to force the Sabbath laws upon itself, because it did not take them with great seriousness (cf. Jer. 17:19-27; Neh. 13:15-22; Ezek. 22:8, 26). Num. 15:32-36 probably indicates that the death penalty is no longer in effect, though the seriousness of Sabbath breaking is not diminished.

We can conclude, then, by saying that there is evidence in the exilic and postexilic literature that the Sabbath occupied an important place in the mind of religious leaders, priests and prophets alike, at the time of this literature. However, there is little or no reason to hold a legalistic view of Sabbath observance as reflected in this literature, although the accumulation of Sabbath laws might easily lead to just such a view; and, as we have noted, Is. 56; 58; Jer. 17; Neh. 13 come close to such a view. On the other hand, we saw in Ezekiel and Nehemiah that the Sabbath is released from association with the law, and that it becomes something more, namely, a sign of the covenant. On the whole, therefore, there is no impoverishment of the Sabbath in this literature, whereby the Sabbath is relegated to "mere law." There is, rather, an enrichment of it, involving the collection of old laws, formulation and reformulation of new laws, as well as creative theological reflection upon them.

IV. TRADITION AND HISTORY

The purpose of this section is to attempt to put some historical
order into the Sabbath traditions and their interpretation. We will
begin by examining the influence of the exile on them, then we shall
discuss the postexilic situation, and finally we shall turn to the pre-
exilic traditions. A concluding statement will sum up the matter in
historical sequence.

The Sabbath and the exile

It is often assumed that the destruction of Jerusalem and the
temple, and the consequent termination of the religious functions
whereby the covenant was actualized, led to the introduction of new
means of identifying the covenant people, notably circumcision and the
Sabbath. The latter, being fundamentally a period of time, could be
celebrated anywhere, even in captivity, without recourse to the temple
and the cultic functions of Jerusalem, so it is claimed. "With the loss
of the holy place the 'holy time' became more important."[1] It is quite

[1]Kraus, Worship in Israel, p. 87. See also von Rad, Genesis, p.
60. That the exile is generally thought to have exerted a radical
influence on the Sabbath is also supported by the views of many encyclo-
pedia and dictionary articles, which usually aim at expressing generally
accepted views. Thus Kutsch, "Sabbat," cols. 1259-60. "Im Exile wurde
wie die Beschneidung so auch die Beobachtung des S. in Abgrenzung
gegenüber der Umwelt zu einem Bekenntnisakt. Seiner gesteigerten
Bedeutung entspricht eine zunehmende Verschärfung des Ruhesgebotes. . .";
K. Steckel, "Sabbat," Calver Bibellexikon, ed by K. Gutbrod, R. Kucklich,
and Th. Schlatter (2nd ed.; Stuttgart: Calver Verlag, 1967), col. 1148:
"Erhöhte Bedeutung gewann er im Exil. Inmitten einer heidnischen
Umgebung wurde seine Beobachtung neben der Beschneidung zum Haupt-
kennzeichnen der Zugehörigkeit zur isr. Bundesgemeinde, vgl. Hes. 20:

obvious that the vast majority of references to the Sabbath occur in the exilic and postexilic literature, but then the greater part of the Old Testament literature is generally assigned to this period also, including the three large historical works (Dtr., P, Chr.), and most of the cultic legislation. If the exile thus saw increased literary activity, in the form both of history writing and of legal collections, it is not so startling that we should also find more references to the Sabbath during this period. However, the further assertion of a relationship between the Sabbath and the lost holy place is not thereby demonstrated. In fact, we find that the holy place (the temple) and the institutions associated with it retained an extraordinarily important place in the religious thought of the exiled community, and even served to relay ideas about the covenant. Although the temple, Zion, and the kingship were brought to an end,[1] or at least were not presently in existence, the cultic regulations and the religious significance associated with these institutions did not lose their impact on the thinking of the

12. Darum schärfte das nachexilische Gesetz seine Begehung der Gemeinde als heiligernste Pflicht ein. . . ." Cf. Morgenstern, "Sabbath," p. 139; Willy Rordorf, "Sabbat," Biblisch-Historisches Handwörterbuch, ed. by Bo Reicke and Leonhard Rost (Göttingen: Vandenhoeck & Ruprecht, 1966), III, 1634. An interesting illustration is provided by Skinner and Muilenburg who seem to have their better judgment overruled by this generally accepted view: "The truth is that in this, as in many other cases, the real turning-point was not the deportation of the people but the suppression of the popular ritual by Josiah's reformation. None the less it is important to observe that, for whatever reason, a profound transformation of the character of the Sabbath emerges in the writings of the Exilic and post-exilic period" ("Sabbath," p. 866).

[1] Jer. 41:5 indicates that some of the cultic functions were carried on after the temple was supposedly "destroyed."

exiled community.[1]

The Sabbath itself had received a serious wound with the destruction of Jerusalem and with the resultant exile, for we have seen that in pre-exilic times it was not just a day on which man and beast refrained from work, but also a religious feast celebrated at the cult centers which in late pre-exilic times were no doubt gradually absorbed in the central Jerusalem sanctuary.[2] If, therefore, the exilic emphasis of the Sabbath (holy time) is considered to have provided a substitute for the lost holy place, we should expect that the exilic Sabbath literature would emphasize abstinence from work on this day, since that is the most non-cultic aspect of the Sabbath traditions. But this is not what we find, certainly not in Ezekiel who, together with Deutero-Isaiah, was in especially close touch with the religious situation of the exiled

---

[1]The temple, for example, was under severe attack by some pre-exilic prophets, notably Jeremiah (ch. 7), but it played an important role in the thinking of the exilic prophet Ezekiel (chs. 40ff.). P was preoccupied with the sacral institutions of the temple and projected them into the early period of Israel's history. Zion and the Davidic kingship figure prominently in Deutero-Isaiah and the Deuteronomistic historian, as well as in the early postexilic prophets, viz., Zechariah. It is quite true that the destruction of the city and the temple, and the deportation of the people, brought Yahwism and the covenant under severe strain. Cf. Ronald E. Clements, God and Temple (Philadelphia: Fortress Press, 1965), pp. 100ff.; Janssen, Juda in der Exilzeit, pp. 58ff. However, it seems that this crisis was overcome precisely through a fervent hope in the restoration of temple, city, and the throne of David. The loss of the holy place gave rise to powerful efforts to restore it, not to make a substitute for it. For the relevant literature, see Ackroyd, Exile and Restoration.

[2]The reform movements under Hezekiah and Josiah had contributed to this development. At the time of Jeremiah the Jerusalem temple occupied a central role in the religious consciousness of the people (Jer. 7), although many local cult centers undoubtedly remained in use all the same (Jer. 2:20; 3:2, 23), perhaps providing outlets for the kind of religious activity which was not tolerated in Jerusalem.

community. Far from emphasizing the Sabbath as holy time, in distinction from the lost holy place, Ezekiel associates the Sabbath with holiness generally, and with the holy place and holy things in particular.[1] It is more accurate, therefore, to say that all spheres of holiness received renewed attention by Ezekiel. The same may be said about P. The frequent occurrences of Sabbath references here need not be attributed to the deprivation of the temple, at which occasion holy time is to have gained significance, for P is as interested in holy things, the sacred services, and the holy place, as in holy time. The main concern of the priestly legislation incorporated in P, as well as of Ezekiel, is with the holy versus the profane and the clean versus the unclean, i.e., with cultic matters.[2]

We can distinguish three areas in which the exile may have changed the role of the Sabbath in the life of the community. (1) The cultic aspects of Sabbath observance connected with the temple were of necessity terminated.[3] It has been suggested that the synagogue

---

[1]Ezek. 20:12 passim understands the Sabbath as an institution which was given by Yahweh to Israel and which she must keep holy; Ezek. 22:8 associates the Sabbath with holy things (presumably the sacred paraphernalia and function of the temple); Ezek. 23:38 speaks of a defiled sanctuary and a profaned Sabbath in the same breath; Ezek. 46: 1-6 describes the particular Sabbath celebrations in the restored temple.

[2]Cf. Joachim Begrich, "Die priesterliche Tora," in Gesammelte Studien zum Alten Testament (Munich: Chr. Kaiser Verlag, 1964), pp. 232-60, especially pp. 238ff.; Koch, Die Priesterschrift von Exodus 25 bis Leviticus 16, pp. 96ff. To P the salvation of Israel, says Koch, depends on a well ordered cult. Ackroyd, Exile and Restoration, pp. 91ff.

[3]We are here referring to the exiled community. It would be extremely interesting to know how the Sabbath functioned among the people who remained in Judah, and for whom 586 B.C. meant just another

institution originated in congregational practices during the exile, and that the Sabbath celebration was associated with them. However, we have no clear evidence of an exilic synagogue, nor of a communal Sabbath celebration during the exile, and any conclusions concerning such Sabbath activities are based on the simple and natural assumption that an isolated community living in a ghetto situation and refraining from working on the Sabbath would naturally seek fellowship on that day.[1] (2) It has furthermore been proposed that the Sabbath, together with the rite of circumcision, became a unique and identifying mark of the Israelite covenant community, one which unified and characterized the community at a time when deportation and death had done much to obliterate it.[2] There is not much evidence that it functioned as an external sign of the Jew, or was intended to do so, as it happened in later times.[3] Nevertheless, it did serve as a sign to the members of the community, whereby they indicated to each other that they had entered the covenant, but that was not for the information of the outsiders. It is

---

lost war. It is likely that they maintained some cultic activity at the ruined temple (see Jer. 41:5) and it is just possible that it was the descendants of these people whom Nehemiah observed working in the fields on the Sabbath (Neh. 13:15-16). The returned Jews who dwelt in Jerusalem were, of course, not more faithful to the Sabbath, as the same account indicates (Neh. 13:17).

[1]See above, pp. 147-48.

[2]Cf. Bentzen, Den israelitiske Sabbats Oprindelse og Historie, p. 61. "Its [the exilic comminity's] great interest in the cult, which is to keep Israel pure from heathen contamination, leads to the new great significance for the Sabbath as the sign of the Jew." Also Noth, "The Laws in the Pentateuch," p. 66; Ringgren, Israelite Religion, p. 298.

[3]In Hellenistic times, for example, circumcision became an external sign as well, and in the Christian era the Sabbath has functioned much the same way.

doubtful that it could possibly have been an effective external sign,
for the Babylonians themselves had in their calendar a system of
religious days which undoubtedly were in use at this time. According to
this calendar system, approximately every seventh day was set aside as a
day on which at least certain people in the community (king, prophet,
and physician) must not perform their normal functions. One additional
day, the šabattu day, may have coincided with one of the above mentioned
days, and its name is similar to that of the Hebrew šabbāt.[1] Although
these days did not occur exactly every seventh day, they did so by
approximation, and like the Sabbath they involved abstinence from work
and had some religious implications.[2] Consequently, the seventh-day
Sabbath was not such a remarkable institution in a Babylonian environment. (3) Finally and most importantly, it has been proposed that the
Sabbath began to occupy a greater role in Israel's theological thinking
during this period. The most significant results of this reflection on
the Sabbath are said to be (a) the association of the Sabbath and the
creation; (b) the function of the Sabbath as a sign and a covenant; (c)
the "legalization" of the Sabbath, i.e., the Sabbath became a matter of

---

[1]The relationship between the šabattu day and the ûmê lemnûti
has not been established, but by the time of the Assyrian reform calendar (seventh century B.C.) the latter occurred on the 7., 14., 21., 24.,
19. days of the month, and the šabattu day was identified with the day
of the full moon, or the 14.-15. day of the month, thus possibly coin-
ciding with one of the ûmê lemnûti. However, we have no evidence that
the latter were ever called šabattu. See above, n. 2, pp. 94-95.

[2]The work restrictions were placed on the king, the prophet, and
the physician in particular. We do not know if there was a general
diminishing of activity. See above, n. 1, pp. 96-97. But these days
were also evil days (ûmu lemnu) when one sought to pacify the anger of
the gods.

law as a result of the preoccupation with the collection and amplification of Torah during this period.

We shall now test the proposed new roles of the Sabbath in these
three areas by the traditions and interpretations we examined in section
III of this study. Our question is simply, what effects did the exile
and its accompanying events have on the Sabbath according to the Sabbath
literature of the exilic writers and the Sabbath traditions which they
adopted?[1]

In the first place, we learn very little about the religious
observances of the Sabbath. As we noted above, there is no indication
that Sabbath assemblies were held. At the same time, we learn that the
Sabbath was understood to be closely associated with the now lost
temple, and we may presume, therefore, that the exiles considered an
appropriate Sabbath celebration to be a temple celebration.[2] This also

---

[1]The postexilic literature should be used with caution, especially that which is dated in the late fifth century B.C. or later, for
we are here in an altogether different situation which may itself have
given rise to new practices on, and interpretations of, the Sabbath. To
the material written under the shadow of the exile we may count that
which is dated in the sixth century B.C. The reality of the destruction
of Jerusalem and the deportation (a generally known consequence of a
national defeat at the time) probably began to take shape at the end of
the seventh century B.C., and certainly by 605 B.C., when the neo-
Babylonian military power had been established in the west; and its
impact continued into the fifth century B.C., until with Ezra and
Nehemiah the center of Jewish religious thought was being re-established
in Jerusalem.

[2]This is implied in Lam. 2:6 and Ezek. 22:8, 26; 23:38. Also
the projected new temple will be the center of Sabbath observance (Ezek.
44:24; 45:17; 46:1-5). The priestly laws assume the same relationship
between Sabbath and temple. Lev. 23:3 identifies the Sabbath as a "holy
convocation" along with the other appointed feasts celebrated before the
priests at the holy place. Num. 28:9-10 and Ezek. 46:4-5 enumerate the
sacrifices to be brought on the Sabbath, and Ezek. 45:17 regulates that
the prince (the projected political leader) shall provide the

means that a proper Sabbath should be celebrated as a day of joy and festivity.[1] It did, of course, remain a day (every seventh) on which no work was allowed,[2] and it is only natural to ask what the community did on this day, and to suggest that it assembled in homes and perhaps elsewhere for religious services of some kind.

Now it would indeed be a stroke of ingenuity if the exiled community could have transformed this Sabbath into a day of sheer holy time and, moreover, have made it into one of the main signs of the community's covenant relationship; but the evidence for such a view of the Sabbath is weakened by the fact that both P and Ezekiel associate this Sabbath with the holy temple. It is the temple Sabbath with its holy time, abstention from work, and sacred offerings which became a sign for Israel. We may say that the Sabbath was exiled with the people, and like them it had to adjust to new circumstances; but it did not lose its attachment to Jerusalem.[3]

The second area in which the Sabbath supposedly gained new

---

offerings. Finally, Ezek. 46:2-5 stipulate the mode of the execution of these offerings in the temple structure.

[1]See above, pp. 124-25. Cf. Morgenstern, "Sabbath," p. 139.

[2]Jer. 17:19-27; Is. 58:13; Ex. 31:14-15.

[3]This does not mean that the Sabbath was not celebrated in a non-cultic fashion in Babylonia; it probably was, as were undoubtedly some of the other festal occasions during the year. See above, pp. 147-48. Bentzen speaks of a hjemmesabbat (home Sabbath) on which neighbors and friends would gather in someone's home for celebration or study or worship (Den israelitiske Sabbats Oprindelse og Historie, p. 62). We may also assume that many exiles abandoned Sabbath observance and dissociated themselves from their religious traditions generally. However, we cannot be certain of this. We are only informed about the attitude of the relatively few among them who returned, and they were probably the poorest and most pious.

significance is more difficult to evaluate. It is claimed that circumcision and the Sabbath became identifying marks of the covenant community. Here we must remember that both P (Ex. 31:13, 17) and Ezekiel (Ezek. 20:12, 20) call the Sabbath a sign, not of a true Israelite, or of an Israelite in exile, but of the covenant relationship. We have no indication that the Sabbath was intended to identify the exiles in a foreign land in which a seventh-day Sabbath was after all not a very suitable identifying mark, as we have suggested above.

This leaves us with the third area in which we may detect an influence of the exile on the Sabbath. The exile, it has been proposed, might have led Israel to reflect upon the Sabbath. What kind of reflection do we find?

First, there is the association of the Sabbath and creation which appears only in P (Gen. 2:1-3; Ex. 20:11; 31:17). We have proposed that this is very likely a pre-exilic tradition, but the fact remains that it appears in the creation account in P and in the Sabbath laws which conclude the announcement of the construction of the tabernacle and which precede the account of its erection, also in P. It has been proposed that the creation Sabbath appears in literature from the exilic period, because Israel (P) learned about creation with a concluding rest from the Babylonians,[1] or because a reason was needed for the new prominence achieved by the Sabbath institution at this time,[2] but neither of these explanations is satisfactory. Firstly, there is really

---

[1]For the relevant material, see above, pp. 174-82.

[2]See above, n. 1, p. 65.

no evidence that Israel borrowed religious and intellectual ideas
extensively from their captors,[1] and secondly, because the creation
Sabbath motif is in fact not used as part of, or support for, a new
Sabbath program.[2] What then can account for the presence of this motif
in the exilic literature? Does it depend on a pre-exilic tradition?

The fourth commandment (Ex. 20:8-11) is probably pre-exilic, and
it makes use of the creation Sabbath motif.[3] Ex. 31:17 seems to use the

---

[1]This applies particularly to the segment of the exiles which
was responsible for creatively preserving their religious heritage.
There may have been more borrowing on the part of Israel in the Assyrian
period through the royal cult in Jerusalem. It seems, however, that the
exile caused Israel to be separate from other nations and not to adopt
their ideas extensively. Cf. G. Ernest Wright, Biblical Archaeology
(2nd rev. ed.; Philadelphia: Westminster Press, 1962), p. 45.

[2]Gen. 2:1-3 completely misses the opportunity to enforce the
weekly Sabbath institution among men. Ex. 20:11 gives a reason for the
six-seven day work schedule, but does not trace the origin of the Sabbath to the creation week. Ex. 31:17 comes perhaps closest to tracing
the weekly Sabbath to the creation Sabbath, but its appearance here
seems to be more conventional than creative, perhaps patterned after the
structure of Ex. 20:8-11.

[3]There are several reasons for holding this position. (1) Ex.
20:8-11 must stand in some kind of relation to Dt. 5:12-15 which, as
part of D, must be pre-exilic. (2) Nielsen (The Ten Commandments, pp.
39-41) has argued that Dt. 5:12-15 depend structurally upon Ex. 20:9-11
and, therefore, must be younger. Granted that it is much easier to
establish a relationship between the two than to determine the direction
of this relationship, it is nevertheless correctly observed that Dt. 5:
12-15 contain expansions and that its "reason" for the Sabbath is less
forceful than the one in Ex. 20:8-11, and is clearly of Deuteronomic
provenance. Nielsen further maintains that the explicatory ʿal-kēn
(therefore), Dt. 5:15b, is modelled upon Ex. 20:11, since it functions
so much more effectively in the latter than in the former case. (3) The
fourth commandment in both Exodus and Deuteronomy is very artistically
structured, a fact which suggests that Ex. 20:11 is not merely an
addition to a previously composed shorter law. Rather, all three verses
(vss. 8-11) form a tightly knit unit. See above, pp. 169-77. There are
indications which lead us to believe that P was not responsible for this
composition. (a) The introductory command begins with zākôr (remember),
while every instance of this type of Sabbath law in P has šāmôr (keep,
observe), e.g., Ex. 31:13, 14, 16; Lev. 19:3, 30; 26:2. (b) Ex. 31:17,

same motif very casually, and yet with the intention of providing a climax to a series of Sabbath regulations. From these occurrences of the motif we have concluded that the creation Sabbath is a pre-exilic tradition which was at the disposal of P. It was the creation account framed by the seven-day scheme with which P began his history. Hereby something new and distinctive was said about the beginning of the world. The creator in this account did not rest (enter an _otiositas_), but ceased to create, and subsequently blessed and hallowed the day on which this task was completed. Such a picture of creation is only remotely related to what Israel might have learned in captivity; and we have suggested that she did in fact not learn it there, but knew it prior to the exile. At the same time, the creation Sabbath is not unrelated to the weekly Sabbath, as Ex. 20:11; 31:17 emphasize. On the contrary, it suggests that the Sabbath is a universal institution which preceded Israel herself, and it also adds a personal touch to Israel's view of Yahweh who stopped his work and was refreshed. We suspect, therefore, that P's interest in the creation Sabbath tradition is partly a rebuttal of certain motifs in the Babylonian creation accounts, and partly an emphasis on the importance and universal quality of the Sabbath institution. The

which undoubtedly comes from P, stands closer to Gen. 2:1-3 (P) than to Ex. 20:11, e.g., it operates with a two-part cosmos, and it uses the verb šbt. (c) The second part of the fourth commandment ("Six days you shall labor, and do all your work") differs slightly from the standard P formulations of the same law ("Six days shall work be done") and reminds one a little of the old law in Ex. 34:21. See above, n. 2, pp. 168-69. These pointers seem to indicate that Ex. 20:8-11, including the creation Sabbath motif, is pre-exilic, and earlier than the parallel material in P. This does not exclude the possibility that priestly circles were responsible for the fourth commandment in its present form, but it does indicate that the content of the commandment was not formulated by P, but is earlier.

creation Sabbath was not a new concept of the exiled community, which was eagerly preserving, restoring, and re-evaluating its traditions, but not creating new ones.

A second characteristic of exilic Sabbath literature is the characterization of the Sabbath as a sign and a covenant (Ex. 31:13, 16, 17; Ezek. 20:12, 20). It also occurs indirectly, we noted, in several other passages, viz., Jer. 17:19-26; Is. 56:2-6; 58:13. This appears to be a characterization of the Sabbath which should be attributed directly to the exile, for we do not find the Sabbath used this way in pre-exilic texts. The same theme may be detected in Lev. 25:34-35, 43; II Chr. 36:21 which indicate that the proper relationship between Israel and her land involves the observance of the sabbatical year, the land's Sabbath. Only one pre-exilic passage, Dt. 5:14-15, is able somehow to associate the Sabbath and Israel's covenant; but this may be more accidental than real.[1] About the time of the exile Israel thus began to think about the Sabbath in a new way. How can we account for this?

The answer which is most often given is that the circumstances of the exile brought the Sabbath institution to prominence, while at the same time, law (Torah) became the most forceful institution of the exiled religious community.[2] These two developments contributed to the

---

[1] We have suggested that the reference to Yahweh's deliverance (Dt. 5:15) is primarily related to the humanitarian expansion in vs. 14b and only secondarily to the Sabbath command itself. In other words, the sequence of thought in Dt. 5:12-15 is: Sabbath institution, humanitarian concern, exodus deliverance, and not Sabbath institution, exodus deliverance, humanitarian concern. See above, p. 134.

[2] This view is based largely on the opinion that the postexilic community and later Judaism centered all religious thinking and functions around Torah, particularly in the sense that a broken covenant

strict Sabbath regulations and to the understanding of Sabbath keeping
as a guarantee of the covenant.

This answer must, however, remain an undemonstrated hypothesis.
We have agreed that the exilic situation was not particularly congenial
to Sabbath keeping, at least not in the form whereby exilic writers conceived of genuine Sabbath keeping. There can be no doubt, however, that
some type of Sabbath observance was maintained, undoubtedly abstention
from work and perhaps some congregational activity. But the religious
leaders (prophet, priest, and historian) in the exile were not advocat-
ing a new "bloodless" cult suited for the exilic situation. They were
fervently looking for a return and for the restoration of Jerusalem and
the temple with all its cultic activities. The religious institutions
which were maintained in the exile must thus have been considered incom-
plete and temporary, and not at all ideal to bring even the Sabbath to
prominence.

As for the law (Torah), it is not easy to determine its role in
the community precisely. There was a great interest in the law at this
time,[1] but we must agree with Ackroyd that such an interest need not

---

relationship could be restored by a meticulous observance of Torah. But
this view is foreign to the late Old Testament literature. The most
personal statements about man's relationship to God (Job, Ecclesiastes,
and even the Psalms) make no mention of this. "There is no basis in the
Old Testament for the well-known idea which Lutheranism exalted to
almost canonical status, that Israel was compelled by God's law to an
ever greater zeal for the law. . . ." Gerhard von Rad, Old Testament
Theology, Vol. II: The Theology of Israel's Prophetic Traditions, trans.
by D. M. G. Stalker (New York: Harper & Row, Publishers, 1965), p. 405.

[1]The formulation of D and H, as well as the collection of
priestly laws, testify to this.

imply legalism.[1] We have further noted that the exilic Sabbath literature is not legalistic in its treatment of the Sabbath laws. On the
contrary, we saw that the Sabbath was elevated above "mere law" as a
special institution.[2] It is a short step from this position to some
sort of legalistic view of it, a step which Is. 56:2-6; 58:13 are perhaps nearly stumbling into, though not necessarily. It has not happened
in the postexilic passage, Neh. 13:15-22, for here we have merely one
aspect of Nehemiah's reform, and the Sabbath law is simply meeting a
particular instance of Sabbath breaking.[3] Jer. 17:19-26, which is
undoubtedly earlier than Neh. 13, did also, we have suggested, originate
in a specific situation in which the Sabbath was disregarded. The
elaboration of its fairly simple Sabbath command (vss. 21-22) comes very
close to a suggestion that Sabbath keeping is merely a function of the
greater concern with Israel's national survival, so that the Sabbath has
been reduced to a concern with law for the sake of Israel's salvation.
But in the process the Sabbath is cut loose from its original setting
and is used merely as a springboard to introduce a favorite theme. That
this could happen does, of course, testify to the impact of the Sabbath
on the writer of this passage. However, we cannot conclude from the

---

[1]_Exile and Restoration_, p. 155. The primary function of law in
the understanding of the exilic community was to indicate that there is
no aspect of life which lies outside the control of God, not that it
provided a way of coming to terms with God.

[2]See above, pp. 229-34.

[3]I.e., the question reflected in Neh. 13:15-22 is not, how shall
Israel obey the Sabbath law? But rather, what shall be done about the
current Sabbath breaking? The situation is concerned with Sabbath
keeping, not Sabbath legislation.

literature in question that the exilic period reduced the Sabbath to "mere law," and at the same time elevated law to the foremost religious institution of the community. Nevertheless, we cannot deny that the Sabbath received much attention and reached prominence in the exilic literature. How can this be accounted for?

The answer to this question may well be found in hints made by recent studies of the exile and the Sabbath, namely, that the so-called exilic Sabbath is really pre-exilic.[1] Unfortunately, we have little or no direct evidence; but there are perhaps a few pointers in this direction. (1) Ezek. 20:11-12 understands the giving of the Sabbath as something special which happened at Sinai, in addition to the giving of the law. If one can believe the setting of the chapter, the real exile beginning in 586 B.C. had not yet taken place and could, therefore, not have contributed to the transformation of the Sabbath. (2) We have noted that the Sabbath laws in P (Ex. 31:12-17; 35:2-3; Lev. 19:3, 30; 23:3; 26:2) follow traditional patterns which date back into pre-exilic times. (3) Dt. 5:12-15 comes from this same period, and so does possibly also Ex. 20:8-11. (4) The creation Sabbath, we have suggested, is probably also a pre-exilic tradition.

If this renewed interest in the Sabbath can be traced back into pre-exilic times, we must ask if there is any specific period in which this could have happened. The answer must of necessity be in the form of an intelligent guess; but it does seem that the Assyrian period, more precisely the period from the reign of Hezekiah to that of Josiah, would

---

[1]Cf. Ackroyd, Exile and Restoration, pp. 85ff.; Skinner and Muilenburg, "Sabbath," p. 866.

offer a good setting for what we may call the creative period of the Old Testament Sabbath traditions. (1) It was a time of close contact with the Mesopotamian powers, a contact whose influences were being curtailed by the reform movements of Hezekiah and Josiah. (2) It was a time when Israel was at once losing and struggling for her identity politically, religiously, and culturally.[1] (3) Deuteronomy was an attempt to find this identity by reaching back into the Mosaic age and resurrecting old traditions. H attempted to restore long forgotten ethical and cultic laws. P sought to rewrite the history of Israel around the covenant with Abraham, and to collect Israel's legal traditions. (4) The many Sabbath laws in P and H also fit into this general period. Some of them are traditional laws preserved intact, or expanded to meet the present situation. The commands to observe the Sabbath and to keep it holy are suitable in a time when the institution suffered general neglect. The identification of the seventh day as a holy Sabbath, solemn rest, holy to Yahweh, and a holy convocation would also be suitable in a time when Yahwism was being rescued from severe attacks which were mediated largely

---

[1] See II Kg. 16:10-20. A vassal of the Assyrian king had to pay tribute both to the king and to his gods. Cf. II Chr. 28:23. II Kg. 21 gives the impression that King Manasseh was prepared to extend his tribute to his Assyrian overlord, by undertaking religious practices of Assyrian orientation, beyond what his political obligations called for. Many of the religious innovations may not have represented conscious deviations from the national religion on the part of the innovator, despite the opinions of Deuteronomy and the prophets to the contrary. Nevertheless, the impact of Assyrian religion and the occult were no doubt great under the reign of Manasseh. Cf. John Bright, A History of Israel (Philadelphia: Westminster Press, 1959), p. 290. It is worth noting also that Assyria was capable of exerting other than sheer political and military influence at this time. The great Ashurbanipal library suggests that the Assyrian rulers were interested in the literary arts and religion.

through foreign cultic influences. In short, the emphasis on the Sabbath should be understood as one reaction against foreign cultic and religious influences. (5) There was also prophetic activity at this time. Nahum, speaking sometime before 612 B.C., announced: "Behold, on the mountains the feet of him who brings good tidings, who proclaims peace! Keep your feasts, O Judah, fulfill your vows, for never again shall the wicked come against you."[1] Zephaniah, who probably spoke a few years earlier,[2] found Israel totally corrupt, because she had accepted foreign cult objects and practices.[3]

In a situation like this we can imagine how the Sabbath could be taken up for new and vigorous consideration. It was a weekly feast day celebrated at the temple, not a yearly festival. That in itself made it unique. As providing a framework of the creation account, it had produced a distinctly Israelite creation narrative, quite different from the undoubtedly well known Babylonian varieties. Because of the practice of congregating at the temple on this day, the Sabbath provided unique opportunities for cementing Israel as a distinct and tightly knit community. The humanitarian concerns and the salvation historical associations connected with it furthered this objective. It might have been one of the few, perhaps the only, uniquely Israelite feast in this

---

[1]Nah. 1:15.

[2]The book of Zephaniah is generally placed before the Josianic reform, because it seems to portray an unreformed situation in Judah. Cf. Eissfeldt, Introduction, p. 424; Fohrer, Introduction, p. 456. Later dates have been suggested, but they have not been generally accepted. Cf. J. P. Hyatt, "The Date and Background of Zephaniah," JNES, VII (1948), 25-29; D. L. Williams, "The Date of Zephaniah," JBL, LXXXII (1963), 77-88.

[3]Zeph. 1:4-6.

period. We know that the passover was not celebrated regularly,[1] and
that there were numerous occasions for engaging in non-Israelite worship
at the time.[2] We know that the Sabbath received attention and expansions in D, and perhaps also in Ex. 20, at this time. It is possible
that Jer. 17:19-27 depends on a prophetic oracle about the Sabbath from
this time, and we know that Ezekiel could hold a high view of the Sabbath from the beginning of the exile. It is, therefore, quite possible
that priestly and Levitical circles, like those who promoted the
Deuteronomic material, gave instruction in Sabbath observance, exhorted
the laity to keep it, and have found this institution of great importance for the community whose identity and self-understanding as a
covenant community had been under such a severe strain in this period,
and which was now seeing the foreboding of a new and worse disaster.
The renewed interest in the Sabbath which we find in exilic literature
is, therefore, likely to have begun in the late pre-exilic reaction to
non-Israelite, especially Assyrian, religious and cultic influences, a
reaction which was epitomized in the Deuteronomic reform. There just
does not seem to be enough reason, nor evidence, for assuming that all
this interest in the Sabbath which we find reflected in P and Ezekiel
could have arisen during the captivity.

This position should not lead us to minimize the importance
attributed to the Sabbath by the exiles. It merely suggests that the

---

[1]II Kg. 23:21-23.

[2]II Kg. 21 reports the existence of high places, altars,
ᵓasherôth, worship of heavenly bodies, child sacrifice, mediums,
wizards. Some of these were available in the temple compound. Cf.
Ezek. 8:7-18; II Kg. 16:10-20.

creative period for the Sabbath traditions is pre-exilic. Ezekiel
depends on these traditions, and so does P with little or no modification introduced.[1] Among these traditions we would count the various
forms of Sabbath laws, the creation Sabbath, and the association of
Sabbath and covenant. The Deuteronomistic historian and Deutero-Isaiah,
on the other hand, make no use of the Sabbath traditions, although both
were highly creative theologians and addressed the theological problems
of the exiled community. The Sabbath traditions, we believe, were
important to the exiled community, but not uniquely so. This is also
the impression we get from Is. 56:2-6, where the concern with the Sabbath is surpassed by the concern with some practical problems of the
religious community. Only Is. 58:13 and Jer. 17:19-27 indicate a somewhat distinct preoccupation with the institution, but not a fanatical
one, by a long mile.[2]

All told, the exile seems to have provided an occasion for the
pre-exilic Sabbath traditions and interpretations to solidify. As the

---

[1]Exceptions to this may be found in Gen. 2:1-3 and Ex. 16:22-30.
Though the creation Sabbath is probably older than P, we do not know
what form it took in the creation account. In Ex. 20:11; 31:17 it is
already released from the creation and put to use in the Sabbath legislation. It is possible that P used the creation Sabbath motif
creatively in Gen. 2, but unfortunately we cannot distinguish material
behind the present account. The manna story is radically reworked by P,
although, as we have noted, it employs traditional Sabbath material.

[2]Is. 58:13 is really opposing the commonly accepted cultic and
religious views of the Sabbath. Assuming as we have done that Is. 58:
13 is an indigenous part of the chapter as a whole, we must understand
the prophet to denounce any casual religious observances with no moral
or spiritual content. He is appealing to his listeners to do what they
have not been doing, namely, take the Sabbath seriously as Yahweh's day
and as a day of joy.

exile progressed and the restoration began, other aspects of Israelite
religion began to claim the attention of the community, and the Sabbath
reverted to its earlier role as a temple feast, a religious institution
which some people found it inconvenient to observe. But it was no
longer a creative force in the religious understanding of the community,
as it must have been in the late seventh century B.C. and perhaps even
earlier.

The postexilic Sabbath

We must now look at the community of the fifth century B.C.
which moved out from under the dark cloud of the exile only to face far
more threatening situations of social and political disarray, economic
disaster, and spiritual lethargy.[1] The sources, as far as the Sabbath
question is concerned, are primarily Nehemiah and the Chronicler. Of
course, the community also had access to the Sabbath literature in the
Pentateuch, especially the numerous priestly materials. However, we
have argued that the historical situation responsible for the latter is
the late pre-exilic and the exilic time, and it is likely that the community of the latter part of the fifth century paid little attention to
it. This is certainly the impression we get from the Nehemiah references.
Is. 56; 58; Jer. 17 probably fit better into the transition period
between the exile and the restoration or, in the case of Jer. 17, perhaps in the exilic situation.

The account in Neh. 13 portrays a community which has no concern

----

[1]Cf. Jacob M. Myers, "The Kerygma of the Chronicler," _Interpre-
tation_, XX (1966), 261.

for the Sabbath. The farmers in Judah who openly worked on the Sabbath may well be Judeans who had not been in Babylon, but they must be Jews whom Nehemiah expected to keep the Sabbath, for he had observed them closely, and the passage describes their Sabbath breaking in detail. Moreover, they are distinguished from the Tyrian tradesmen who are identified as foreigners, whether or not they actually resided in Judah. It is remarkable that these farmers are not even blamed for their activities. Either Nehemiah considered them outside his jurisdiction, or he had given up their case. He only warns them against selling their crop and wares in Jerusalem on the Sabbath. The other guilty party consisted of the nobles of Judah and Jerusalem, probably rulers who were responsible for the actions of the community at large by virtue of their social and political position. They accepted the situation, probably even participated in Sabbath breaking, and they were not prepared to correct it. In fact, Sabbath breaking was so accepted in Jerusalem that the traders did not even take Nehemiah seriously when he closed the city gate on the Sabbath, but continued their business outside the wall. It took military force to convince all parties that Nehemiah meant for the Sabbath to be observed.

At the same time we are given to believe that the community was acquainted with the Sabbath and had access to Sabbath traditions. Neh. 10:31 refers to a situation similar, or identical, to the one we find in Neh. 13. We have not been able to determine whether it preceded or followed chapter 13 historically, but it knows Sabbath keeping to be one of the religious obligations of the covenant people. Neh. 9:13-14 reminds us of Ezek. 20:12-13. The Sabbath is made known at Sinai in addition to the giving of the law, and thus it plays a specific role in the history of the covenant people.

In the light of the fact that the Sabbath traditions and the common Sabbath regulations must have been known to the community, its total neglect of the institution in Neh. 13 suggests that the Sabbath was not an integral part of the fifth century B.C. Judean community.

This picture of the Sabbath is contradicted by the Chronicler for whom it plays an important role in the temple services and serves to explain the destruction of the land in connection with the captivity (II Chr. 36:21). Now it is generally agreed today that although the Chronicler has been shown to be historically accurate and informative on many points,[1] the main importance of his writings lies in their theological content, their message.[2] This message is directed to the community living around 400 B.C. in Judah, and it appears to have at least two foci: (1) an affirmation of the central role of the Davidic dynasty for the survival of the nation; (2) a concern with cultic matters and with the purity of the community.[3]

The several references to the Sabbath, except one (II Chr. 36:21), fall under (2) above. There is no indication, however, that the

---

[1]Myers summarizes as follows: "He did not deliberately distort history to fit his purpose; he employed those phrases that were apropos and, at numerous points, he manifestly relied on sources sometimes more accurate than those used by the Deuteronomist." I Chronicles, p. xxx. Several studies supporting this conclusion are listed in the bibliography of Myers, I Chronicles, pp. xciff.

[2]Cf. Peter R. Ackroyd, "History and Theology in the Writings of the Chronicler," CThM, XXXVIII (1967), 501-515; Myers, "The Kerygma of the Chronicler," pp. 259-73; Robert North, "Theology of the Chronicler," JBL, LXXXII (1963), 369-81.

[3]Cf. Myers, "The Kerygma of the Chronicler," pp. 262ff.

Sabbath should be observed in order that the purity of the community may be preserved, or that the covenant may be established, or that the laborers may have rest. It always appears simply as a day on which cultic activity is taking place.[1] In all these occurrences the Sabbath is taken for granted and mentioned rather incidentally. Thus it is mentioned in connection with other feast days, and its services are recounted in connection with other cultic functions placed upon the temple personnel, notably the Levites whom the Chronicler favors. Because of this situation we cannot draw any conclusions as to the role of the Sabbath among the population generally, and we have no reason to believe that it was taken more seriously than in Neh. 13. Whether or not the cultic role of the Sabbath in Chronicles is founded on real or ideal practices is not clear, but they may be real. That the Levites in particular were responsible for the proper observance of the Sabbath is also implied in Neh. 15:22.

We have only one illustration of any kind of theological reflection on the Sabbath by the Chronicler, namely, II Chr. 36:21. Here the exile having lasted seventy years is interpreted as one long Sabbath for the land, making up for lost sabbatical years during a 490 year period. We have found this theme also in Lev. 26, but without the seventy year motif. Apparently this interpretation of the Sabbath was current in exilic and postexilic times. We have suggested that it may be an outcome of the understanding of the Sabbath as a covenant. The sabbatical

---

[1]The bread was prepared for the tables (I Chr. 9:32). The levitical temple singers were busy on this day (I Chr. 23:30-31). Special offerings were presented (II Chr. 2:4; 8:13; 31:3).

year functions, according to the Chronicler's interpretation, as the land's covenant with Israel, and it holds redemptive powers for the land and its occupants. The exile, as one long accumulated sabbatical year, is thus explained as a punishment for the people, but a redemption for the land with the Sabbath as the concept of mediation. There is a relationship here between the Sabbatical year and the Sabbath, as also Jer. 17:19-27 and Neh. 13:15-22 may imply, but it is not developed. The exile did not become a Sabbath with redemptive powers for the community, nor did the restoration from captivity. We suspect that the Chronicler here has combined the seventy year theme from Jeremiah and the sabbatical year as discussed in Lev. 26, in an effort to understand the captivity and the destruction of the land.

The postexilic literature does not demonstrate a community so preoccupied with the Sabbath as the postexilic community is sometimes accused of being.[1] There is evidence of general disrespect for the Sabbath in Nehemiah, while the Chronicler takes it for granted as one of the common temple feast days. It does not appear in the wisdom literature, perhaps because the Sabbath had become largely a cultic institution with which the wisdom literature was not concerned, nor is it present in the postexilic prophets and the Psalms. We must assume, however, that the Sabbath institution eventually came to play a very important part in

---

[1] It is generally assumed that the prominence gained by the Sabbath during the exile continued and was solidified in postexilic times and into the period of the developing Judaism. The fact that so little is made of it in fifth and fourth century literature is attributed to the fact that the Sabbath was generally respected and observed. Cf. Bentzen, Den israelitiske Sabbats Oprindelse og Historie, p. 81.

Jewish life in subsequent times. It appears as such in Maccabean literature.[1] However, the creative period of the Biblical Sabbath traditions
had gone, and had given place to an institution of primarily cultic
orientation although work was prohibited on it. For illustrations of
strict Sabbath observance and renewed theological preoccupation with it,
we must look beyond the Old Testament literature.

The pre-exilic Sabbath

We have already suggested that the great preoccupation with the
Sabbath in exilic literature, notably in P, had its beginning in pre-
exilic times and was part of the general reaction against foreign
influences on Israelite religious and cultic life during the Assyrian
period. The Sabbath, however, was in existence long before this time;
in fact, it had probably gone through a history of its own in pre-exilic
times. Unfortunately, the textual evidence is very scarce.

We have already proposed that Levitical and priestly circles
were responsible for resurrecting, reformulating, and reinterpreting the
Sabbath traditions before the exile. It was from the fund of traditions
preserved by these circles that H, Ezekiel, and P drew their Sabbath
material. In it we find commands to keep the Sabbath, prohibitions of
work on it, the Sabbath formula, characterization of the seventh day as
Yahweh's day, the creation Sabbath, and the Sabbath as a sign and a
covenant.

Moving back, we have three texts from the latter part of the
eighth century which describe the Sabbath as a feast day in the temple

---

[1]Cf. I Macc. 2:29-41.

(Hos. 2:11; Am. 8:5; Is. 1:13). Here the Sabbath appears as a well
established religious feast day which, along with other festivals, is so
closely associated with both the southern and the northern states that
the prophets can proclaim Yahweh's rejection of Israel by announcing the
termination of these sacred seasons. The Sabbath is in no way singled
out, however, as representing Israelite religion, piety, or the covenant
in particular. It is but one among other days of celebration. Am. 8:5
suggests that although the Sabbath was a standard part of Israel's
religious life, and a generally accepted one, there was impatience with
its prohibitions against work. This then must have been an integral
feature of the Sabbath. The regulations for cessation of work on the
seventh day, though not stated in these passages, must have been known
before, perhaps in the form of the Sabbath laws we find in Ex. 20:9-10;
23:12; 34:21. We do not know, unfortunately, what the eighth century
prophets would have considered appropriate Sabbath keeping. They were
clearly not concerned with restoring the Sabbath, but with correcting
evil carried out on it, or in conjunction with it. Hos. 2:11 and Is.
1:13 seem to indicate that the Sabbath was a joyous and festal occasion,
celebrated without moral and religious responsibility. Is. 1:13
announces that as such the Sabbath is of no interest to Yahweh, and Hos.
2:11 threatens that Yahweh will remove the Sabbath celebrations from
Israel. There is no attempt made to reinterpret the Sabbath in humanitarian or ethical terms. Am. 8:5 comes closest to this, but does not
carry it out. It seems that the Sabbath has solidified as a cultic
institution with which the concerns of eighth century prophecy have very
little, if anything, in common.

A few more Sabbath texts surface in the mid-ninth century (II Kg. 4:23; 11:4-12), but they are not very informative. We may conclude from the latter that the Sabbath was a temple festival on which large crowds gathered in the temple courts, very much the way Is. 1:13 pictures the occasion. II Kg. 4:23 hints that Sabbath keeping in communities which were either too isolated to make a temple visit possible, or which simply did not worship at the temple, involved visiting a seer and releasing laborer and beast from work.

The original manna story is attributed to JE and thus was in existence during the early part of the monarchy. We have seen that it is very difficult to separate the early parts of Ex. 16:22-30 from the later expansions; but if we begin with the introduction to the old part of the account (vss. 4-5), we find the Sabbath understood particularly in terms of the six-seven-day scheme. The people are commanded to gather a day's portion of food daily for six days, except on the sixth day, when they will gather a double portion to last for two days. The concluding verses, probably also from the old account (vss. 29-30), further explain that the double portion of food on the sixth day was given for the purpose of providing food on the seventh day, on which day the people were to stay at home and not gather food, because this day is the Sabbath. The old account assumes the existence of the Sabbath; and the manna schedule is simply complying with the Sabbath regulation, as well as providing a test case for it.

Ex. 34:21 understands the Sabbath solely in terms of the weekly schedule of rest and work, here with reference to agricultural work. We have no indication of assemblies at the sanctuaries, or journeys to holy

men. This is the more startling since the Sabbath law here is sur-
rounded by regulations regarding festivals on which all males must
appear before Yahweh, i.e., at the sanctuary. Ex. 23:12, assuming that
it has not been expanded in later times, makes explicit the humanitarian
concern with the laborer on the Sabbath. Both laws may well reach back
into pre-monarchial times. It is very likely that the fourth commandment existed in the form of a Sabbath formula, regulating the six days
of work and the seventh day of rest, at this time. We have also proposed that the categorical prohibitions ending in the austere môt yûmāt
characterize the Sabbath or seventh day in this period. The earliest
Sabbath traditions are basically work regulations. But although there
is a humanitarian interest imbedded in them, they are not just labor
laws in the modern sense of the term, as is demonstrated by the understanding, or at times misunderstanding, which these early traditions
were able to bring to Israel's cultic and religious experiences.

This is as far as the Old Testament takes us, as we explore the
Sabbath traditions. The question of pre-Israelite Sabbath traditions,
i.e., traditions which ancient Hebrew or other peoples fostered, is
approached both from the side of the Old Testament and from outside this
literature. From the Old Testament side it is asked, what is the basis
for prohibiting work on the seventh day? From the outside it is asked
if comparable prohibitions are known elsewhere.

We have already noted that comparative studies (looking at the
Sabbath from the outside) provide very interesting illustrations of the
Israelite phenomenon portrayed in the Old Testament, but no explanations

of it.[1] The illustrations which are presently available just do not bridge the gap between the Sabbath traditions of the Old Testament and similar traditions preserved elsewhere in the literature of other peoples.

The view from the Old Testament does not take us very far either. It has been suggested that the categorical prohibitions of work on the Sabbath are very old, although they now appear in P. It is also obvious that the Sabbath formula appears on the Old Testament scene fully developed. So perhaps they preceded the Old Testament literature, its traditions, and even its people. But what then gave rise to them? Here the Old Testament is not helpful. There is no evidence that the lunar phases were responsible, or the planets, or the full moon. We do not hear of any social or economic institutions which could provide the chronological framework for this phenomenon. And the old agricultural festivals, some lasting seven days, just cannot claim responsibility for the seven-day week, as even Kiker admits.[2] There is no magical or mythical or metaphysical area of Israel's experience which can adequately account for it. Is it possible that some early form of a taboo responsible for this day can be detected in the Old Testament? Ex. 35:3 and Num. 15:32-36 are curious passages; they both appear in P, and if they are very old traditions, their original context is now lost. They simply prohibit the making of fires on the Sabbath (Num. 15:32-36 may be concerned with "the work" of gathering sticks in preparation for a fire), but they cannot be attributed to a Kenite fire taboo with any degree of

---

[1]See above, p. 8.   [2]See above, n. 1, p. 119.

certainty. Moreover, such an association would contribute little to our understanding of the Sabbath, for our knowledge of the Kenites is very limited.

This leaves us with the conclusion that the Sabbath is older than the Old Testament, and probably also older than Israel, but with our present sources we cannot trace the Sabbath beyond the Old Testament itself. It appears in the earliest strata of the Old Testament as the seventh day on which work is prohibited. We do not know the forces which were at work in the beginning to motivate the origin of the Sabbath. There may have been several, e.g., a need for rest, a humanitarian concern, a taboo, or a belief that the powers of earth, beast, and man must be regularly restored through a period of rest. The Old Testament itself is scarcely aware of such forces as motivations for the original Sabbath, although it may know of them in a muted form. This ignorance concerning the origin of the Sabbath is openly admitted in Gen. 2:1-3 which introduce this day as one of God's creative works.

Summary and conclusion

We can now attempt to summarize the history of the Sabbath traditions in the Old Testament literature.

The earliest traditions reach behind the beginning of the major literary works considered by scholars to have been initiated at the time of the establishment of the monarchy. This takes us back into pre-monarchial times and perhaps to the pre-settlement period. Two major themes stand out in these early traditions: (1) The regulations for the six days of work and the seventh day of rest; (2) the prohibition against performing any work on the seventh day at the risk of death. These traditions may well be pre-Mosaic, but we cannot be certain of this. The oldest stratum of Ex. 16 remembers that the six-seven day scheme was available to the Hebrews who escaped Egyptian slavery, and that gathering the manna in the wilderness was conditioned by this already existent scheme. We are not able within the Old Testament to press behind it, to a different one which might have inspired its development.

It has been suggested repeatedly that the early Sabbath traditions were characterized by a taboo of some kind. The prohibition against making fires, the possible association of Sabbath and lunar phases, the prohibition against leaving one's house (Ex. 16:29), and the strict prohibitions against work have led to this conclusion; but none of the arguments are really persuasive.[1] The Old Testament does not understand the Sabbath as a taboo day, even in the oldest stratum. The only explanation we have for the Sabbath phenomenon is the humanitarian orientation of some early and some late passages.[2] Nevertheless, there may have been deeper religious implications in the regulations for the Sabbath. It is indistinguishable from the number seven in the early traditions, and it is possible that its significance as that which is "complete" or that which "completes" or "delimits" played a role in

---

[1] We have suggested in this thesis that the prohibitions against making fires are really work prohibitions, that the command to stay in one's house is designed to keep Israel from gathering manna, i.e., work, and that the strict prohibitions against work are no indication that a taboo is involved, but that they can derive from many other interests, viz., serious religious or humanitarian considerations.

[2] Ex. 20:9-10; 23:12; Dt. 5:13-14; II Kg. 4:23.

these traditions; but this is never stated directly. We have also
mentioned the possibility of a sacral view of the work and rest of man
and beast, and of the earth's production and regeneration; but it is
found only on the fringes of the Old Testament traditions, if it is
there at all. Similarly, we have suggested that the late and frequent
characterization of the seventh day (Sabbath) as holy suggests a dimension of divine ownership and respect, fear, and recognition regarding it
on the part of man.

These early Sabbath traditions may not have used the word
šabbāt for the seventh day. It seems as if that day is always associated with cessation of work, whereas šabbāt has festal qualities,
although the former is not purely secular, as we have seen, and the
latter is not purely sacred in character. It is possible that šabbāt
came to be used about the seventh day as it became gradually more insti-
tutionalized, but certainly already in early monarchial times, or
perhaps even earlier. There is nowhere any distinction between the two
in Old Testament literature. The early laws do, however, use the verb
šbt to characterize man's relationship to that day. It is likely that
the noun is derived from the verb, meaning the day which delimits
(namely, the seven-day period and work).

In monarchial times, on the other hand, there is no doubt about
the naming of the seventh day. It retains its characterization as
seventh day, a day without work; but it is now spoken of simply as the
Sabbath. In ninth and eighth century texts, the Sabbath is a holy feast
day celebrated at the sanctuaries and at the temple. It was apparently
totally absorbed in the cult, possibly at the expense of its

humanitarian orientation (Am. 8:5).

In the latter part of the monarchy, the humanitarian concern is reiterated by means of some important additions to the fourth commandment. The Sabbath must also have been the object of some theological reflection, for it is now associated with the salvation history of Israel, i.e., the exodus event. When, therefore, the exilic literature abounds in Sabbath references, while the exile does not provide any good explanation for such a suddenly increased preoccupation with the Sabbath, we have proposed that this great interest in the Sabbath traditions, as reflected in P and Ezekiel particularly, began prior to the exile, possibly in connection with the reform movement of Hezekiah and continuing with interruptions into the reign of Josiah. This reform aimed at restoring old traditions and emphasizing the characteristically Israelite oriented aspects of the cult. The Sabbath qualified in both respects. The old six-seven-day scheme was restored and expanded with the explicit identification of the Sabbath and the seventh day so that it was both a day without work and a feast day. The temple Sabbath and the seventh day without work for man and beast had not always kept good company (cf. Am. 8:5), although they occurred on the same day. Now their identification was reaffirmed in priestly laws, used undoubtedly for instructing the laity. The importance of the Sabbath was further emphasized with the additions "to Yahweh," "holy," "a solemn rest." The command to "keep the Sabbath" further emphasized the importance of this institution in these circles.

The interest in the Sabbath is further illustrated by the creation Sabbath theme. We do not know when the creation account was first

framed by the week ending in the Sabbath, but it does not appear to be a
product of P, as we have suggested here.

Finally, we have the identification of the Sabbath as a sign and
covenant between Yahweh and Israel. That appears in the priestly laws
and in Ezekiel and is always associated with the Sinai event.

The exilic literature apart from Ezekiel and P does not mention
the Sabbath. It is not discussed by the Deuteronomistic historian or in
Deutero-Isaiah. P does, of course, contain many Sabbath references; but
they seem to consist primarily of traditional material, collected and
modified to fit into the general concerns of P. One exception is the
story of the manna, but even here we have found that traditional material is used in P's reconstruction of the old account. Besides, the
manna story was always associated with the Sabbath, or at least with the
six-seven-day scheme. In the latter part of the sixth century, when the
exile was beginning to dissolve itself with the occurrence of several
return movements, the Sabbath was again not prominent. It is not mentioned in the important prophetic literature by Haggai and Zechariah.
Is. 56:2-6 suggests that the community was faced with far more pressing
problems to which the question of Sabbath observance was subordinated.
Nevertheless, it did not go entirely unnoticed during the exile and
immediately thereafter. Jer. 17:19-27 probably belongs to this time,
but as we have suggested earlier, it may be based on authentic Jeremiah
material. If so, its elaborate emphasis on Sabbath observance is simply
a reworking of a genuine Jeremiah oracle by one of the prophet's
disciples with the intention of providing a theological explanation of
the catastrophe in 586 B.C. Is. 56:2-6 shows that the Sabbath was a

part of exilic religion, even an important part, but at the same time it is here brought to the service of an even more pressing problem facing the covenant community, namely, the problem of the relationship of foreigners and eunuchs to the covenant. Is. 58:13, from the same period, has a high view of the Sabbath; but even it is partially curtailed by the ethical orientation of the chapter as a whole.

There is no good evidence that the exile was a particularly creative period for the Old Testament Sabbath traditions, nor can it be affirmed that the Sabbath institution came to play a new and important role at this time. The Sabbath laws were collected, the creation Sabbath was used to support the Sabbath laws in Ex. 31:17 (Ex. 20:8-11 may well be pre-exilic), and the Sabbath sign helped explain the national catastrophe. Moreover, there can be no doubt that festal and cultic qualities continued to be associated with the day. It was still a temple Sabbath, but we have no evidence to support the view that the Sabbath returned to a taboo day during or after the exile,[1] or that its fundamental character changed radically.[2] It was a time of solidification and sedimentation of the Sabbath traditions.

In postexilic times, i.e., in the fifth and fourth centuries B.C., we learn little about the Sabbath. Neh. 10, 13 indicate that it was generally and systematically neglected, although some attempts at reformation were made, and some success was achieved, even if by force

---

[1]Cf. Bentzen, Den israelitiske Sabbats Oprindelse og Historie, pp. 85-86. This position is also held by the scholars who detect an influence on the Sabbath from the Babylonian ûmê lemnûti.

[2]E.g., from a monthly day (the day of the full moon) to a weekly day, or from a feast day to a taboo day, or the like.

and public confession. The Chronicler considered the Sabbath an
important part of the temple cult; and although we need not assume that
the Chronicler was more programmatic and idealistic than realistic, we
can, nevertheless, not conclude that the Sabbath played a great role in
the community of his time. It may well have been largely a day for the
Levites to observe together with the people who stopped their work on
this day and who chanced to be in the temple, while the main part of the
secular population offered it only "benign neglect." At any rate, we
have no indication that the Sabbath was a matter of major consequence to
the newly established Jerusalem community, which was not as scrupulous
about its religious obligations as we might have expected (cf. Malachi).
On the other hand, we can be certain that the reforms of Ezra and Nehemiah had important consequences for the future of the community's
religious life, including its Sabbath observance; but unfortunately we
have no information concerning the immediate effects of these reforms.
However, the frequent inclusion of the Sabbath among the prominent
temple festivals in Chronicles may indicate that it was on its way back
into a prominence which was to continue until it again became a factor
of major significance in the community, or at least the pious persons
within it, during the third and second centuries B.C.

Retrospect and prospect

Finally, we may look at the Sabbath literature from the perspective of its tradition-history. It becomes clear at the outset that
this literature consists of far more transmitted traditional material
than of creative compositions. We have seen that, though the three old

types of Sabbath laws were expanded in P, they were not basically changed. The creation Sabbath tradition is also stable, and the later tradition identifying the Sabbath as a sign and a covenant is remarkably permanent. The so-called creative period of the Sabbath traditions is, therefore, not creative in the strict sense of the word. It rather provided an occasion for the embattled community and its spiritual leaders to reach back into the pool of traditions associated with the beginnings of the community, and to refurbish these and to apply them to the new situation at hand. The creation Sabbath itself is actually not a new Sabbath tradition, but simply the application of the traditional six-seven-day scheme to God's creative activities. As such, it contributed to a demythologizing of the common Near Eastern creation motifs. That the creation Sabbath, being a very powerful Sabbath tradition, should achieve a status independent of the creation account (Ex. 20:11; 31:17) is only natural, but we find no further development of the creation Sabbath motif, except perhaps for the enigmatic expression that Yahweh not only ceased from his work, but also was refreshed on this day (Ex. 31:17), if that is indeed a secondary development.

Also, the Sabbath regulations of the late period, though expanded and embellished, do not really go beyond the early terse laws commanding work on the six days, and prohibiting it on the seventh day. And finally, the passages identifying the Sabbath as a sign for Israel or as a covenant, notably in Ex. 31 and Ezek. 22; 23, are so much alike that they are frequently considered to stand in a literary relationship. This view has been rejected by this study in favor of a position which holds that these passages depend on common traditions.

This may then lead to some final conclusions regarding the Old Testament Sabbath traditions. (1) In the earliest times of the literary history of the Old Testament, dating back perhaps to pre-monarchial times, we already find Sabbath traditions which regulate work and rest in a seven-day schedule, which enforce the observance of these regulations both with punitive measures and with hortatory remarks; which associate the Sabbath with some sacral and cultic motifs; and which may well have been aware of humanitarian principles involved in the abstention from work. These ways of understanding the Sabbath are not the result of lengthy developments under the influence of a developed cultic system, prophetic religion, or foreign (Mesopotamian) influences, as earlier studies, mentioned in the introduction, have suggested. On the contrary, they are present in the earliest traditions; and they can be traced in the scanty descriptions of the Sabbath institution in the literature of the early monarchy. (2) The renewed interest in the Sabbath during the later part of Old Testament history should be understood as a renewed interest in the old Sabbath traditions. Our analysis of these traditions has pointed to a consistency in their basic structure and content that leads to this conclusion. These later Sabbath traditions should not be attributed to the need of the exiled community for a Sabbath institution of holy time to compensate for the lost holy place (the temple), as is so commonly done. On the one hand, these traditions do not reflect the existence of such an exilic Sabbath institution for which this community had no particular use, as we have argued above; and on the other hand, they seem to have been formed prior to the exile. For this reason, the renewed interest in the Sabbath should not be placed during the exile, but some time prior to it. The Assyrian period, approximately from the reign of Hezekiah to that of Josiah, would seem to provide the most appropriate occasion for such a creative engagement with the Sabbath traditions. It was at this time, and not during the exile, that Israel reached back into her fund of traditions and resurrected the many Sabbath traditions, expanded them, reapplied them, and enlarged their impact on the community's life and self-understanding. (3) The exile itself was an anticlimax for the interest in the Sabbath and was not, as we have often been led to believe, the great occasion for a new concern with this institution and new thoughts about it. This judgment holds true for the immediate postexilic period also.

This study has not said the last word about the Old Testament Sabbath. By its definition, it has been of a descriptive nature and has been limited to a description of the Sabbath traditions. The theological significance of these, and of their history, is largely untouched and remains to be explored. The origin of the Sabbath and its traditions has not yet been found, and the search still goes on. The judgment that the creative period of the Sabbath traditions is primarily pre-exilic rather than exilic and postexilic must be tested against an examination of other aspects of Old Testament religious and literary activities of this period. But these and other questions lie beyond the scope of this investigation.

WORKS CITED

Dictionaries and Lexicons

The Assyrian Dictionary. Chicago: The Oriental Institute, 1956--.

Brown, Francis; Driver, S. R.; and Briggs, Charles A. Hebrew and English Lexicon of the Old Testament. Oxford: Clarendon Press, 1907.

Gesenius, Wilhelm, and Buhl, Frants. Hebräisches und aramäisches Handwörterbuch über das Alte Testament. 17th ed. Berlin: Springer-Verlag, 1949.

Jastrow, Morris. A Dictionary of the Targumin, the Talmud Babli and Yerushalmi, and the Midrashic Literature. New York: Title Publishing Company, 1943.

Koehler, Ludwig, and Baumgartner, Walter. Lexicon in Veteris Testamenti Libros. Leiden: E. J. Brill, 1958.

Commentaries and Other Studies of the

Old Testament Literature

Commentaries

Baentsch, Bruno. Exodus-Leviticus. HK, Pt. 1, Vol. II, 1. Göttingen: Vandenhoeck & Ruprecht, 1903.

Batten, Lorin W. The Books of Ezra and Nehemiah. ICC, Vol. XII. New York: Charles Scribner's Sons, 1913.

Beer, Georg, and Galling, Kurt. Exodus. HAT, Vol. III. Tübingen: Verlag von J. C. B. Mohr (Paul Siebeck), 1939.

Benzinger, I. Die Bücher der Chronik. KHC, Vol. X. Tübingen: Verlag von J. C. B. Mohr (Paul Siebeck), 1901.

_____. Die Bücher der Könige. KHC, Vol. XI. Tübingen: Verlag von J. C. B. Mohr (Paul Siebeck), 1899.

Bertholet, Alfred. Die Bücher Esra und Nehemia. KHC, Vol. XIX. Tübingen: Verlag von J. C. B. Mohr (Paul Siebeck), 1902.

_____, and Galling, Kurt. Hesekiel. HAT, Vol. XIII. Tübingen: Verlag von J. C. B. Mohr (Paul Siebeck), 1936.

Bowman, Raymond A. "Introduction and Exegesis to Ezra and Nehemiah." The Interpreter's Bible. Vol. III. Edited by George A. Buttrick. New York: Abingdon Press, 1954.

Bright, John. Jeremiah. AB, Vol. XXI. New York: Doubleday & Company, Inc., 1965.

Budde, Karl. Die biblische Urgeschichte: Gen. 1-12, 5 untersucht. Giessen: J. Ricker, 1883.

Cassuto, Umberto. A Commentary on the Book of Genesis. Pt. I: From Adam to Noah Genesis I-VI8. Translated by I. Abrahams. Jerusalem: Magnes Press, Hebrew University, 1961.

Condamin, Albert. Le livre de Jérémie. Paris: Librairie Lecoffre, 1936.

Cook, George A. The Book of Ezekiel. ICC, Vol. XXI. Edinburgh: T. & T. Clark, 1951.

Cornill, Carl H. Das Buch Jeremia. Leipzig: Chr. Herm. Tauchnitz, 1905.

Curtis, Edward L., and Madsen, Albert A. The Books of Chronicles. ICC, Vol. XI. New York: Charles Scribner's Sons, 1910.

Duhm, Bernhard. Das Buch Jeremia. KHC, Vol. XI. Tübingen: Verlag von J. C. B. Mohr (Paul Siebeck), 1910.

_____. Das Buch Jesaja übersetz und erklärt. HK, Pt. II, Vol. I. 4th ed. Göttingen: Vandenhoeck & Ruprecht, 1922.

Eichrodt, Walther. Der Prophet Hesekiel: Kapitel 19-48. ATD, Vol. XXII, Pt. 2. Göttingen: Vandenhoeck & Ruprecht, 1966.

Elliger, Karl. Leviticus. HAT, Vol. IV. Tübingen: J. C. B. Mohr (Paul Siebeck), 1966.

Elmslie, W. A. L. "Introduction and Exegesis to 1-2 Chronicles." The Interpreter's Bible. Vol. III. Edited by George A. Buttrick. New York: Abingdon Press, 1954.

Fohrer, Georg, and Galling, Kurt. Ezechiel. HAT, Vol. XIII. Tübingen: Verlag von J. C. B. Mohr (Paul Siebeck), 1955.

Galling, Kurt. Die Bücher der Chronik, Esra, Nehemia. ATD, Vol. XII. Göttingen: Vandenhoeck & Ruprecht, 1954.

Glahn, Ludwig. Der Prophet der Heimkehr: Jesaja 40-66. Copenhagen: Levin & Munksgaard, 1934.

Gray, George B. The Book of Isaiah: I-XXXIV. ICC, Vol. XVIII. Edinburgh: T. & T. Clark, 1912.

_____. Numbers. ICC, Vol. IV. New York: Charles Scribner's Sons, 1903.

Gunkel, Hermann. Genesis übersetz und erklärt. HK, Pt. 1, Vol. I. 5th ed. Göttingen: Vandenhoeck & Ruprecht, 1922.

Haller, Max. Die fünf Megilloth. HAT, Vol. XVIII. Tübingen: Verlag von J. C. B. Mohr (Paul Siebeck), 1940.

Harper, William R. Amos and Hosea. ICC, Vol. 23. New York: Charles Scribner's Sons, 1905.

Heinisch, Paul. Das Buch Leviticus. HS, Pt. 1, Vol. 3. Bonn: Peter Hanstein Verlagsbuchhandlung, 1935.

Hölscher, Gustav. "Die Bücher Esra und Nehemia." Die Heilige Schrift des Alten Testaments. Vol. II. Edited by E. Kautzsch. Tübingen: Verlag von J. C. B. Mohr (Paul Siebeck), 1923.

Holzinger, Heinrich. Genesis. KHC, Vol. I. Tübingen: Verlag von J. C. B. Mohr (Paul Siebeck), 1898.

Hyatt, J. Philip. "Introduction and Exegesis to Jeremiah." The Interpreter's Bible. Vol. V. Edited by George A. Buttrick. New York: Abingdon Press, 1956.

Kaiser, Otto. Der Prophet Jesaja: Kapitel 1-12. ATD, Vol. XVII. Göttingen: Vandenhoeck & Ruprecht, 1963.

Kraus, Hans-Joachim. Klagelieder (Threni). BK, Vol. XX. Neukirchen-Vluyn: Neukirchener Verlag, 1956.

_____. Psalmen. BK, Vol. 15, 1-2. Neukirchen-Vluyn: Neukirchener Verlag, 1960.

Leslie, Elmer A. Jeremiah: Chronologically Arranged, Translated, and Interpreted. Nashville: Abingdon Press, 1954.

Marsh, John. "Introduction and Exegesis to Numbers." The Interpreter's Bible. Vol. II. Edited by George A. Buttrick. New York: Abingdon Press, 1953.

Marti, Karl. Das Buch Jesaja. KHC, Vol. X. Tübingen: Verlag von J. C. B. Mohr (Paul Siebeck), 1900.

278

_____. Das Dodekapropheton. KHC, Vol. XIII. Tübingen: Verlag von J. C. B. Mohr (Paul Siebeck), 1904.

Matthews, Isaac G. Ezekiel. Philadelphia: American Baptist Publication Society, 1939.

Meek, Theophile J. "Introduction and Exegesis to Lamentations." The Interpreter's Bible. Vol. VI. Edited by George A. Buttrick. New York: Abingdon Press, 1956.

Muilenburg, James. "Introduction and Exegesis to Isaiah 40-66." The Interpreter's Bible. Vol. V. Edited by George A. Buttrick. New York: Abingdon Press, 1956.

Myers, Jacob M. Ezra, Nehemiah. AB, Vol. XIV. New York: Doubleday & Company, Inc., 1965.

_____. I Chronicles. AB, Vol. XII. New York: Doubleday & Company, Inc., 1965.

_____. II Chronicles. AB, Vol. XIII. New York: Doubleday & Company, Inc., 1965.

Noth, Martin. Exodus: A Commentary. Translated by J. S. Bowden. Philadelphia: Westminster Press, 1962.

_____. Leviticus: A Commentary. Translated by J. E. Anderson. Philadelphia: Westminster Press, 1965.

_____. Das vierte Buch Mose: Numeri. ATD, Vol. VII. Göttingen: Vandenhoeck & Ruprecht, 1966.

Rad, Gerhard von. Deuteronomy: A Commentary. Translated by D. Barton. Philadelphia: Westminster Press, 1966.

_____. Genesis: A Commentary. Translated by John H. Marks. Philadelphia: Westminster Press, 1961.

Rudolph, Wilhelm. Das Buch Ruth, Das Hohe Lied, Die Klagelieder. KAT, Vol. XVII. Gerd Mohn: Gütersloher Verlagshaus, 1963.

_____. Chronikbücher. HAT, Vol. XXI. Tübingen: Verlag von J. C. B. Mohr (Paul Siebeck), 1955.

_____. Esra und Nehemia samt 3. Esra. HAT, Vol. XX. Tübingen: Verlag von J. C. B. Mohr (Paul Siebeck), 1949.

_____. Hoshea. KAT, Vol. XIII, Pt. 1. Gerd Mohn: Gütersloher Verlagshaus, 1966.

_____. Jeremia. HAT, Vol. XII. 2nd ed. Tübingen: Verlag von J. C. B. Mohr (Paul Siebeck), 1958.

Rylaarsdam, J. Coert. "Introduction and Exegesis to Exodus." The Interpreter's Bible. Vol. I. Edited by George A. Buttrick. New York: Abingdon Press, 1952.

Simpson, Cuthbert A. "Introduction and Exegesis to Genesis." The Interpreter's Bible. Vol. I. Edited by George A. Buttrick. New York: Abingdon Press, 1952.

Snaith, Norman H. "Introduction and Exegesis to 1-2 Kings." The Interpreter's Bible. Vol. III. Edited by George A. Buttrick. New York: Abingdon Press, 1954.

Speiser, E. A. Genesis. AB, Vol. I. New York: Doubleday & Company, Inc., 1964.

Torrey, Charles C. The Second Isaiah. New York: Charles Scribner's Sons, 1928.

Weiser, Artur. Das Buch Jeremia, Kapitel 1-25:13. ATD, Vol. XX. 5th ed. Göttingen: Vandenhoeck & Ruprecht, 1966.

_____. "Klagelieder." Ringgren, Helmer; Weiser, Artur; and Zimmerli, Walther. Spruche, Prediger, Das Hohe Lied, Klage-lieder, Das Buch Ester. ATD, Vol. XVI. 2nd ed. Göttingen: Vandenhoeck & Ruprecht, 1967.

Welch, Adam C. The Book of Jeremiah. London: National Adult School Union, 1928.

Westermann, Claus. Das Buch Jesaja: Kapitel 40-66. ATD, Vol. XIX. Göttingen: Vandenhoeck & Ruprecht, 1966.

_____. Genesis. BK, Vol. I. Neukirchen-Vluyn: Neukirchener Verlag, 1966--.

Wildberger, Hans. Jesaja. BK, Vol. X. Neukirchen-Vluyn: Neukirchener Verlag, 1965--.

Wolff, Hans Walter. Dodekapropheton 1: Hoshea. BK, Vol. XIV. 2nd ed. Neukirchen-Vluyn: Neukirchener Verlag, 1965.

Zimmerli, Walther. Ezechiel. BK, Vol. XIII. Neukirchen-Vluyn: Neukirchener Verlag, 1969.

Books and monographs

Baltzer, Klaus. Das Bundesformular. WMANT, No. 4. 2nd ed. Neukirchen-Vluyn: Neukirchener Verlag, 1964.

Beyerlin, Walter. Origins and History of the Oldest Sinaitic Traditions. Translated by S. Rudman. Oxford: Basil Blackwell, 1961.

Boecker, Hans Jochen. Redeformen des Rechtslebens im Alten Testament. WMANT, No. 14. Neukirchen-Vluyn: Neukirchener Verlag, 1964.

Cazelles, Henri. Études sur le code de l'alliance. Paris: Letouzey et Ané, 1946.

Driver, Samuel R. An Introduction to the Literature of the Old Testament. Meridian Books. New York: World Publishing Company, 1956.

Eissfeldt, Otto. Hexateuch-Synopse. Leipzig: J. H. Hinrichs'sche Buchhandlung, 1922.

_____. The Old Testament: An Introduction. Translated by Peter R. Ackroyd. New York: Harper and Row, Publishers, 1965.

Feucht, Christian. Untersuchungen zum Heiligkeitsgesetz. Berlin: Evangelische Verlagsanstalt, 1964.

Fohrer, Georg. Elia. AThANT, No. 53. 2nd ed. Zürich: Zwingli-Verlag, 1968.

_____. Die Hauptprobleme des Buches Ezechiel. BZAW, No. 72. Berlin: Verlag Alfred Töpelmann, 1952.

_____. Introduction to the Old Testament. Translated by David E. Green. Nashville: Abingdon Press, 1968.

Gerstenberger, Erhard. Wesen und Herkunft des "apodiktischen Rechts." WMANT, No. 20. Neukirchen-Vluyn: Neukirchener Verlag, 1965.

Gese, Helmut. Der Verfassungsentwurf des Ezechiel, Kap. 40-48: Traditionsgeschichtlich Untersucht. Tübingen: J. C. B. Mohr (Paul Siebeck), 1957.

Gottwald, Norman K. Studies in the Book of Lamentations. SBT, No. 14. London: SCM Press Ltd., 1954.

Heintrich, Volkmar. Ezechielprobleme. BZAW, No. 61. Giessen: Verlag von Alfred Töpelmann, 1932.

Hölscher, Gustav. Hesekiel der Dichter und das Buch. BZAW, No. 39. Giessen: Verlag von Alfred Töpelmann, 1924.

Hooke, Samuel H. In the Beginning. The Clarendon Bible: Old Testament, Vol. VI. Oxford: Clarendon Press, 1947.

Jahn, Gustav. Die Bücher Esra (A und B) und Nehemia. Leiden: E. J. Brill, 1909.

Jepsen, Alfred. Untersuchungen zum Bundesbuch. BWANT, No. 41. Stuttgart: Verlag W. Kohlhammer, 1927.

Jeremias, Jörg. Theophanie: Die Geschichte einer alttestamentlichen Gattung. WMANT, No. 10. Neukirchen-Vluyn: Neukirchener Verlag, 1965.

Kellermann, Ulrich. Nehemia: Quellen, Überlieferung, und Geschichte. BZAW, No. 102. Berlin: Verlag Alfred Töpelmann, 1967.

Kilian, Rudolph. Literarkritische und formgeschichtliche Untersuchung des Heiligkeitsgesetzes. Bonn: Peter Hanstein's Verlag GMBH, 1963.

Koch, Klaus. The Growth of the Biblical Tradition: The Form-Critical Method. Translated by S. M. Cupitt. New York: Charles Scribner's Sons, 1969.

_____. Die Priesterschrift von Exodus 25 bis Leviticus 16: Eine überlieferungsgeschichtliche und literarkritische Untersuchung. FRLANT, No. 71. Göttingen: Vandenhoeck & Ruprecht, 1959.

Kornfeld, Walter. Studien zum Heiligkeitsgesetz (Lev. 17-26). Vienna: Herder Verlag, 1952.

Lohfink, Norbert. Das Hauptgebot: Eine Untersuchung literarischer Einleitungsfragen zu Dtn 5-11. Analecta Biblica, Investigationes Scientificae in Res Biblicas, No. 20. Rome: Pontificio Instituto Biblico, 1963.

Long, Burke O. The Problem of Etiological Narrative in the Old Testament. BZAW, No. 188. Berlin: Verlag Alfred Töpelmann, 1968.

Malina, Bruce J. The Palestinian Manna Tradition: The Manna Tradition in the Palestinian Targums and Its Relationship to the New Testament Writings. Leiden: E. J. Brill, 1968.

Mendenhall, George E. Law and Covenant in Israel and the Ancient Near East. Pittsburg: The Presbyterian Board of Colportage of Western Pennsylvania, 1955. Also in BA, XVII (1954), 26-46, 49-76.

Menes, Abram. Die vorexilischen Gesetze Israels. BZAW, No. 50.
Giessen: Verlag von Alfred Töpelmann, 1928.

Miller, John W. Das Verhältnis Jeremias und Hesekiels sprachlich und
theologisch untersucht. Assen: Van Gorcum & Comp., 1955.

Mowinckel, Sigmund. Le Décalogue. Paris: Librairie Félix Alcan, 1927.

————. Studien zu dem Buche Ezra-Nehemia. Vol. I: Die nachchronistische Redaktion des Buches. Die Listen: Skrifter utgitt av
det Norske Videnskaps-Akademi i Oslo, II. Hist.-Filos. Klasse.
Ny Serie, No. 3. Oslo: Universitetsforlaget, 1964.

————. Studien zu dem Buche Ezra-Nehemia. Vol. II: Die Nehemia-
Denkschrift. Skrifter utgitt av det Norske Videnskaps-Akademi i
Oslo, II. Hist.-Filos. Klasse. Ny Serie, No. 1. Oslo:
Universitetsforlaget, 1964.

————. Studien zu dem Buche Ezra-Nehemia. Vol. III: Die
Ezrageschichte und das Gesetz Moses. Skrifter utgitt av det
Norske Videnskaps-Akademi i Oslo, II. Hist.-Filos. Klasse. Ny
Serie, No. 7. Oslo: Universitetsforlaget, 1965.

————. Zur Komposition des Buches Jeremia. Kristiania [Oslo]:
Jacob Dybwad, 1914.

Nielsen, Eduard. The Ten Commandments in New Perspective: A Traditio-
historical Approach. Translated by David J. Bourke. SBT,
Second Series, No. 7. London: SCM Press Ltd., 1968.

Noth, Martin. Überlieferungsgeschichte des Pentateuch. Stuttgart:
W. Kohlhammer Verlag, 1948.

————. Überlieferungsgeschichtliche Studien. Halle: Max Niemeyer
Verlag, 1943.

Otzen, Benedikt. Studien über Deuterosacharja. Acta Theologica Danica,
Vol. VI. Copenhagen: Prostant Apud Munksgaard, 1964.

Rabast, Karlheins H. Das apodiktische Recht im Deuteronomiun und im
Heiligkeitsgesetz. Berlin-Hermsdorf: Heimatdienstverlag, 1948.

Rad, Gerhard von. Die Priesterschrift im Hexateuch literarisch
untersucht und theologisch gewertet. BWANT, No. 65. Stuttgart-
Berlin: Verlag W. Kohlhammer, 1934.

————. Studies in Deuteronomy. Translated by D. Stalker. SBT,
No. 9. London: SCM Press, Ltd., 1953.

Rendtorff, Rolf. Die Gestze in der Priesterschrift: Eine
gattungsgeschichtliche Untersuchung. FRLANT, N.F., No. 44.

Göttingen: Vandenhoeck & Ruprecht, 1954.

Reventlow, Henning Graf. Gebot und Predigt im Dekalog. Gerd Mohn: Gütersloher Verlagshaus, 1962.

_____. Das Heiligkeitsgesetz formgeschichtlich untersucht. WMANT, No. 6. Neukirchen-Vluyn: Neukirchener Verlag, 1961.

Rudolph, Wilhelm. Der "Elohist" von Exodus bis Josua. BZAW, No. 68. Berlin: Verlag von Alfred Töpelmann, 1938.

Schmidt, Werner, H. Die Schöpfungsgeschichte der Priesterschrift: Zur Überlieferungsgeschichte von Genesis I1-II4a und II4b-III24. WMANT, No. 17. 2nd ed. Neukirchen-Vluyn: Neukirchener Verlag, 1967.

Schulz, H. Das Todesrecht im Alten Testament. Studien zur Rechtsform der Mot-Jumat-Sätze. BZAW, No. 114. Berlin: Verlag Alfred Töpelmann, 1969.

Stamm, Johann Jakob, and Andrew, Maurice E. The Ten Commandments in Recent Research. SBT, Second Series, No. 2. London: SCM Press Ltd., 1967.

Steck, Odil H. Überlieferung und Zeitgeschichte in den Elia-Erzählungen. WMANT, No. 26. Neukirchen-Vluyn: Neukirchener Verlag, 1968.

Steinmann, Jean. Le prophète Jérémie: Sa vie, son ouvre et son temp. Paris: Les Éditions du Cerf, 1952.

Torrey, Charles C. The Composition and Historical Value of Ezra-Nehemiah. Giessen: J. Richer'sche Buchhandlung, 1896.

Volz, Paul. Studien zum Text des Jeremia. Leipzig: J. C. Hinrichs'sche Buchhandlung, 1920.

Weiser, Artur. The Old Testament: Its Formation and Development. Translated by Dorthea M. Barton. New York: Association Press, 1961.

Welch, Adam C. The Work of the Chronicler. London: Oxford University Press, 1939.

Wellhausen, Julius. Die Composition des Hexateuchs und der historischen Bücher des Alten Testaments. 2nd ed. Berlin: Druck und Verlag von Georg Reimer, 1889.

284

Articles

Ahlemann, Frieder. "Zur Esra-Quelle." ZAW, LIX (1942-43), 77-98.

Albright, William F. "The Date and Personality of the Chronicler."
JBL, XXXIX (1920), 104-24.

Alt, Albrecht. "The Origins of Israelite Law." Essays on Old Testament
History and Religion. Translated by R. A. Wilson. Anchor
Books. New York: Doubleday & Company, Inc., 1968.

Auerbach, Elias. "Die babylonische Datierung im Pentateuch und das
Alter des Priesterkodex." VT, II (1952), 334-42.

Bertholet, Alfred. "Zum Schoepfungsbericht in Genesis 1." JBL, LIII
(1934), 237-40.

Bright, John. "The Date of the Prose Sermons of Jeremiah." JBL, LXX
(1951), 15-35.

Eissfeldt, Otto. "Goethes Beurteilung des kultischen Dekalogs von Ex.
34 im Lichte der Pentateuchkritik." ZThK, LXIII (1966), 135-44.

Elliger, Karl. "Sinn und Ursprung der priesterlichen Geschichtserzählung." ZThK, XLIX (1952), 121-43.

Fohrer, Georg. "Das sogenannte apodiktisch formulierte Recht und der
Dekalog." KuD, XI (1965), 49-74.

_____. "Jesaja 1 als Zusammenfassung der Verkündigung Jesajas."
ZAW, LXXIV (1962), 251-68.

Fraenkel, Siegmund. "Zur Wurzel רצד." ZAW, XIX (1899), 181.

Freedman, David N. "The Chronicler's Purpose." CBQ, XXIII (1961),
436-42.

Hammershaimb, Erling. "Ezekiel's View of the Monarchy." Some Aspects
of Old Testament Prophecy from Isaiah to Malachi. Arhus:
Rosenkilde og Bagger, 1966.

Harrelson, Walter. "The Celebration of the Feast of Booths According to
Zech xiv 16-21." Religions in Antiquity: Essays in memory of
Erwin Ramsdell Goodenough. Edited by Jacob Neusner. Studies in
the History of Religions, Vol. XIV. Leiden: E. J. Brill, 1968.

Hempel, Johannes. "Priesterkodex": Paulys Realencyclopädie der
classischen Altertumswissenschaft. Neue Bearbeitung, Vol. XXII,
Pt. 2. Stuttgart: Alfred Druckenmüller Verlag, 1954, cols.
1943-67.

Hoffmann, Georg. "Versuche zu Amos." ZAW, III (1883), 87-126.

Hölscher, Gustav. "Das Buch der Könige: Seine Quellen und seine
Redaktion." Eucharisterion, H. Gunkel zum 60. Geburtstage, I.
Edited by Hans Schmidt. FRLANT, No. 36. Göttingen: Vanden-
hoeck & Ruprecht, 1923.

Humbert, Paul. "Die literarische Zweiheit der Priester-Codex in der
Genesis (Kritische Untersuchungen der These von von Rad)." ZAW,
LVIII (1940-41), 30-57.

_____. "La relation de Genèse 1 et du Psaume 104 avec la liturgie du
Nouvel-An israélite." RHPhR, XV (1935), 1-27. Also in
Opuscules d'un Hébraïsant. Neuchatel: Secrétariat de
L'Université, 1958.

Hvidberg, Flemming. "The Canaanite Background of Gen. I-III." VT, X
(1960), 285-94.

Hyatt, J. Philip. "The Beginning of Jeremiah's Prophecy." ZAW, LXXVIII
(1966), 204-14.

_____. "The Date and Background of Zephaniah." JNES, VII (1948),
25-29.

_____. "Moses and the Ethical Decalogue." Encounter, XXVI (1965),
199-206.

_____. "Were There an Ancient Historical Credo in Israel and an
Independent Sinai Tradition?" Translating & Understanding the
Old Testament. Essays in Honor of Herbert Gordon May. Edited
by Harry Thomas Frank and William L. Reed. Nashville: Abingdon
Press, 1970.

Jacob, Benno. "The Decalogue." JQR, XIV (1923-24), 141-87.

Jepsen, Alfred. "Beiträge zur Auslegung und Geschichte des Dekalogs."
ZAW, LXXIX (1967), 277-304.

_____. "Nehemia 10." ZAW, LXVI (1954), 87-106.

Kapelrud, Arvid S. "The Date of the Priestly Code." ASTI, III (1964),
58-64.

Kessler, Werner. "Die literarische, historische und theologische
Problematik des Dekalogs." VT, VII (1957), 1-16.

Kilian, Rudolf. "Apodiktisches und kasuistisches Recht im Licht
ägyptischer Analogien." BZ, N.F. VII (1963), 185-202.

_____. "Die Totenerweckungen Elias und Elisas - eine Motivwanderung?" BZ, N.F. X (1966), 44-56.

Koch, Klaus. "Die Eigenart der priesterschriftlichen Sinaigesetzgebung." ZThK, LV (1958), 36-51.

Köhler, Ludwig. "Der Dekalog." ThR, N.F. I (1929), 161-84.

Kuhl, Curt. "Zum Stand der Hesekiel-Forschung." ThR, XXIV (1956-57), 1-53.

Liebreich, Leon J. "The Impact of Nehemiah 9:5-37 on the Liturgy of the Synagogue." HUCA, XXXII (1961), 227-37.

Lohfink, Norbert. "Zur Dekalogfassung von Dt. 5." BZ, N.F. IX (1965), 17-32.

May, Herbert G. "Towards an Objective Approach to the Book of Jeremiah: The Biographer." JBL, LXI (1942), 139-55.

Morgerstern, Julian. "The Book of the Covenant." HUCA, V (1928), 1-151.

_____. "The Decalogue of the Holiness Code." HUCA, XXVI (1955), 1-27.

_____. "The Oldest Document of the Hexateuch." HUCA, IV (1927), 1-138.

_____. "Two Compound Technical Terms in Biblical Hebrew." JBL, XLIII (1924), 311-20.

Mowinckel, Sigmund. "Psalm Criticism Between 1900 and 1935 (Ugarit and Psalm Exegesis)." VT, V (1955), 13-33.

_____. "Die vorderasiatischen Königs-und Fürsteninschriften." Eucharisterion H. Gunkel zum 60. Geburtstage, I. Edited by Hans Schmidt. FRLANT, No. 36. Göttingen: Vandenhoeck & Ruprecht, 1923.

_____. "Zur Geschichte der Dekaloge." ZAW, LV (1937), 218-35.

Myers, Jacob M. "Some Considerations Bearing on the Date of Joel." ZAW, LXXIV (1962), 178-90.

Noth, Martin. "The Laws in the Pentateuch: Their Assumptions and Meaning." The Laws in the Pentateuch and Other Studies. Translated by D. R. Ap-Thomas. Philadelphia: Fortress Press, 1966.

Pfeiffer, Robert H. "The Oldest Decalogue." JBL, XLIII (1924), 294-310.

Phillips, Anthony. "The Case of the Woodgatherer Reconsidered." VT, XIX (1969), 125-28.

Rad, Gerhard von. Das Formgeschichtliche Problem des Hexateuch. BWANT, Fourth Series, No. 26. Stuttgart: W. Kohlhammer Verlag, 1938. E. T. "The Form-Critical Problem of the Hexateuch." The Problem of the Hexateuch and Other Essays. Translated by E. W. Trueman Dicken. New York: McGraw-Hill Book Company, 1966.

_____. "The Levitical Sermon in I and II Chronicles." The Problem of the Hexateuch and Other Essays. Translated by E. W. Trueman Dickens. New York: McGraw-Hill Book Company, 1966.

_____. "Die Nehemia-Denkschrift." ZAW, LXXVI (1964), 176-87.

Reventlow, Henning Graf. "Kultisches Recht im Alten Testament." ZThK, LX (1963), 267-304.

Ringgren, Helmer. "Är den bibliska skapelsberättelsen en kulttext?" SEÅ, XIII (1948), 9-21.

Rost, Leonhard. "Der Schöpfungsbericht der Priesterschrift." CuW, X (1934), 172-78.

Rowley, H. H. "The Book of Ezekiel in Modern Study." BJRL, XXXVI (1953-54), 146-90. Also in Men of God: Studies in Old Testament History and Prophecy. London: Thomas Nelson and Sons Ltd., 1963.

_____. "Moses and the Decalogue." BJRL, XXXIV (1951-52), 81-118. Also in Men of God: Studies in Old Testament History and Prophecy. London: Thomas Nelson and Sons Ltd., 1963.

Rudolph, Wilhelm. "Die Einheitlichkeit der Erzählung vom Sturz der Atalja (2 Kön 11)." Festschrift Alfred Bertholet zum 80. Geburtstag. Edited by Walter Baumgartner, et al. Tübingen: J. C. B. Mohr (Paul Siebeck), 1950.

_____. "Problems of the Books of Chronicles." VT, IV (1954), 401-09.

Schmidt, Hans. "Mose und der Dekalog." Eucharisterion: H. Gunkel zum 60. Geburtstage, I. Edited by Hans Schmidt. FRLANT, No. 36. Göttingen: Vandenhoeck & Ruprecht, 1923.

Schwally, Friedrich. "Miscellen." ZAW, XI (1891), 257.

Stamm, Johann Jakob. "Dreissig Jahre Dekalogforschung." ThR, N.F. XXVII (1961), 189-239, 281-305.

Thiel, Winfried. "Erwägungen zum Alter des Heiligkeitsgesetzes." ZAW, LXXXI (1969), 40-73.

Vink, J. G. "The Date and Origin of the Priestly Code in the Old Testament." Oudtestamentlische Studiëen, Vol. XV. Edited by P. A. H. De Boer. Leiden: E. J. Brill, 1969.

Voort, A. van der. "Genèse I, 1 à II, 4a et le Psaume CIV." RB, LVIII (1951), 321-47.

Watts, John D. W. "Infinitive Absolute as Imperative and the Interpretation of Exodus 20:8." ZAW, LXXIV (1962), 141-45.

Weingreen, J. "The Case of the Woodgatherer (Numbers XV 32-36)." VT, XVI (1966), 361-64.

Welch, Adam C. "The Source of Nehemiah IX." ZAW, XLVII (1929), 130-37.

Williams, D. L. "The Date of Zephaniah." JBL, LXXXII (1963), 77-88.

Zimmerli, Walther. "Die Eigenart der prophetischen Rede des Ezechiel: Ein Beitrag zum Problem an Hand von Ez. 14:1-11." ZAW, LXVI (1954), 1-26.

_____. "The Word of God in the Book of Ezekiel." JThC, IV (1967), 1-13.

Studies Dealing with Near Eastern or Israelite Religion, History, Texts, Languages, and Other Matters

Books and monographs

Ackroyd, Peter R. Exile and Restoration: A Study of Hebrew Thought of the Sixth Century B.C. Philadelphia: Westminster Press, 1968.

Albrektson, Bertil. History and the Gods: An Essay on the Idea of Historical Events as Divine Manifestations in the Ancient Near East and in Israel. Lund: Gleerup, 1967.

Albright, William Foxwell. From the Stone Age to Christianity: Monotheism and the Historical Process. Anchor Books. 2nd ed. New York: Doubleday & Company, 1957.

_____. Yahweh and the Gods of Canaan: A Historical Analysis of Two Contrasting Faiths. New York: Doubleday & Company, Inc., 1968.

Barth, Jakob. Die Nominalbildung in den semitischen Sprachen. Leipzig: J. C. Hinrichs'sche Buchhandlung, 1894.

Bauer, Hans, and Leander, Pontus. Historische Grammatik der hebräischen Sprache des Alten Testamentes. Hildesheim: Georg Olms Verlagsbuchhandlung, 1962.

Bright, John. A History of Israel. Philadelphia: Westminster Press, 1959.

Cate, Robert L. "An Investigation into the Origin of the Triliteral Root System of Hebrew Verbs." Unpublished Th.D. dissertation, Southern Baptist Theological Seminary, 1959.

Childs, Brevard S. Memory and Tradition in Israel. SBT, No. 37. London: SCM Press Ltd., 1962.

Clay, Albert T. The Origin of Biblical Traditions: Hebrew Legends in Babylonia and Israel. Yale Oriental Series. Researches, Vol. XII. New Haven: Yale University Press, 1923.

Clements, Ronald E. God and Temple. Philadelphia: Fortress Press, 1965.

Cox, Harvey. The Secular City: Secularization and Urbanization in Theological Perspective. New York: Macmillan Company, 1965.

Delitzsch, Friedrich. Babel und Bibel. 3rd ed. Leipzig: J. C. Hinrichs'sche Buchhandlung, 1903.

_____. Babel und Bibel. 5th ed. Leipzig: J. C. Hinrichs'sche Buchhandlung, 1905.

Eerdmans, Bernardus D. The Religion of Israel. Leiden: Universitaire Pers, 1947.

Ehrlich, Ernst L. Die Kultsymbolik im Alten Testament und im nachbiblischen Judentum. Stuttgart: Anton Hiersemann, 1959.

Eliade, Mircea. The Sacred and the Profane: The Nature of Religion. Translated by Willard R. Trask. Harper Torchbooks. New York: Harper & Row, Publishers, 1961.

Engnell, Ivan. Studies in Divine Kingship in the Ancient Near East. 2nd ed. Oxford: Basil Blackwell, 1967.

Gaster, Theodor H. Thespis. Anchor Books. New ed. New York: Doubleday & Company, Inc., 1961.

Gesenius, Wilhelm, and Kautzsch, Emil. Hebrew Grammar. Translated by A. E. Cowley. 2nd ed. Oxford: Clarendon Press, 1910.

Goudoever, J. van. Biblical Calendars. 2nd rev. ed. Leiden: E. J. Brill, 1961.

Graham, William G., and May, Herbert G. Culture and Conscience: An Archaeological Study of the New Religious Past in Ancient Palestine. Chicago: University of Chicago Press, 1936.

Gray, John. The Legacy of Canaan: The Ras Shamra Texts and their Relevance to the Old Testament. SVT, Vol. V. 2nd rev. ed. Leiden: E. J. Brill, 1965.

Gressmann, Hugo, ed. Altorientalische Texte zum Alten Testament. 2nd ed. Berlin: Verlag Walter de Gruyter & Co., 1926.

Gunkel, Hermann. Schöpfung und Chaos in Urzeit und Endzeit: Eine religionsgeschichtliche Untersuchung über Gen 1 und Ap Joh 12. Göttingen: Vandenhoeck & Ruprecht, 1895.

Harrelson, Walter. From Fertility Cult to Worship. New York: Doubleday & Company, Inc., 1969.

Heidel, Alexander. The Babylonian Genesis: The Story of Creation. Phoenix Books. 2nd ed. Chicago: University of Chicago Press, 1951.

Heidel, William Arthur. The Day of Yahweh: A Study of Sacred Days and Ritual Forms in the Ancient Near East. New York: Century Co., 1929.

Hölscher, Gustav. Geschichte der israelitischen und jüdischen Religion. Giessen: Verlag von Alfred Töpelmann, 1922.

_____. Geschichtsschreibung in Israel: Untersuchungen zum Jahvisten und Elohisten. Lund: C. W. K. Gleerup, 1952.

Hooke, Samuel H., ed. Myth and Ritual: Essays on the Myth and Ritual of the Hebrews in Relation to the Cultural Pattern of the Ancient East. London: Oxford University Press, 1933.

_____. The Origins of Early Semitic Ritual. London: Oxford University Press, 1938.

Janssen, Enno. Juda in der Exilzeit: Ein Beitrag zur Frage der Entstehung des Judentums. FRLANT, No. 69. Göttingen: Vandenhoeck & Ruprecht, 1956.

Johns, C. H. W. Assyrian Deeds and Documents. Vol. II. London: George Bell and Sons, 1901.

Johnson, A. R. The Cultic Prophet in Ancient Israel. Cardiff: University of Wales Press, 1962.

Keller, Carl A. Das Wort OTH als "Offenbarungszeichen Gottes": Eine philologisch-theologische Begriffsuntersuchung zum Alten

Testament. Basel: Buchdruckerei E. Hoenen, 1946.

Kittel, Rudolf. _Geschichte des Volkes Israel_. 6th ed. Stuttgart: Verlag Friedrich Andreas Perthes A.-G., 1923.

König, Eduard. _Geschichte der alttestamentlichen Religion_. 2nd ed. Gütersloh: Druck und Verlag von C. Bertelsmann, 1915.

Kraus, Hans-Joachim. _Worship in Israel: A Cultic History of the Old Testament_. Translated by G. Buswell. Richmond, Va.: John Knox Press, 1966.

Kuenen, Abraham. _The Religion of Israel_. Translated by A. H. May. London: Williams and Norgate, 1874.

Lambert, W. G., and Millard A. R. _Atra-Ḥasīs: The Babylonian Story of the Flood_. Oxford: Clarendon Press, 1969.

Landsberger, Benno. _Der kultische Kalender der Babylonier und Assyrer_. Leipzig: J. C. Hinrichs'sche Buchhandlung, 1915.

Langdon, Stephen. _Babylonian Menologies and the Semitic Calendars_. London: Oxford University Press, 1935.

Lauterbach, Jacob Z. _Rabbinic Essays_. Cincinnati: Hebrew Union College Press, 1951.

Lods, Adolphe. _Histoire de la littérature hebraïque et juive_. Paris: Payot, 1950.

_____. _Israel: From Its Beginning to the Middle of the Eighth Century_. Translated by S. H. Hooke. New York: Alfred A. Knopf, 1932.

Mahler, Eduard. _Handbuch der jüdischen Chronologie_. Leipzig: Buchhandlung Gustav Fock, G.m.b.H., 1916.

Marti, Karl. _Geschichte der israelitischen Religion_. 5th ed. Strassburg: Friedrich Bull Verlagsbuchhandlung, 1907.

Meissner, Bruno. _Babylonien und Assyrien_, II. Heidelberg: Carl Winters Universitätsbuchhandlung, 1925.

Meyer, Eduard. _Geschichte des Altertums_. Vol. II, 2: _Der Orient vom zwölften bis zur Mitte des achten Jahrhunderts_. 3rd ed. J. G. Cotta'sche Buchhandlung Nachfolger, 1953.

Mowinckel, Sigmund. _Psalmenstudien II_. Amsterdam: Verlag P. Schippers, 1961.

_____. The Psalms in Israel's Worship. Translated by D. R. Ap-Thomas. New York: Abingdon Press, 1962.

Newman, Murray L., Jr. The People of the Covenant: A Study of Israel from Moses to the Monarchy. Nashville: Abingdon Press, 1962.

Nielsen, Ditlef. Die altarabische Mondreligion und die mosaische Überlieferung. Strassburg: Verlag von Karl J. Trübner, 1904.

_____, ed. Handbuch der altarabischen Altertumskunde. Vol. I: Die altarabische Kultur. Copenhagen: Nyt Nordisk Forlag, Arnold Busck, 1927.

Nilsson, Martin P. Primitive Time-Reckoning. Lund: C. W. K. Gleerup, 1920.

Nowack, Wilhelm. Lehrbuch der hebräischen Archaologie, I. Freiburg und Leipzig: J. C. B. Mohr, 1894.

Oesterley, W. O. E., and Robinson, Theodore H. Hebrew Religion: Its Origin and Development. 2nd rev. ed. London: Macmillan Company, 1937.

Östborn, Gunnar. Tōrā in the Old Testament: A Semantic Study. Lund: Håkon Ohlssons Boktrycheri, 1945.

Otto, Rudolf. The Idea of the Holy: An Inquiry into the Non-Rational Factor in the Idea of the Divine and Its Relation to the Rational. Translated by John W. Harvey. A Galaxy Book. New York: Oxford University Press, 1958.

Pedersen, Johannes. Israel: Its Life and Culture, I-IV. London: Oxford University Press, 1926-40.

Pfeiffer, Robert H. Religion in the Old Testament: The History of a Spiritual Triumph. New York: Harper & Brothers, 1961.

Pritchard, James B., ed. Ancient Near Eastern Texts Relating to the Old Testament. 2nd ed. Princeton: Princeton University Press, 1955.

Procksch, Otto. Theologie des Alten Testaments. Gütersloh: C. Bertelsmann Verlag, 1950.

Quast A. "Analyse des Sündenbewusstseins Israel nach dem Heiligkeitsgesetz." Unpublished Dr. Theol. dissertation, University of Göttingen, 1957.

Rad, Gerhard von. Das Gottesvolk im Deuteronomium. BWANT, No. 47. Stuttgart: W. Kohlhammer Verlag, 1929.

_____. Old Testament Theology. Vol. I: The Theology of Israel's Historical Traditions. Translated by D. M. G. Stalker. New York: Harper & Row, Publishers, 1962.

_____. Old Testament Theology. Vol. II: The Theology of Israel's Prophetic Traditions. Translated by D. M. G. Stalker. New York: Harper & Row, Publishers, 1965.

Rendtorff, Rolf. Studien zur Geschichte des Opfers im Alten Testament. WMANT, No. 24. Neukirchen-Vluyn: Neukirchener Verlag, 1967.

Ringgren, Helmer. Israelite Religion. Translated by D. E. Green. Philadelphia: Fortress Press, 1966.

Rowley, H. H. From Joseph to Joshua: Biblical Traditions in the Light of Archaeology. London: Oxford University Press, 1950.

_____. Worship in Ancient Israel: Its Form and Meaning. Philadelphia: Fortress Press, 1967.

Sayce, A. H. The "Higher Criticism" and the Verdict of the Monuments. 3rd ed., rev. New York: E. & J. B. Young & Co., 1894.

Schottroff, Willy. "Gedenken" im Alten Orient und im Alten Testament: Die Wurzel zākar im semitischen Sprachkreis. WMANT, No. 15. Neukirchen-Vluyn: Neukirchener Verlag, 1964.

Segal, Judah B. The Hebrew Passover: From the Earliest Times to A.D. 70. London Oriental Series, No. 12. London: Oxford University Press, 1963.

Sellin, Ernst. Geschichte des israelitisch-jüdischen Volkes, I. Leipzig: Quelle & Meyer, 1924.

Smith, George. Assyrian Discoveries: An Account of Explorations and Discoveries on the Site of Nineveh, During 1873 and 1874. New York: Scribner, Armstrong, and Co., 1875.

Snaith, Norman H. The Jewish New Year Festival: Its Origin and Development. London: Society for Promoting Christian Knowledge, 1947.

Strack, Hermann L., and Billerbeck, Paul. Kommentar zum Neuen Testament aus Talmud und Midrasch, IV, Part II. Munich: C. H. Beck'sche Verlagsbuchhandlung Oscar Beck, 1922-28.

Ungnad, Arthur. Babylonische Briefe aus der Zeit der Hammurapi-Dynastie. Leipzig: J. C. Hinrichs'sche Buchhandlung, 1914.

_____, and Matouš, Lubor. Grammatik des Akkadischen. 4th ed. Munich: Verlag C. H. Beck, 1964.

294

Vaux, Roland de. _Ancient Israel_. Vol. I: _Social Institutions_. New
        York: McGraw-Hill Book Company, 1965.

_____. _Ancient Israel_. Vol. II: _Religious Institutions_. New York:
        McGraw-Hill Book Company, 1965.

_____. _Studies in Old Testament Sacrifice_. Cardiff: University of
        Wales Press, 1964.

Vogt, Hubertus C. M. _Studie zur nachexilischen Gemeinde in Esra-
        Nehemia_. Werl: Dietrich Coelde Verlag, 1966.

Vriezen, Th. C. _The Religion of Israel_. Translated by H. Hoskins.
        London: Lutterworth Press, 1967.

Weber, Max. _Gesammelte Aufsätze zur Religionssoziologie_. Vol. III:
        Das antike Judentum. Tübingen: Verlag von J. C. B. Mohr (Paul
        Siebeck), 1923.

Webster, Hutton. _Rest Days: A Sociological Study_. The University
        Studies of the University of Nebraska, Vol. XI. Lincoln:
        Published by the University, 1911.

_____. _Rest Days: A Study in Early Law and Morality_. New York:
        Macmillan Company, 1916.

Wright, G. Ernest. _Biblical Archaeology_. 2nd rev. ed. Philadelphia:
        Westminster Press, 1962.

Würthwein, Ernst. _Der ʿAmm-ha-ʾarez im Alten Testament_. BWANT, No. 69.
        Stuttgart: W. Kohlhammer Verlag, 1936.

Articles

Ackroyd, Peter R. "History and Theology in the Writings of the
        Chronicler." _CThM_, XXXVIII (1967), 501-15.

Balkan, Kemal. "The Old Assyrian Week." _Studies in Honor of Benno
        Landsberger on his Seventy-Fifth Birthday April 12, 1965_.
        Edited by H. Güterbock and Th. Jacobsen. Chicago: University
        of Chicago Press, 1965.

Bauer, J. B. "Die literarische Form des Heptaemeron." _BZ_, N.F. I.
        (1957), 273-77.

Begrich, Joachim. "Die priesterliche Tora." _Gesammelte Studien zum
        Alten Testament_. Munich: Chr. Kaiser Verlag, 1964.

Berry, George R. "The Hebrew Word ᚱᚺᚷ." _JBL_, L (1931), 207-10.

Borger, Reikele. "An Additional Remark on P. R. Ackroyd, JNES, XVII, 23-27." JNES, XVIII (1959), 74.

Brinkman, J. A. "New Evidence on Old Assyrian ḫumuštum." Orientalia, XXXII (1963), 387-94.

_____. "Note on Old Assyrian Ḫamuštum." JNES, XXIV (1965), 118-20.

Dussaud, René. "Yahwé, fils de El." Syria, XXXIV (1957), 232-42.

Eichrodt, Walther. "The Law and the Gospel." Interpretation, XI (1957), 23-40.

Eissfeldt, Otto. "Die Wohnsitze der Götter von Ras Shamra." Kleine Schriften, II. Edited by R. Sellheim and F. Maass. Tübingen: J. C. B. Mohr (Paul Siebeck), 1963.

Engnell, Ivan. "'Knowledge' and 'Life' in the Creation Story." Wisdom in Israel and in the Ancient Near East. Presented to Professor Harold Henry Rowley. Edited by M. Noth and D. Winton Thomas. SVT, Vol. III. Leiden: E. J. Brill, 1955.

Galling, Kurt. "Erwägungen zur antiken Synagoge." ZDPV, LXXII (1956), 163-78.

Gray, John. "The Hebrew Conception of the Kingship of God: Its Origin and Development." VT, VI (1956), 268-85.

Gunneweg, A. H. J. "Sinaibund und Davidsbund." VT, X (1960), 335-41.

Hehn, Johannes. "Zur Bedeutund der Siebenzahl." Vom Alten Testament: Festschrift Karl Marti. Edited by K. Budde. BZAW, No. 41. Giessen: Verlag von Alfred Töpelmann, 1925.

Jensen, P. "Assyrio-hebraïca." ZA, IV (1889), 274-78.

Kapelrud, Arvid S. "The Number Seven in Ugaritic Texts." VT, XVIII (1968), 494-99.

Koch, Klaus. "Word und Einheit des Schöpfergottes in Memphis und Jerusalem: Zur Einzigartigkeit Israels." ZThK, LXII (1965), 251-93.

Kraus, Hans-Joachim. "Zum Gesetzesverständnis der nachprophetischen Zeit." Kairos, XI (1969), 122-33.

Kutsch, Ernst. "Erwägungen zur Geschichte der Passafeier und des Massotfestes." ZThK, LV (1958), 1-35.

_____. "מִקְרָא." ZAW, LXV (1953), 247-53.

_____. "Die Wurzel ⁊‎𝔶‎⅃‎ im Hebraischen." VT, II (1952), 57-69.

Lambert, W. G. "A New Look at the Babylonian Background of Genesis." JThS, N.S. XVI (1965), 287-300.

Landsberger, B., and Wilson, J. W. Kinnier. "The Fifth Tablet of Enuma Eliš." JNES, 20 (1961), 154-79.

Lewy, Julius, and Lewy, Hildegard. "The Origin of the Week and the Oldest West Asiatic Calendar." HUCA, XVII (1942-43), 1-152.

Loewenstamm, Samuel E. "The Seven Day-Unit in Ugaritic Epic Literature." IEJ, XV (1965), 121-33.

Menes, Abram. "Temple und Synagoge." ZAW, L (1932), 268-76.

Morgenstern, Julian. "The Chanukka Festival and the Calendar of Ancient Israel." HUCA, XX (1947), 1-136.

Muilenburg, James. "Holiness." The Interpreter's Dictionary of the Bible. Edited by G. A. Buttrick, et al. New York: Abingdon Press, 1962, II, 616-25.

Myers, Jacob M. "The Kerygma of the Chronicler." Interpretation, XX (1966), 259-73.

Nielsen, Eduard. "The Levites in Ancient Israel." ASTI, III (1964), 16-27.

North, Robert. "Theology of the Chronicler." JBL, LXXXII (1963), 369-81.

Noth, Martin. "God, King, and Nation in the Old Testament." The Laws in the Pentateuch and Other Studies. Translated by D. R. Ap-Thomas. Philadelphia: Fortress Press, 1966.

Peters, John P. "The Wind of God." JBL, XXX (1911), 44-54.

Pettazzoni, R. "Myths of Beginning and Creation-Myths." Essays on the History of Religion. Translated by H. J. Rose. Numen Supplement, No. 1. Leiden: E. J. Brill, 1954.

Plöger, Otto. "Siebzig Jahre." Festschrift Friedrich Baumgärtel zum 70. Geburtstag, 14. Januar, 1958. Edited by Leonard Rost. Erlangen: Universitätsbund, 1959.

Rad, Gerhard von. "The City on the Hill." The Problem of the Hexateuch and Other Essays. Translated by E. W. Trueman Dickens. New York: McGraw-Hill Book Company, 1966.

_____. "The Promised Land and Yahweh's Land in the Hexateuch." The Problem of the Hexateuch and Other Essays. Translated by E. W. Trueman Dickens. New York: McGraw-Hill Book Company, 1966.

_____. "There Remains Still a Rest for the People of God: An Investigation of a Biblical Conception." The Problem of the Hexateuch and Other Essays. Translated by E. W. Trueman Dickens. New York: McGraw-Hill Book Company, 1966.

_____. "Typological Interpretation of the Old Testament." Translated by John Bright. Essays on Old Testament Hermeneutics. Edited by Claus Westermann and James Luther Mays. Richmond, Va.: John Knox Press, 1963.

Rost, Leonhard. "Sinaibund und Davidsbund." ThLZ, LXXII (1947), 129-34.

Sayce, A. H. "Assyriological Notes--No. 3." PSBA, XIX (1877), 280-92.

Sekine, Masao. "Davidsbund und Sinaibund bei Jeremia." VT, IX (1959), 47-57.

Welch, Adam C. "The Share of N. Israel in the Restoration of the Temple Worship." ZAW, XLVIII (1930), 175-87.

Wildberger, Hans. "Israel und sein Land." EvTh, XVI (1956), 404-22.

Zimmerli, Walther. "Das Gesetz im Alten Testament." Gottes Offenbarung: Gesammelte Augsätze zum Alten Testament. Munich: Chr. Kaiser Verlag, 1963.

_____. "Erkenntnis Gottes nach dem Buch Ezechiel." Gottes Offenbarung: Gesammelte Aufsätze zum Alten Testament. Munich: Chr. Kaiser Verlag, 1963.

_____. "Sinaibund und Abrahambund (Ein Beitrag zum Verständnis der Priesterschrift)." ThZ, XVI (1960), 266-88. Also in Gottes Offenbarung: Gesammelte Aufsätze zum Alten Testament. Munich: Chr. Kaiser Verlag, 1963.

Studies on the Sabbath Institution, the Sabbath Texts,

and Etymological Questions

Books and monographs

Beer, Georg. Schabbath: Der Mischnatractat "Sabbat." Tübingen: J. C. B. Mohr (Paul Siebeck), 1908.

Bentzen, Aage. Den israelitiske Sabbats Oprindelse og Historie indtil

Jerusalems Erobring aar 70 E. Kr. Copenhagen: J. H. Schultz
Forlagsboghandel A/S, 1923.

Bohn, Friedrich. Der Sabbat im Alten Testament und im altjüdischen
religiösen Aberglauben. Gütersloh: Druck und Verlag von
C. Bertelsmann, 1903.

Bostrup, Paul O. Den israelitiske Sabbats Oprindelse og Karakter i
Foreksilsk Tid. Copenhagen: G. E. C. Gads Forlag, 1923.

Campiche, Roger. "Le Sabbat dans l'Ancient Testament." Doctoral
dissertation, University of Geneva, 1935.

Congdon, Roger D. "Sabbatic Theology." Unpublished Th.D. dissertation,
Dallas Theological Seminary, 1949.

Dupont-Sommer, A. Sabbat et parascève à Éléphantine d'après des ostraca
araméens inédits. Paris: Imprimerie Nationale, 1950.

Hehn, Johannes. Siebenzahl und Sabbat bei den Babyloniern und im Alten
Testament. Leipzig: J. C. Hinrichs'sche Buchhandlung, 1907.

Heschel, Abraham J. "The Sabbath: Its Meaning for Modern Man." The
Earth is the Lord's and the Sabbath. Harper Torchbooks. New
York: Harper & Row, Publishers, 1966.

Jenni, Ernst. Die theologische Begründung des Sabbatgebotes im Alten
Testament. Theologische Studien, No. 46. Zollikon-Zürich:
Evangelischer Verlag AG., 1956.

Kiker, Charles W. "The Sabbath in the Old Testament Cult." Unpublished
Th.D. dissertation, Southern Baptist Theological Seminary, 1968.

Lotz, Wilhelm. Questions de Historia Sabbati. Leipzig: J. C.
Hinrichs, 1883.

Meesters, J. H. Op zoek naar de oorsprong van de Sabbat. Studia
Semitica Neerlandica, No. 7. Assen: Van Gorcum & Company,
N.V., 1966.

Meinhold, Johannes. Sabbat und Sonntag. Wissenschaft und Bildung,
Vol. 45. Leipzig: Verlag von Quelle & Meyer, 1909.

_____. Sabbat und Woche im Alten Testament. Göttingen: Vandenhoeck
und Ruprecht, 1905.

Rordorf, Willy. Sunday: The History of the Day of Rest and Worship in
the Earliest Centuries of the Christian Church. Translated by
A. A. K. Graham. Philadelphia: Westminster Press, 1968.

Yamashiro, George. "A Study of the Hebrew Word Sabbath in Biblical and Talmudic Literatures." Unpublished Ph.D. dissertation, Harvard University, 1955.

Articles

Barnes, W. Emery. "Prophecy and the Sabbath: A Note on the Teaching of Jeremiah." JThS, XXIX (1928), 386-90.

Botterweck, G. Joh. "Der Sabbat im Alten Testamente." ThQ, CXXXIV, 134-47 and 448-57.

Budde, Karl. "Antwort auf Johannes Meinholds 'Zur Frage.'" ZAW, XLVIII (1930), 138-45.

_____. "The Sabbath and the Week: Their Origin and their Nature." JThS, XXX (1929), 1-15.

Brown, Francis. "The Sabbath in the Cuneiform Records." The Presbyterian Review, III (1882), 688-700.

Cannon, W. W. "The Weekly Sabbath." ZAW, XLIX (1931), 325-27.

Cazelles, Henri. "Ex 34, 21 traite-t-il du Sabbat?" CBQ, XXIII (1961), 223-26.

Dupont-Sommer, A. "L'ostracon araméen du Sabbat (Collection Clermont-Ganneau No. 152)." Semitica, II (1949), 29-39.

Eerdmans, Bernadus D. "Der Sabbath." Vom Alten Testament: Festschrift Karl Marti. Edited by Karl Budde. BZAW, No. 41. Giessen: Verlag von Alfred Töpelmann, 1925.

Eichrodt, Walther. "Der Sabbat bei Hesekiel: Ein Beitrag zur Nachgeschichte des Prophetentextes." Lex Tua Veritas: Festschrift für Hubert Junker. Edited by H. Gross and F. Mussner. Trier: Paulinus-Verlag, 1961.

Féret, H. N. "Le sources bibliques." Le jour du Seigneur: Mystique et pratique du dimanche. Congrèss (2e) National de Pastorale Liturgique, Lyon, 1947. Paris: R. Laffont, 1948.

Gaster, Theodore H. "Le jour du repos." Evidences, XLIII (1954), 43-48.

Hehn, Johannes. "Zur Sabbatfrage." BZ, XIV (1917), 198-213.

Hirschfeld, H. "Remarks on the Etymology of Šabbāth." JRAS, LIII (1896), 353-59.

Hulst, A. R. "Bemerkungen zum Sabbatgebot." Studia Biblica et Semitica:

Theodoro Christiano Vriezen Dedicata. Edited by W. C. van Unnik and A. S. van der Woude. Wageningen: H. Veenman & Zonen N.V., 1966.

Jastrow, Morris. "On הַשַּׁבָּת מִמָּחֳרָת (The Day after the Sabbath)." AJSL, XXX (1913-14), 94-110.

_____. "The Original Character of the Hebrew Sabbath." AJTh, II (1898), 312-52.

Johns, C. H. W. "The Babylonian Sabbath." ExT, XVII (1905-6), 566-67.

Kohler, Kaufmann. "The Sabbath and Festivals in Pre-Exilic and Exilic Times." Studies, Addresses, and Personal Papers. New York: Block Publishing Co., 1931.

Kornfeld, Walter. "Der Sabbath im Alten Testament." Der Tag des Hern. Edited by Hermal Peichl. Vienna: Verlag Herder, 1958.

Kraeling, E. J. "The Present Status of the Sabbath Question." AJSL, XLIX (1932-33), 218-28.

Kutsch, E. "Sabbat." Die Religion in Geschichte und Gegenwart. Edited by Kurt Galling, et al. 3rd ed. Tübingen: J. C. B. Mohr (Paul Siebeck), 1958, V, 1258-60.

Lotz, Wilhelm. "Sabbat." Realencykopädie für protestantische Theologie und Kirche. Edited by A. Hauck. Leipzig: J. C. Hinrichs'sche Buchhandlung, 1906, XVII, 283-91.

Mahler, Eduard. "Der Sabbat: Seine etymologische und chronologisch-historische Bedeutung." ZDMG, LXII (1908), 33-79.

Meek, Theophile J. "The Sabbath in the Old Testament: Its Origin and Development." JBL, XXXVIII (1914), 201-12.

Meinhold, Johannes. "Die Entstehung des Sabbats." ZAW, XXIX (1909), 81-112.

_____. "Zur Sabbatfrage." ZAW, XLVIII (1930), 121-38.

Morgenstern, Julian. "Sabbath." Interpreter's Dictionary of the Bible. Edited by G. A. Buttrick, et al. New York: Abingdon Press, 1962, IV, 135-41.

North, Robert. "The Derivation of Sabbath." Biblica, XXXVI (1955), 182-201.

Pinches, Theophilus G. "Sapattu, the Babylonian Sabbath." PSBA, XXVI (1904), 51-56.

Rordorf, Willy. "Sabbat." Biblisch-Historisches Handwörterbuch. Edited by Bo Reicke and Leonhard Rost. Göttingen: Vandenhoeck & Ruprecht, 1966, III, 1633-35.

Schrenk, Gottlob. "Sabbat oder Sonntag." Judaica, II (1946), 169-89.

Shapiro, David S. "The Sabbatical Year." Tradition, VII (1965), 45-56.

Skinner, John, and Muilenburg, James. "Sabbath." Hasting's Dictionary of the Bible. Edited by F. C. Grant and H. H. Rowley. Rev. ed. New York: Charles Scribner's Sons, 1963, pp. 866-67.

Slonim, M. B. "The Gender of Sbt (Sabbath) in the Hebrew Bible." JBL, LXX (1951), iv-v.

Steckel, K. "Sabbat." Calver Bibellexikon. Edited by K. Gutbrod, R. Kucklich, and Th. Schlatter. 2nd ed. Stuttgart: Calver Verlag, 1967, pp. 1147-49.

Torrey, Charles C. "Recent Hebrew Lexicography." AJSL, XXXIII (1916-17), 53.

Toy, Crawford H. "The Earliest Form of the Sabbath." JBL, XVIII (1899), 190-94.

Tur-Sinai, N. H. "Sabbat und Woche." BiOr, VIII (1951), 14-24.

Vriezen, Th. C. "Kalender en Sabbat." NThSt, XXIII (1940), 172-95.

Zimmern, Heinrich. "Nochmals Sabbat." ZDMG, LVIII (1904), 458-60.

_____. "Sabbath." ZDMG, lVIII (1904), 199-202.